Amalia Holst: On the Vocation of Woman to Higher Intellectual Education

BSHP NEW TEXTS IN THE HISTORY OF PHILOSOPHY

The aim of this series is to encourage and facilitate the study of all aspects of the history of philosophy, including the rediscovery of neglected elements and the exploration of new approaches to the subject. Texts are selected on the basis of their philosophical and historical significance and with a view to promoting the understanding of currently under-represented authors, philosophical traditions, and historical periods. They include new editions and translations of important yet less well-known works which are not widely available to an anglophone readership. The series is sponsored by the British Society for the History of Philosophy (BSHP) and is managed by an editorial team elected by the Society. It reflects the Society's main mission and its strong commitment to broadening the canon.

General editors
Maria Rosa Antognazza
Michael Beaney
Mogens Lærke (managing editor)

ALSO PUBLISHED IN THE SERIES

Félix Ravaisson: French Philosophy in the Nineteenth Century
Edited with an English translation by Mark Sinclair

Leibniz: General Inquiries on the Analysis of Notions and Truths
Edited with an English translation by Massimo Mugnai

Amalia Holst

On the Vocation of Woman to Higher Intellectual Education

Edited with an English translation by
ANDREW COOPER

Great Clarendon Street, Oxford, OX2 6DP,
United Kingdom

Oxford University Press is a department of the University of Oxford.
It furthers the University's objective of excellence in research, scholarship,
and education by publishing worldwide. Oxford is a registered trade mark of
Oxford University Press in the UK and in certain other countries

© Andrew Cooper 2023

The moral rights of the author have been asserted

All rights reserved. No part of this publication may be reproduced, stored in
a retrieval system, or transmitted, in any form or by any means, without the
prior permission in writing of Oxford University Press, or as expressly permitted
by law, by licence or under terms agreed with the appropriate reprographics
rights organization. Enquiries concerning reproduction outside the scope of the
above should be sent to the Rights Department, Oxford University Press, at the
address above

You must not circulate this work in any other form
and you must impose this same condition on any acquirer

Published in the United States of America by Oxford University Press
198 Madison Avenue, New York, NY 10016, United States of America

British Library Cataloguing in Publication Data
Data available

Library of Congress Control Number: 2023936264

ISBN 978–0–19–284594–8

DOI: 10.1093/oso/9780192845948.001.0001

Printed and bound by
CPI Group (UK) Ltd, Croydon, CR0 4YY

Contents

Acknowledgements   vii
Introduction   ix
Note on translation   lix

On the Vocation of Woman to Higher Intellectual Education   1

Preface   7

1. Does Higher Education of the Mind Contradict the Proximate Calling of Woman as Wife, Mother, and Housewife?   9
2. Woman Considered as Wife   43
3. The Educated Woman as Mother   68
4. The Educated Woman as Housewife   93
5. On the Education of Woman in the Unmarried State   105

Appendix 1: Biographical References   111
Appendix 2: Reviews of Holst's Work   117

Notes   127
Bibliography   147
Index   155

Acknowledgements

Working on this edition has opened several exciting collaborations and many debts of gratitude. I am immensely grateful to Dalia Nassar and Kristin Gjesdal for initially encouraging me to write about Amalia Holst. It is a privilege to build on their pioneering work, which has enriched the field of German philosophy by attending to the writings of women philosophers. I thank Susan Richter and Jörg Rathjen for aiding my attempt to verify claims that Holst received a doctorate from the University of Kiel. Special thanks to Alexandra Lilley for pushing me to take on the project, to Emily Aitkin for helping me feel the sting of Holst's critique of misogyny, and to the Women in the History of Philosophy reading group at the University of Warwick for bringing the text to life. Several others have supported the project and given helpful advice along the way, including Nigel Warburton, Alison Stone, Corey Dyck, Christine Mayer, Stephen Cooper, and Tobias Keiling. I thank the anonymous reviewers of the complete manuscript; their insightful comments on the introduction and translation were extremely helpful as I revised the text. And I am especially grateful to Simon Gansinger, who patiently worked through the translation to correct oversights and errors. All remaining faults are my own.

This project was enabled by the generous financial support of the Leverhulme Trust, the Department of Philosophy at the University of Warwick, and the British Society for the History of Philosophy. I am grateful to the staff members of several libraries for helpful advice and archival work, including The British Library, Universitätsbibliothek Frankfurt am Main, Staats- und Universitätsbibliothek Hamburg, Universitätsbibliothek Kiel, and the University of Warwick Library. It has been a pleasure to work with the series editors of BSHP New Texts in the History of Philosophy, Mogens Lærke, Maria Rosa Antognazza, and Michael Beaney. I thank my editor at Oxford University Press, Peter Momtchiloff, for efficiently guiding the text through the various stages to publication. And I am grateful to Oxford University Press for granting permission to build on material that was originally published as 'Amalia Holst' in *The Oxford Handbook for Nineteenth-Century Women Philosophers in the German Tradition* (2023), edited by Kristin Gjesdal and Dalia Nassar.

Andrew Cooper
Tufnell Park, London

Introduction

Amalia Holst (1758–1829) was a dedicated pedagogue and an outspoken philosopher. Her daring book *On the Vocation of Woman to Higher Intellectual Education* (*Über die Bestimmung des Weibes zur höhern Geistesbildung*, 1802) exposed a striking paradox at the heart of the German Enlightenment.[1] While the celebrated figures of the Enlightenment made significant gains in unearthing the social conditions of human freedom, they failed to advance either the political status or the education of women.[2] Immanuel Kant defined intellectual autonomy as the mark of Enlightenment, yet he deemed that a woman's mind is constituted differently to that of a man. If a woman were to pursue the higher education of her mind, Kant declared, she would 'destroy the merits that are proper to her sex'.[3] Johann Gottlieb Fichte demonstrated that free activity is the final end of every self-determining I. Yet, like Kant, he also held that 'the minds of men and women are, by nature, very different'.[4] While a man's education should include speculative philosophy, so that he grasps the principles of his knowledge, a woman's education should not disrupt her natural feeling for the good and the true. Instead, it should consist of practical training for the domestic duties to which nature has destined her. Against the backdrop of revolution in France, which dissolved natural bonds and threatened the role of the family in civic life, there was an explosion of texts across the German states on 'the vocation of woman' (*die Bestimmung des Weibes*), which called on central tenets of the Enlightenment to secure the subordinate status of

---

[1] In her pioneering study of Holst's writings, Carol Strauss Sotiropoulos presents the widening gap between the ideal of freedom and the social status of women as a form of irony. While this may be a fair historical assessment, Holst's contention is that the gap is paradoxical; the suppression of women is the final contradiction to be overcome in the progress of reason. See Sotiropoulos, 'Scandal Writ Large', 98.

[2] A rare exception to this failure is Theodor von Hippel. See Section 3.2.

[3] Kant, *Observations on the Feeling of the Beautiful and the Sublime*, 2:229. Later in his career, and despite his close friendship with Hippel, Kant argued that a learned woman is fraudulent: she uses books 'in the same way as her watch...which she carries so that people will see that she has one, though it is usually not running or not set by the sun'. Kant, *Anthropology from a Pragmatic Point of View*, 7:307.

[4] Fichte, *Grundlage des Naturrechts nach Prinzipien der Wissenschaftslehre*, 135. I follow Michael Baur's translation in Fichte, *Foundations of Natural Right*, 304.

women by philosophical means.[5] Holst's book stages a bold interjection. It seeks to unveil the double standards of her male interlocutors and establish the priority of reason before gendered roles.

Holst recognized that the Enlightenment project, when left in the hands of one sex, does not advance human freedom but in fact reproduces the coercion it purports to overcome. Drawing from her practical experience as a teacher, she sought to expose the contradictions she encountered in the leading pedagogies of the movement. One of her primary targets was a progressive group of reformers known as the Philanthropinists (*Menschenfreunde*) who aimed to realize the Enlightenment's slogan *Sapere aude!* (Dare to know!) by replacing the cerebral, authoritative legacy of scholastic education with a noncoercive environment aligned with the student's natural capacities. Their reform project was not peripheral to the German Enlightenment. In the midst of deep social and political change occurring across the German states, the schooling system offered a key site of reform for those seeking to instantiate the Enlightenment's emancipatory ideals while avoiding the radical upheaval unfolding in France.[6] Inspired by Jean-Jacques Rousseau's *Emile, or On Education* (*Émile, ou De l'éducation*, 1762) and pioneered by Johann Bernhard Basedow's model school in Dessau (the Philanthropin, founded in 1774), Philanthropinism gained the support of the leading philosophers of the day. Kant acted as the primary fundraiser for the Philanthropin in the 1770s, declaring that 'never before has a more just demand been made on the human species, and never before has such a great and more self-extending benefit been unselfishly offered'.[7]

Holst too was convinced that the ideals of the Enlightenment required a new movement in education tailored to the student's natural capacities.

---

[5] In her study of women's intellectual and political participation during the French Revolution, Geneviève Fraisse argues that 'in this passage from the old to the new regime, at the very moment of the rupture, the rights of man were not those of woman, not out of forgetfulness but out of an internal necessity that we must try to discern'; Fraisse, *Muse de la Raison*, 15. Exploring Fraisse's thesis in the British context, Eileen O'Neill argues that philosophy itself altered in years following the revolution such that it became harder for women to be recognized as philosophers. O'Neill defines this alteration as the 'oxymoron problem': by definition, women could not be identified as philosophers; O'Neill, 'Disappearing Ink', 20. In what follows I argue that a similar case can be made in the German context.

[6] For a study of gender and education in the construction of the modern German state, see Mayer, 'Bildungsentwürfe und die Konstruktion der Geschlechterverhältnisse zu Beginn der Moderne'.

[7] Kant, *Gesammelte Schriften*, II 447. Kant published two essays in support of the Philanthropin in the *Königsbergische gelehrte und politische Zeitung*, which have been reprinted in the Akademie Ausgabe (II 445–52). For a discussion of Kant's curious attraction to Basedow's project, see Louden, 'Kant and Basedow on the Need to Transform Education'.

Yet her ongoing struggle to advance the education of women alerted her to a form of coercion that remained lodged at the heart of the movement. While the Philanthropinists claimed that education must enable each student's rationality to develop on its own course, they restricted the curriculum for girls to subjects that were strictly necessary for their 'threefold vocation' (*dreifache Bestimmung*). As Karl Friedrich Pockels put it,

> The vocation of a woman is to become a wife, a mother, and a housewife, in fact, a *pure wife*, a *perfect mother*, and a *prudent housewife*. It is to this end that girls must study. Everything that does not contribute to her vocation leads away from it, and makes her an unnatural sight.[8]

The Philanthropinists envisaged the education of women as a vital part of reform. Yet they maintained that the duties prescribed by a woman's vocation place normative constraints on her intellect. A woman's education must be restricted to knowledge that will enable her to please her husband, raise her children well, and manage a good home. Areas of knowledge that extend beyond this end are not only unnecessary but also dangerous, for they entice her to neglect the duties bestowed on her by nature. These attitudes were not restricted to the Philanthropinists but were repeated and even refined by many of the major philosophers of the German Enlightenment, not least Kant and Fichte but also Mendelssohn, Schleiermacher, Humboldt, and Hegel, to name just a few.

In the opening pages of *On the Vocation of Woman*, Holst challenges the elevated position assumed by men who have 'dared to set a limit that our minds may not transgress in the field of knowledge' (p. 9). She begins her argument by issuing a fiery demand to the male gatekeepers of women's education:

> In the name of our sex, I challenge men to justify the right they have presumed for themselves, which holds back an entire half of humankind, barring them from the source of the sciences and allowing them at most to skim their surface. (p. 10)

---

[8] Pockels, *Versuch einer Charakteristik des weiblichen Geschlechts*, II 332. Pockels is in fact citing a letter by Christian Friedrich Sintenis entitled 'On Learned Women' ('Über gelehrte Weiber', 1796), which was widely circulated among German literati in the mid-1790s; Sintenis, *Briefe über die wichtigsten Gegenstände der Menschheit*, III 273. See Holst's response to the letter, beginning on p. 44.

Holst's demand resonates with the work of several women writers across Europe, including Olympe de Gouges, Mary Wollstonecraft, and Germaine de Staël. Yet in contrast to the early feminists we celebrate today, whose works were published in multiple editions and translated into several European languages, Holst's book had little success.[9] Following its initial publication, *On the Vocation of Woman* received just three reviews, all appearing in journals based in Holst's home town of Hamburg.[10] None of her reviewers acknowledge the merits of her project or take her argument seriously. Holst's book did not outstrip its original print run, nor was it recognized as a notable feminist text until the twentieth century.[11]

Understanding why *On the Vocation of Woman* has been overlooked—both then and now—confronts us with a darker side of the German Enlightenment that, until recently, has been neglected. Over the past few decades, scholars have become increasingly aware that women were not only excluded from the fruits of the Enlightenment but also erased from the historiography of German philosophy.[12] Sabrina Ebbersmeyer, for instance, traces the deliberate removal of women from anthologies of German philosophy, beginning in the late eighteenth century and extending to the present day. She presents a sobering analysis in which the absence of women's voices has less to do with the opportunities available to women than with a sustained attempt to 'keep women out of academia in general and out of philosophy in particular'.[13] *On the Vocation of Woman* provides further evidence in support of Ebbersmeyer's claim, for it demonstrates that the absence of women in the historiography of German philosophy is not due to a lack of powerful texts by women. Indeed, Holst was alive to the obstacles facing women philosophers at the turn of the nineteenth century

---

[9] Wollstonecraft's *A Vindication of the Rights of Woman* (1792) was immediately translated into major European languages and reached a third English edition just four years after its initial publication. Staël's novel *Corinne ou l'Italie* (1807) was widely translated within the year of its publication, and by 1872 had gone through more than forty printings. Though Gouges's *Declaration of the Rights of Woman and the Female Citizen* (1791) was not immediately translated, its contents were widely discussed across Europe, especially after her public execution in 1793. See Johns, 'Translations'.

[10] The three reviews are included in Appendix 2.

[11] Gertrud Bäumer was the first to acknowledge Holst as an important figure in the history of German feminism in Volume 1 of *Handbuch der Frauenbewegung* (1901). *On the Vocation of Woman* was not reprinted until Berta Rahm's edition in 1983.

[12] See O'Neill, 'Early Modern Women Philosophers and the History of Philosophy'; Ebbersmeyer, 'From a "memorable place" to "drops in the ocean"'; Nassar and Gjesdal, 'Editors' Introduction'.

[13] Ebbersmeyer, 'From a "memorable place" to "drops in the ocean"', 444. See also O'Neill, 'Early Modern Women Philosophers', 186.

and set out to repudiate a repeated claim made by her male peers that the very idea of a learned woman is contradictory. At one point she frames her argument in response to a public letter entitled 'On Learned Women' ('Über gelehrte Weiber', 1796), in which the theologian and popular writer Christian Friedrich Sintenis declares that

> a so-called learned woman is and remains either a laughable or an adverse creature. Either her learnedness is not right, or, even if it were, then she is not right as a *woman*. If the latter, then as a woman she is a non-woman, something monstrous, and if this is how she is found in her natural state, she deserves merely to be *gaped at* and certainly never *admired*.[14]

A so-called learned woman is a laughable creature, Sintenis quips, for by becoming learned she loses the essential characteristics of her femininity. Feminine qualities do not lie in the cultivation of moral and epistemic virtues but in the untarnished innocence a woman possesses from childhood. Elsewhere he attests that it 'is just as absurd to imagine a woman philosopher as it is to imagine a woman standing in rank as a soldier'.[15] The image of a woman philosopher is absurd, for, qua philosopher, a woman would no longer be a woman; a woman philosopher is a contradiction in terms. Sintenis's letter is, of course, polemical. Yet it does nothing but extend a widely held view to its unsavoury conclusions. Holst railed against the pervasive drive to curb women's education, yet her attempt to shift public opinion had limited success.[16]

By making Holst's *On the Vocation of Woman* available to the anglophone audience, this translation provides students and scholars of German philosophy with a timely resource for developing a richer understanding of their field, and general readers with access to a powerful early feminist text that reveals the opportunities and difficulties facing women philosophers at the turn of the nineteenth century. From the opening pages, the reader encounters a stylistically dexterous and philosophically astute writer who

---

[14] Sintenis, *Briefe über die wichtigsten Gegenstände der Menschheit*, III 280–1. It seems that Holst first encountered Sintenis's letter cited in Pockels's *Versuch einer Charakteristik des weiblichen Geschlechts*, II 296–345. Pockels elaborates on Sintenis's argument in several places, indicating his support of the author's satirical portrait of the learned women.
[15] Pockels, *Versuch einer Charakteristik des weiblichen Geschlechts*, II 332.
[16] The difficulties facing Holst's project exemplify the observation made by John Stuart Mill and Harriet Taylor eighty years later: one who wants to criticize a principle that is held almost universally has 'more difficulty in obtaining a trial, than any other litigants have in getting a verdict'; Mill, *The Subjection of Women*, 120.

constantly reformulates her position in anticipation of her readers' demands. The dialogical character of the text requires some level of familiarity with the central concepts of the German Enlightenment if its contribution to the philosophical debates of the period is to be fully appreciated.[17] My aim in this introduction is thus to provide sufficient context for readers to feel the rhetorical force of Holst's book. Section 1 presents a brief sketch of Holst's life, writings, and the state of pedagogy in the German states at the end of the eighteenth century. Section 2 provides a summary of the text and reconstructs several of its major arguments. Section 3 examines its early reception and identifies several sources that inspired Holst to write.

1 Life and Context

1.1 Amalia Holst, née von Justi

Little is known about Holst's life save the obituaries and biographical entries that appeared in local magazines and compendia of German writers in the years following her death in 1829. These are included in Appendix 1. The entries repeat themselves at several points, sometimes reproducing false information (e.g. the publication date of *On the Vocation of Woman*). Their authors acknowledge a lack of familiarity with the major events of Holst's life, and, at times, contradict each other (e.g. on the question of Holst's doctorate). Such discrepancies suggest that Holst's eulogists had little information to go by, and perhaps that they did not expect their efforts to have enduring significance.

The entries agree on the following. Johanna Paulina Amalia von Justi was born on 10 February 1758 to Johann Heinrich Gottlob von Justi and his second wife, Johanna Maria Magdalena Merchand.[18] Her precise birthplace is unclear. On the cover page to *On the Vocation of Woman*, Holst describes herself as 'a child of the Prussian states' (p. 5), and the announcement of her

---

[17] For an account of the dialogical character of women's writing at the turn of the nineteenth century and the role this played in excluding women writers from philosophy's canon, see Pollok, 'The Role of Writing and Sociability for the Establishment of a Persona', 196–7.

[18] Holst's full name appears on the announcement of her marriage, which is reproduced in Rahm's edition of *Über die Bestimmung des Weibes* (see Rahm, 'Nachwort', 155). Her chosen first name is spelled in several different ways by her eulogists (Amalie, Amelie, Amalia) and she changes between 'Amalia' and 'Amalie' when signing the letters published in Lindemann's *Musarion*. I follow the spelling of 'Amalia' from the cover page of *On the Vocation of Woman* (see p. 1).

marriage states that she is 'aus Berlin'. Yet it is likely that Holst was born in Altona, just outside Hamburg, where her father kept a residence and was working at the time of her birth.[19] The family moved to Berlin in 1760 and then, shortly after, to Bernau, just north of the city. Johann von Justi was a leading cameralist and self-described 'state adventurer' (*Staatsabenteurer*), rising to fame across Europe through an active life of writing, public administration, and state entrepreneurship. Before entering public service, he published several radical essays in which he advocated for civic reform through the increasing involvement of women in public offices. In 'Proposal on the Establishment of a Female Jury' ('Vorschlag von Errichtung eines weiblichen Schöffenstuhls', 1745), he proposed to erect civil courts administered and elected by women officials.[20] In 'Proposal on the Establishment of an Academy for Women' ('Vorschlag von Errichtung einer Akademie vor das Frauenzimmer', 1747), he argued that it would be impossible to instantiate the goals of Enlightenment without the establishment of 'a rational education for the female sex'.[21] In the years leading up to Amalia's birth, Justi taught German language and rhetoric in Vienna and then economics at the University of Göttingen (indeed, he was the first to do so). He founded several journals on social and political matters and published an astonishing sixty-seven books on economics and political science (*Staatswissenschaft*).[22] Yet Justi was not a scholar in the traditional sense. His writings were motivated by a restless drive to reform and centralize the Prussian economy, a trait that attracted the attention of Frederick the Great, who, upon hearing of his achievements in 1765, appointed Justi as Prussian captain of mines and financial expert in the management of state property. While he was a neglectful husband during his first marriage and constantly moved between positions during his second, Amalia was evidently attached to her father.[23]

A difficult chapter unfolded for the family in 1768 when Justi was accused of embezzling state funds, a fate met by several prominent cameralists of the

---

[19] Justi left Göttingen in 1757 to take up a position in Denmark; his residence in Altona was close to the Danish-German border at the time. See Rahm, 'Nachwort', 156.
[20] Justi, 'Vorschlag von Errichtung eines weiblichen Schöffenstuhls', 131.
[21] Justi, 'Vorschlag von Errichtung einer Akademie vor das Frauenzimmer', 312.
[22] For a survey of Justi's writings, see Reinert, 'Johann Heinrich Gottlob von Justi', 33.
[23] Justi's first wife, Gertrud, left him in June 1756 because 'her husband no longer maintained her'; cited in Reinert, 'Johann Heinrich Gottlob von Justi', 40. His estate was in such disarray that one of his maids at the time claimed that she had not been paid for five years. Amalia's affection for her father is nevertheless evident in her correspondence with Beckmann. See Beckmann, *Vorrath kleiner Anmerkungen über mancherley gelehrte Gegenstände*, 549–50.

time, including Georg Heinrich Zincke and Johann Friedrich Pfeiffer. While the accusations were never substantiated, Justi died as a prisoner in Küstrin in 1771, when Amalia was 13.[24] This episode left her mother in a prolonged state of grief, which prevented Amalia from publishing a collection of her father's letters that she hoped would explain the unfortunate situation and clear her father's name.[25] The charge was formally revoked when it became clear that Justi's estate could not repay his fine of 2,878 thaler,[26] and the king took personal responsibility for completing the education of his six children.[27]

The details of Amalia's adult life are somewhat more substantive. She moved to Hamburg in 1791, married Dr Johann Ludolf Holst in 1792 at the age of 33, and had three children, Emilie, Mariane, and Eduard. Johann Holst was a lawyer, and directed a pedagogical institute in Hamburg-St Georg. Amalia Holst clearly imbibed her father's entrepreneurial spirit and tenacious drive for reform. She was engaged in teaching from the age of 15 (possibly as a governess in Bernau), and quickly became convinced that it 'is only through the higher education of women that the ennoblement of humanity as a whole is achieved'.[28] From 1792 to 1802 she was headmistress of the preschool Johann directed, and went on to establish three schools for girls (*Erziehungsinstitute*) in Boizenburg, Hamburg, and Parchim.[29] An obituary appearing in the *Freimütiges Abendblatt* offers a striking insight into her teaching practice:

---

[24] Backhaus argues that it was Justi's aide who was in fact guilty of embezzlement. When Justi was appointed by Frederick II as captain of mines, his appointee noted that Justi had weak eyesight and could not manage the bookkeeping. Thus Frederick appointed an aide to manage the documentation of state expenditures. See Backhaus, 'Introduction', xi.
[25] See Beckmann's account of this episode in the first entry of Appendix 1.
[26] As a comparison, Justi's yearly salary in 1765 was 2,000 thaler. Reinert, 'Johann Heinrich Gottlob von Justi', 42.
[27] Backhaus, 'From Wolff to Justi', 18.
[28] One of the few insights we have of Holst's career before she was married is a letter written in 1802 to the Enlightener August Hennings, asking for his assistance to found an educational institute in Hamburg. As she lays out her credentials, Holst states that she has been engaged in education 'since her fifteenth year'. Holst, 'Brief an August Hennings (Hamburg, 29 May 1802)'. For a discussion of Holst's known letters, see Dyck, 'Amalia Holst on the Education of the Human Race'.
[29] Several of Holst's eulogists record that she started a school in Boizenburg, before returning briefly to Hamburg and then starting another school in Parchim (see pp. 113–14). In her edition of *Über die Bestimmung des Weibes*, Rahm includes a baptismal record of Holst's granddaughter Mathilde, which states that Holst was leading an educational institute in Parchim in 1819 (and also identifies her as a 'Doktorin'); Rahm, 'Nachwort', 154. While Holst states in her letter to Hennings that she intends to start a school in Hamburg, there is debate about whether her plans were realized.

her school was held in general esteem, for she did not educate her female students merely for domestic service, or for society, or for the so-called refined side of life. Rather, she educated them for life as a whole and opened the wellspring in spirit and mind for a loving and intelligent fulfilment of everything that the female vocation demands of woman in religious and cosmopolitan respects. Household management and maternal care, faithfulness in large and small matters, sensitivity and strength, sense and understanding to delight the circle of society, the propensity to do the right thing, the skill to do it well and without mishap, quiet charity, modest activity with all the knowledge and artistry of female education, and in all this a noble feeling that does not allow the sense of the infinite to be lost in earthly activity, and in which the mind remains free and firm above the colourful essence of all worldly activity: that is what distinguished those who remained in her hands and were left to her guidance until they reached a certain goal. Many parents, young women, husbands, and mothers certainly still thank her for this. Her educational work will remain a blessing for generations to come. (p. 113)

This description of Holst's work as a teacher captures a central theme in her writing. The educated woman does not neglect the demands of domestic life but skilfully navigates her duties in a manner that is alive to the spiritual significance of her vocation as a human being. Holst's pedagogical activities were known by several prominent Enlighteners in Hamburg, including August Hennings, Franz August Gottlob Campe (the nephew of Joachim Heinrich Campe), and Elise Reimarus.[30] There is evidence to suggest that Holst's time in Hamburg overlapped with Reimarus, who was aware of Holst's writings even before the publication of *On the Vocation of Woman*.[31] Several of Holst's eulogists claim that she received a doctorate from the University of Kiel in her later life. Yet the lack of conclusive evidence, and

---

[30] Hennings, Campe, and Reimarus were each involved in the pedagogical debates of the late eighteenth century. Hennings edited the journal *Der Genius des neunzehnten Jahrhunderts*, which published several radical essays on women's education; Campe worked as a publisher and bookseller and helped to arrange the publication of Holst's *On the Vocation of Woman*; Reimarus published numerous entries in Joachim Heinrich Campe's *Kleine Kinderbibliothek*.

[31] In a letter dated 1 February 1802, Reimarus wrote to Franz August Gottlieb Campe, who had sent her a copy of Holst's book: 'You had the good grace, dear Herr Campe, to send me the work of Fr[au] Holst, *On the Vocation of Woman*, but since I have always disliked reading about matters so general as the dealings of people or the alleged rights of women, and know the pen of Mad[ame] H[olst], I think it is better to give it back to you without leafing through it.' Cited in Spalding, *Elise Reimarus (1735–1805)*, 216, n. 46.

the counterclaim made by a later biographer, place the claim in doubt.[32] Holst left Hamburg for Parchim in 1813, and her husband died in 1825. In a letter dated 31 October 1824 she wrote to Campe, who had arranged the publication of *On the Vocation of Woman* in Leipzig two decades earlier, requesting his assistance to publish a new manuscript she had recently completed.[33] Campe seems to have denied her request and the manuscript has unfortunately been lost.[34] What the letter reveals, however, is that Holst continued her literary endeavours to the end of her life. She spent her final years with her son on the river Elbe in Groß Timkenberg, where she died 'quietly and gently' in 1829, 71 years old (p. 115).

1.2 Writings

1.2.1 Observations on the Errors of Our Modern Education

Drawing from the practical experience gained as a pioneer in women's education, Holst wrote several texts on pedagogy and the social status of women. Her earliest known work, published anonymously as *Observations on the Errors of Our Modern Education from a Practical Educator* (*Bemerkungen über die Fehler unserer modernen Erziehung von einer praktischen Erzieherin*, 1791), offers the first critique of Philanthropinism by a woman.[35] In the opening chapter of the book, 'Comparison of the Errors Made in Education Before and After the Basedowian Era', Holst surveys the development of modern pedagogy through Locke and Rousseau to her own time in Germany. Until the 1750s, most schools in the German states taught

---

[32] References to Holst's doctorate can be found on the birth certificate of her granddaughter Mathilde (reproduced in Rahm, 'Nachwort', 154) and in several obituaries (pp. 111–14). The entry on Holst in *Das Lexikon der hamburgischen Schriftsteller* disputes the title (p. 114). In his entry on Holst, Jacoby notes that he could not find confirmation of Holst's alleged doctorate. Jacoby, *Beiträge zur deutschen Literaturgeschichte des achtzehnten Jahrhunderts*, 7. I checked the records in *Promotionen und Disputationen* vol. 1 (1637–1804) and vol. 2 (1805–1914) in the university archives at Kiel and found no record of a doctorate under her name.

[33] 'I remember that once, for certain considerations, you also had my *Vocation o[f] W[oman]* published not by yourself but in Leipzig. If you now did the same with this manuscript, and recommended it to some other publisher, then the situation would be resolved and you would greatly appease[?] me.' Holst, 'Holst to Campe, 31 October 1824'.

[34] Holst informs Campe that he has 'upset [her] greatly' because he did 'not want to accept [her] manuscript'. Holst, 'Holst to Campe, 31 October 1824'.

[35] Fronius, *Women and Literature in the Goethe Era*, 206. The tendency of women writers during this period to publish anonymously is not simply a marker of their precarious social position but also a noteworthy feature of their philosophical expression. While Holst does not reveal her name, her gender is evident in the book's title (*von einer praktischen Erzieherin*). See Easley, *First-Person Anonymous*, 7.

the *septem artes liberales* (seven liberal arts), a rule-based programme characterized by rote learning, recitation, and exercises in rhetoric.[36] As it became increasingly apparent that the Latin schools were out of touch with the practical demands of bourgeois life, proponents of Enlightenment began to advocate various strategies of reform. In response to the pedagogical reform unfolding in England and France, for instance, Johann Christoph Gottsched argued that Latin rhetoric should be replaced with a new programme in the vernacular promoting oration and the public exercise of reason.[37] Yet despite Gottsched's efforts to modernize German education, Holst contends that it was Basedow who 'awakened the imitative spirit of the Germans'.[38] In his enormously popular textbook on education, *The Method Book for Fathers and Mothers of Families and Peoples* (*Das Methodenbuch für Väter und Mütter der Familien und Völker*, 1770), Basedow criticized the 'great disorder in the usual style of teaching in schools'.[39] Like Gottsched, he claimed that the Latin system coerced the student's natural faculties into an arcane mould that is 'without reality'.[40] Yet Basedow claimed that Gottsched failed to advance German pedagogy into the modern era, for he simply replaced the rules of rhetoric with an 'astonishing abundance of disgusting verbal cognition [*Verbalerkenntnis*]'. To apply the new insights of the Enlightenment to the German schooling system, Basedow drew from Locke and Rousseau to argue that the education of children must follow 'the natural order of cognition', which begins in sense perception, is developed by the rational ordering of ideas, and only then culminates in the public use of words.[41] Joachim Heinrich Campe, who

---

[36] Lohmann and Mayer, 'Dimensions of Eighteenth-century Educational Thinking in Germany', 116–18.
[37] Gottsched, *Akademische Redekunst, zum Gebrauche der Vorlesungen auf hohen Schulen als ein bequemes Handbuch eingerichtet und mit den schönsten Zeugnissen der Alten erläutert*, Vorrede.
[38] [Holst,] *Bemerkungen über die Fehler unserer Modernen Erziehung*, 13.
[39] Basedow, *Ausgewählte Schriften*, xi, 26.   [40] Basedow, *Ausgewählte Schriften*, xi, 26.
[41] Basedow, *Ausgewählte Schriften*, 18. Basedow contends that Locke's and Rousseau's empiricism demands an anti-authoritarian pedagogy. Locke, for instance, argued that while children are born with minds as blank slates, their bodies nevertheless move according to natural inclinations. The task of education is thus not to provide direct instruction but to work with the child's free capacity for association, which moves from perception to ideas through a process of reflection; Locke, *Some Thoughts Concerning Education*, 75–9. Similarly, Rousseau grounds his account of learning in the child's natural faculties: 'Since everything which enters into the human understanding comes there through the senses, man's first reason is a reason of the senses; this sensual reason serves as the basis for intellectual reason. Our first masters of philosophy are our feet, our hands, our eyes. To substitute books for all that is not to teach us to reason. It is to teach us to use the reason of others. It is to teach us to believe much and never to know anything.' Rousseau, *Emile, Or on Education*, 125.

worked briefly at Dessau before starting his own experimental school in Hamburg, built on Basedow's *Methodenbuch* to argue that a school's curriculum should not begin with an abstract system of words but with the concrete human vocation 'to make oneself and others happy through the proper training and application of all one's powers and abilities in the circle in which and for which providence has caused him to be born'.[42] Campe illustrates the point with an organic analogy. As a gardener must be familiar with the properties of plants if he hopes to cultivate an environment in which they can flourish, so must the teacher have a firm understanding of children's powers and abilities, and the sphere to which they are destined, if he is to provide a classroom in which they can thrive.

In the case of female students, however, Basedow and Campe both argued that the general human vocation to make oneself and others happy must be constrained to a second vocation that is particular to their sex. Basedow included a chapter in the *Methodenbuch* entitled 'On the Different Education of Sons and Daughters', which draws extensively from Rousseau (fifteen pages of direct quotation from *Emile*) to establish that the female sex is 'under the dominion' of men, and that a woman's education should teach her 'to know how to bear this'.[43] In *Fatherly Advice For My Daughter* (*Väterlicher Rath für meine Tochter*, 1789), Campe instructs the young women of the German states that the purpose of their education is to enable them to balance *two* vocations, one general and one particular:

> You are a *human being*—thus destined for everything that the general calling of humanity entails. You are a *woman*—thus destined for and called to everything that woman is to be to man, to humanity, and to civil society. So you have a twofold vocation, one *general* and one *particular*, one as *human being* and one as *woman*.[44]

---

[42] Campe, *Väterlicher Rath für meine Tochter*, 8. Between 1785 and 1792, Campe edited a sixteen-volume standard work of Enlightenment pedagogy, which included new translations of Rousseau's *Émile* and Locke's *Some Thoughts Concerning Education*.

[43] Basedow, *Ausgewählte Schriften*, 159. For a discussion of gender in Basedow's *Methodenbuch*, see Louden, *Johann Bernhard Basedow and the Transformation of Modern Education*, 119–20. Louden notes that while Basedow restricted women's education to their particular vocation in print, his activities, especially after his resignation from the directorship of the Philanthropin in 1785, indicate that he held a more liberal view in practice. Holst, however, would have been unaware of this. Her primary concern is to stem the growing influence of Basedow's *Methodenbuch* on German pedagogy. See Louden, 'Amalia Holst's Critique of Basedow and Campe', 80–1.

[44] Campe, *Väterlicher Rath für meine Tochter*, 5.

By virtue of their status as human beings, women are called to perfect their powers and abilities. The expression of this vocation, however, is qualified by the 'sphere of influence [*Wirkungskreis*]' to which their sex is destined. Campe makes it clear that a woman's sphere of influence is not contingent on present social conditions but determined by fixed and indubitable nature:

> The first and the most necessary thing I have to tell you here, if you have not already noticed it yourself, is this: the sex to which you belong, according to the present condition of our world, lives in a dependent as well as intellectually and physically weaker state, and, as long as the condition of our world remains the same, necessarily must live. God himself willed— and the entire constitution of human societies on earth, to the extent of our knowledge, is tailored to the fact—that it is not woman but man who should be the head. For this purpose, the Creator—as a rule—gave to man the greater muscular strength, the tauter nerves, the more unyielding fibres, the sturdier bone structure; in addition, the greater courage, the bolder spirit of enterprise, the decisive firmness and coolness, and—as a rule I mean—also the unmistakable predispositions to a greater, more farsighted and comprehensive intellect. The entire course of education and life for both sexes in all cultured peoples has been arranged according to this end: the woman is weak, small, delicate, sensitive, timid, smallminded—the man, on the other hand, is strong, firm, bold, persevering, tall, noble and powerful in body, etc.[45]

Campe contends that a woman's physiology manifests a dependent purpose ordained by the Creator. The task of a woman's education is to teach her to carry her dependence gracefully. Perfectibility and dependence combine to form a distinct female vocation: 'to become *happy wives, educating mothers,* and *wise household administrators*'.[46]

In the opening chapter of *Observations*, Holst expresses her support for the recent shift in German pedagogy from the Latin curriculum to a new programme based on the student's natural capacities. Nevertheless, she explains that her extensive experience as a 'practical educator [*praktische Erzieherin*]' has led her to the conviction that the Philanthropinists fail to

---

[45] Campe, *Väterlicher Rath für meine Tochter*, 18–19. Holst evidently has this passage in mind when she criticizes the Philanthropinists for equating physical and intellectual strength (see pp. 11–12).

[46] Campe, *Väterlicher Rath für meine Tochter*, 14–15.

apply the new understanding of education developed by Locke and Rousseau in practice. In the following four chapters of the book, Holst identifies four errors that stifle German pedagogy from entering the new age of learning it promises. Despite claiming to ground the pedagogical context in the natural ordering of cognition, the Philanthropinists overemphasize the use of reasoning with young children and underplay kinaesthetic learning, play, and imitation.[47] They attempt too much too soon, exciting a child's imagination without first laying a proper foundation.[48] They promote the use of general elementary books, which fail to respond to each child's particular needs.[49] And by dressing up their lessons with the latest children's literature, they overstimulate the imagination and stifle the organic maturation of virtue.[50]

While there is nothing overtly gendered about Holst's diagnosis of the errors of modern education, it nevertheless has radical implications for the Philanthropinists' attempt to curtail the education of women. This is particularly evident in her charge that the errors of modern pedagogues reproduce a contradiction that can be traced back to Rousseau.[51] In the first four books of *Emile*, Rousseau outlines the proper education of a young man to illustrate the pedagogical implications of the Enlightenment. His famous opening lines indicate that nature provides the authoritative grounds for education: 'Everything is good as it leaves the hands of the author of things; everything degenerates in the hands of man.'[52] While education should not therefore be reduced to books and scholarship, Rousseau concedes that Emile must nevertheless learn to live in society. Nature provides the normative foundation of his rationality, yet it is culture that realizes and directs his natural capacities. In Book V, Rousseau turns to the education of Sophie, Emile's future wife. 'In everything not connected with sex', he states, 'woman is man.'[53] This is to say that, to the extent that they share the same organs and bodily needs, men and women are equal. Yet he then asserts that nature has fixed a complementarity between the sexes: 'In everything connected with sex, woman and man are in every respect related and in every respect different.'[54] The difficulty of comparing men and women thus 'comes from

---

[47] [Holst,] *Bemerkungen über die Fehler unserer Modernen Erziehung*, 22.
[48] [Holst,] *Bemerkungen über die Fehler unserer Modernen Erziehung*, 34.
[49] [Holst,] *Bemerkungen über die Fehler unserer Modernen Erziehung*, 47.
[50] [Holst,] *Bemerkungen über die Fehler unserer Modernen Erziehung*, 74.
[51] [Holst,] *Bemerkungen über die Fehler unserer Modernen Erziehung*, 32.
[52] Rousseau, *Emile, or On Education*, 37.   [53] Rousseau, *Emile, or On Education*, 357.
[54] Rousseau, *Emile, or On Education*, 357.

the difficulty of determining what in their constitution is due to sex and what is not'. Rousseau draws the line along biological function, claiming that Sophie's education must be oriented towards the duties determined by her reproductive capacities. This is her 'proper purpose', or, in the 1762 German translation, her 'ureigene Bestimmung [innate vocation]'.[55] Thus a perfect woman and a perfect man 'ought not to resemble each other in mind any more than in looks'.[56]

Holst was not the first woman to identify an inconsistency between Rousseau's general theory of education and his depiction of Sophie. In *Adelaide and Theodore* (*Adèle et Théodore*, 1782), Stéphanie de Genlis scoffs at Sophie's education, which would leave her ill-equipped to educate her children, and contends that women must be educated for a higher calling.[57] In *Letters on the Works and Character of J. J. Rousseau* (*Lettres sur les ouvrages et le caractère de J. J. Rousseau*, 1788), Germaine de Staël rejects Rousseau's claim that Sophie's education must be commensurate to her weaker nature and argues that women should be taught to assume a subordinate role out of love.[58] In *Letters on Education* (1790), Catharine Macaulay praises the 'methods which he [Rousseau] prescribes to excite the attention of children, and to set their reasoning faculties in motion', yet insists that his attempt to distinguish between Emile and Sophie's perfection is nothing but the ravings of a 'licentious pedant'.[59] Indeed, in the 1780s and 1790s it was not uncommon for women writers to challenge Rousseau's views on women without rejecting his egalitarian ideals or denying his influence on their formation as pedagogues.

Holst's ambivalence towards Rousseau has a particular inflection in the context of German pedagogy. While she is clearly inspired by his immanent theory of a child's intellectual development, she seeks to expose a contradiction that the Philanthropinists inherit from Rousseau's veneration of nature. Holst contends that by curtailing a student's course of study to their physiology, Rousseau fails to apply the pedagogical theory he presents in the first four books of *Emile*. Drawing from her practical experience, she claims that a teacher cannot foretell a student's needs. It takes extended time to discern a student's natural capacity for learning

---

[55] Rousseau, *Emile, or On Education*, 362. C.f. Rousseau, *Émile oder über die Erziehung*, 417–18.
[56] Rousseau, *Emile, or On Education*, 358.
[57] Genlis, *Adèle et Théodore ou Lettres sur L'éducation*, I 45–6.
[58] [Staël,] *Lettres sur les ouvrages et le caractère de J. J. Rousseau*, 62.
[59] Macaulay, *Letters on Education*, 29, 128–9.

and a teacher's nurturing care to allow it to emerge on its own particular course.[60] Basedow and Campe reproduce the Rousseauian contradiction, for, despite claiming that education should be aligned to the student's natural capacities, they nevertheless prescribe a generic curriculum for every German boy and girl. The contradiction is especially clear in Campe's gendered elementary books, Holst argues, which purport to offer everything a boy or girl needs regarding 'morality, religion, political science, psychology, criticism, and the fine arts'.[61] Campe's elementary books make 'a strange contrast with the principles laid down by this scholar', for they do not cultivate deep and independent learning. Instead, they 'lead the pupil to the spring [of knowledge] too early', leaving them without a feeling for its meaning and significance as they 'rush to the next stream without ever bothering to return'.[62] Holst's contention is that elementary books are poor substitutes for an attentive teacher with a mastery of the sciences, who can introduce their fundamental principles at the right moment in a manner fitting to a student's particular needs. 'The less I can withhold my applause from almost everything Herr Campe presents in this fine treatise,' she concludes, 'the more I have to lament that he goes completely against his own rules in the application.'[63]

The editor of *Observations*, Johann Gottwerth Müller, clearly recognized the explosive nature of Holst's critique of the Philanthropinists. He included a preface in which he defends her position while distancing himself from the content of the text:

> If she is right, then the public owes her a debt of gratitude, that she has so candidly shared her observations and doubts. If she is wrong, then the builders and guardians of the new system of education gain all the more strength from it, if they can make her errors evident. In both cases she deserves to be heard, and all the more so for, as a practical educator, she is entitled to a voice.[64]

Müller saw that Holst's observations of child development, based on the extensive experience she had gained as a teacher, led her to emphasize

---

[60] [Holst,] *Bemerkungen über die Fehler unserer Modernen Erziehung*, 35.
[61] [Holst,] *Bemerkungen über die Fehler unserer Modernen Erziehung*, 38–9.
[62] [Holst,] *Bemerkungen über die Fehler unserer Modernen Erziehung*, 90.
[63] [Holst,] *Bemerkungen über die Fehler unserer Modernen Erziehung*, 38.
[64] Müller, 'Vorrede des Herausgebers', 4–5.

common human capacities before the considerations of sex or social circumstance. By rejecting Campe's gendered qualification of vocation and prioritizing the general human vocation to perfect one's natural capacities, Holst contends that all children, whether boys or girls, should follow a course of education tailored to their particular capabilities. The implication of her argument is that a perfect woman and a perfect man *could* resemble each other in mind, even if their respective physiologies require different kinds of perfection.

In contrast to the negative reception *On the Vocation of Woman* would later receive, *Observations* gained the esteem of the growing community of literary pedagogues. An early reviewer praised the text for showing 'much insight' into the practical demands of teaching (p. 117). Commending the author's learned treatment of the modern pedagogical literature, the reviewer offers a backhanded compliment by noting that there is nothing in 'the flow of ideas, the tone, and the language' to indicate that the author is a woman. One of Holst's eulogists notes that her book was 'received with the greatest approval' and that the scholarly community was immensely interested to discover its authorship when it was revealed by Johann Beckmann in 1806 (p. 114; see p. 111).[65] Beckmann declared that Holst had merited 'the privilege of being called by her own name', for the text demonstrates her standing as a 'scholar' in the field of pedagogy (p. 111).

1.2.2 Letters on Elisa

In 1799 and 1800, Holst published a series of four signed letters in August Lindemann's *Musarion: A Monthly Journal for Ladies* (*Musarion: Eine Monatsschrift für Damen*) in which she criticizes the model of feminine virtue depicted in Karoline von Wobeser's popular novel *Elisa, or Woman as She Ought to Be* (*Elisa, oder das Weib wie es seyn sollte*, 1795).[66] Wobeser was a champion of women's education, and wrote publicly against the restrictions placed on women's social opportunities. In the preface to the second edition of *Elisa* (published in 1798), she laments the elementary books and lessons in virtue that are supposed to constitute a woman's education. 'Half-enlightenment is always harmful,' she declares, 'but why

---

[65] The passage from Beckmann's article on Justi, in which he reveals Holst as the author of *Observations*, is included in Appendix 1.
[66] At the end of the fourth letter, Holst mentions a fifth and concluding letter that does not seem to have appeared. Holst, 'Vierter Briefe über *Elisa, oder das Weib wie es seyn sollte*', 341.

should women always be half-enlightened?'[67] To prove that learnedness does not undermine femininity, she calls for women to pursue 'true virtue' by means of a 'higher education of the mind [*höhere Ausbildung des Geistes*]'. Yet despite Wobeser's incisive prefatory remarks, Holst contends that the novel itself fails to challenge the actual social status of women and, instead, endorses a passive resignation to the complementarian ideal of marriage defended by the Philanthropinists.

Elisa presents the actions of a woman whose education enables her to pursue her own happiness within the unjust institutions that constrain her activities. While her father dies when she is only thirteen, Elisa has already received a thorough training in virtue, such that her moral sense is so firmly established that she is not in danger of straying from the right path. As an act of self-sacrifice to further her sister's happiness, she renounces her youthful love for Hermann von Birkenstein, and agrees to marry the unloved and overlooked Graf von Wallenheim. Despite his unjust whims and unfaithful conduct, she devotes herself to him unswervingly. Relinquishing all hope of material happiness, she displays a fierce sense of duty to Wallenheim and to her children, such that she dies in the consciousness of her absolute virtue as a faithful wife and a loving mother. In the preface, Wobeser explains that she crafted the narrative in such a way 'that pure morality alone, and the principles of positive religion, should form the basis of Elisa's actions'.[68] Elisa's satisfaction is underscored simply by her hope for happiness in the future life.

Holst praises Wobeser's depiction of Elisa's impassioned sense of duty in the face of domestic unhappiness as a moving fable. Yet as 'a contribution to morality', she claims, 'it is misguided'.[69] Holst explains that Wobeser presents feminine virtue as angelic self-sacrifice, such that 'the vocation of woman is a superhuman ideal'.[70] Not only does she overlook the immanent grounding of happiness, which has been wisely established by nature; Wobeser leaves the institution of marriage completely unchallenged:

> The whole atmosphere between Elisa and her husband is not as it should be between esteemed spouses; it is that of a despotic father against his still uneducated daughter. Elisa almost always behaves towards her husband in

---

[67] [Wobeser,] *Elisa, oder das Weib, wie es seyn sollte*, xi. Citations of *Elisa* refer to the third edition, which includes the preface to the second.
[68] [Wobeser,] *Elisa, oder das Weib, wie es seyn sollte*, x.
[69] Holst, 'Erster Brief über *Elisa, oder das Weib wie es seyn sollte*', 352.
[70] Holst, 'Zweiter Brief über *Elisa, oder das Weib wie es seyn sollte*', 32.

this way, not like a woman who knows, in addition to her duties, her dignity and her rights.[71]

The problem with Wobeser's portrayal of Elisa, according to Holst, is that Elisa's self-renunciation in response to Wallenheim's moral failings does not challenge the institutions that deny her the hope of material happiness. Instead, it recommends that women, if they are to be happy, 'must completely give up rational self-love'.[72] In contrast, Holst calls for women to choose carefully whom they marry.[73] Her critique of *Emile* notwithstanding, she recommends Rousseau's novel *Julie, or The New Heloise* (*Julie, ou la Nouvelle Héloïse*, 1761) as a superior exploration of feminine virtue.[74] In contrast to Wobeser's Elisa, Rousseau's Julie undergoes a slow transformation as she checks her passion and ultimately chooses a path that ensures her earthly happiness as an exemplary wife and mother. Like many women writers of her time, Holst identified strongly with Julie's desire for recognition, which outstrips the complementarian vision of marriage in which women are always the yielding party.[75] Julie's thorough education, which includes music, drawing, and foreign languages, gives her the ability not only to conduct herself according to the principles of virtue and humanity but also to feel her own sentiments and express them to her husband and in society. In Holst's comparison of the two novels, Rousseau's depiction of Julie offers a true contribution to morality, for it demonstrates that a woman's self-realization should not diminish but increase her sphere of influence, and, when required, direct her to confront social norms that inhibit mutual respect between husband and wife. Holst concludes by calling her women readers to view Elisa not as a model of feminine virtue but as a pitiable sister who has, through her own misjudgment, been denied fulfilment in this life.

---

[71] Holst, 'Vierter Brief über *Elisa, oder das Weib wie es seyn sollte*', 528.
[72] Holst, 'Erster Brief über *Elisa, oder das Weib wie es seyn sollte*', 347.
[73] 'Tell me who you marry', Holst declares, 'and I will tell you who you are.' Holst, 'Dritter Brief über *Elisa, oder das Weib wie es seyn sollte*', 224.
[74] Holst, 'Zweiter Brief über *Elisa, oder das Weib wie es seyn sollte*', 35; see also 'Dritter Brief über *Elisa, oder das Weib wie es seyn sollte*', 214–16.
[75] Holst's ambivalent relation to Rousseau echoes Staël's critique of Rousseau's caricature of Sophie and her strong identification with his depiction of Julie. See [Staël,] *Lettres sur les ouvrages et le caractère de J. J. Rousseau*, 32–3. In her review of the *Letters*, Wollstonecraft argues that Staël's praise of Julie's character is superficial and moralistic, and that the novel is in fact dangerous as a guide for women. See [Wollstonecraft,] 'Review of translation of *Letters on the Works and Character of J. J. Rousseau*', 360. For a discussion of the ambivalent response of women writers to Rousseau's depictions of Sophie and Julie, see Trouille, *Sexual Politics in the Enlightenment*, 39–45.

1.2.3 *On the Vocation of Woman*

Holst's rhetorical creativity, and her frustration at the barriers obstructing women's education, culminate in *On the Vocation of Woman to Higher Intellectual Education*. The book was published in 1802 by Heinrich Frölich, a precocious bookseller who established a publishing house in 1798 specializing in works of philosophy. Among Frölich's early publications are the journal *Athenäum*, edited by the Brothers Schlegel with the help of Schleiermacher and Novalis, and several works of philosophy by Goethe, Hoffmann, and La Motte-Fouqué. Frölich had received a recommendation from the bookseller Franz August Gottlob Campe, who had been impressed by Holst's pedagogical endeavours in Hamburg's neighbouring towns. What is immediately striking about the book is that it is published under Holst's own name and addressed to the general reading public.[76] In contrast to Holst's first book, in which the editor seeks to alleviate the reader's concerns with the author's gender, there is no editorial preamble. Holst's characteristically direct and combative prose weaves together the scholarly tone of *Observations* and the sisterly familiarity of her letters to call both the male reading public (*O Männer!*) and her women readers (*meine Freundinnen*) to reimagine woman as an unqualified bearer of the human vocation.

While *On the Vocation of Woman* is undoubtedly a landmark in the history of German philosophy, it was not the first defence of female education to be published under a woman's name. In 1742, Dorothea Christiane Erxleben (née Leporin), the first German woman to be awarded a doctoral degree, published *Rigorous Investigation of the Causes that Obstruct the Female Sex from Study* (*Gründliche Untersuchung der Ursachen, die das weibliche Geschlecht vom Studieren abhalten*), in which she exposes the prejudices underpinning the arguments made against the higher education of women and demands that women be admitted to universities.[77] In the opening essay of her book, Erxleben examines the arguments made by those who claim that the cognitive powers of women are insufficient to achieve learnedness (*Gelehrsamkeit*). Drawing from the work of Christian Thomasius and Christian Wolff, she defines learnedness as '*a rigorous cognition of such necessary and useful truths whereby the understanding and the will are improved and, consequently, the true happiness of the human being is*

---

[76] Several women had published works of philosophy under their own name before Holst, including Tullia d'Aragona, Margaret Cavendish, and Mary Astell. In the German states, however, Holst's achievement was extremely rare.

[77] This right was not granted to German women until 1900, although, as in the case of Erxleben, special permission could be granted for degrees to be awarded to women.

promoted.[78] In contrast to the superficial knowledge that women generally receive, learnedness consists of the practical knowledge that makes one capable of distinguishing between truth and falsehood, goodness and evil, and of using that knowledge to promote the happiness of self and others.[79] Appealing to both biblical and metaphysical grounds, Erxleben contends that women are in equal possession of reason to men, and that membership in the class of women has no bearing on the power and extent of one's capacities.

While Holst had heard of Erxleben's work, it appears that she was unaware that the book had been published (see p. 37). She introduces *On the Vocation of Woman* as a response to the 'one-sided instructions [regarding women's education made] by men alone' and justifies her call for a balanced reassessment of women's access to the sciences on the grounds that hitherto 'no woman has stood up and said aloud' that she finds no contradiction between her vocation as a human being and her calling as a woman (p. 9).

By fashioning herself as a lone advocate of women's education, Holst presents her argument in a way that is rhetorically powerful and yet contextually puzzling. She ignores several texts on education by women writers that were evidently known to her, including Wollstonecraft's *A Vindication of the Rights of Woman*, Wobeser's *Elisa*, and Gouges's *Declaration of the Rights of Woman*, and overlooks several others of which she was likely aware, including Mary Astell's *Serious Proposal to the Ladies*, Catherine Macaulay's *Letters on Education*, and Anne Barbauld's 'What is Education?'[80] The framing of her argument suggests that Holst was primarily concerned with the current debate in the German pedagogical literature regarding the vocation of woman. Before turning to Holst's response to the 'one-sided

---

[78] Leporin, *Gründliche Untersuchung der Ursachen, die das weibliche Geschlecht vom Studieren abhalten*, §21. I follow Dyck's translation in Erxleben, *Rigorous Investigation of the Causes that Obstruct the Female Sex from Study*, 44. For a study of Erxleben's account of learnedness in relation to Wolff and Thomasius, see Dyck, 'On Prejudice and the Limits to Learnedness'.

[79] Thomasius, whose work Erxleben invokes throughout her treatise, defines learnedness as follows: 'Learnedness is knowledge through which the human being is made capable of properly distinguishing the true from the false and the good from the bad, and of providing the true (or as the occasion demands, the probable) causes that ground it in order that he might promote his own temporal and lasting welfare, and that of others, in ordinary life and affairs'; Thomasius, *Introduction to the Doctrine of Reason*, 18.

[80] The extent of Holst's knowledge of other available texts on women's education requires further investigation. I have included notes in the translation where I detected resonances with other women writers, including Astell, Macaulay, and Barbauld.

instructions by men alone', it will be helpful to identify the gendered nature of the debate's central concept: *Bestimmung*.

1.3 The *Bestimmung* Debate

Scholars agree that the *Bestimmung* debate—what a human being is and should aspire to be—was one of the defining events in the German Enlightenment.[81] The celebrated philosophers of the movement, including Mendelssohn, Kant, Herder, and Fichte, called on the concept of vocation (*Bestimmung*) to redefine the rights of humanity according to what can be vindicated by reason. The debate originated in Johann Spalding's *Consideration of the Vocation of the Human Being* (*Betrachtung über die Bestimmung des Menschen*, 1748), which was enormously popular and reprinted eleven times during his lifetime. Spalding defends the Enlightenment vision of rational faith, claiming that what one does with one's life must be determined as an instance of *Selbstdenken*.[82] His aim is to couch the project of autonomy in shared anthropological conditions, such that the highest good of a human life involves the perfection of the capacities (*Fähigkeiten*) given by nature.[83] The task of the philosopher is to identify the stages of education (*Bildung*) through which one must progress on the way to maturity, including a transition from morality to religion and reason. These stages inform the structure and orientation of a child's early education (*Erzeihung*) to shape them into a citizen of the world.

While the *Bestimmung* debate has gained extensive attention in recent literature, scholars seldom note that the rights afforded to the human being were not extended to women. In the wake of Spalding's *Vocation of the Human Being*, Rousseau's *Emile* placed the question of education at the heart of social reform.[84] Rousseau's physiological account of woman's proper purpose (or in the German translation, her *ureigene Bestimmung*) appealed to philosophers in Germany who were concerned by the rapid social change occurring in France, which threatened to undermine the

---

[81] Preuss, 'Translator's Introduction'; Zammito, *Kant, Herder, and the Birth of Anthropology*; James, 'Fichte on the Vocation of the Scholar and the (Mis)Use of History'; Printy, 'The Determination of Man'.
[82] Zammito, *Kant, Herder, and the Birth of Anthropology*, 166.
[83] Spalding, *Betrachtung über die Bestimmung des Menschen*, 82.
[84] Rousseau's *Émile, ou De l'éducation* immediately appeared in German translation as *Emile oder Über die Erzeihung* (1762), and played a vital role in the *Bestimmung* debate. See Hermann, *Aufklärung und Erziehung*, 99.

foundational role of the family in civic life. The final decade of the eighteenth century saw an explosion of texts on the vocation of woman, including Ernst Brandes's *On Women* (*Ueber die Weiber*, 1787), Christoph Meiners's *History of the Female Sex* (*Geschichte der weiblichen Geschlecht*, 1788–1802), Joachim Heinrich Campe's *Fatherly Advice For My Daughter* (*Väterlicher Rath für meine Tochter*, 1789), Johann Ludwig Ewald's *The Art of Becoming a Good Girl, Wife, Mother, and Housewife* (*Die Kunst, ein gutes Mädchen, eine gute Gattin, Mutter und Hausfrau zu werden*, 1802), and Karl Friedrich Pockels's *Characteristics of the Female Sex* (*Versuch einer Charakteristik des weiblichen Geschlechts*, 1797–1802). While these texts acknowledge that men and women are both in possession of two vocations—a general vocation as humans and a particular vocation as members of a sex—they did not envisage the respective tasks of balancing to be equal. According to Rousseau's complementarian account of gendered roles,

> There is no parity between the two sexes in regard to the consequence of sex. The male is male only at certain moments. The female is female her whole life or at last during her whole youth. Everything constantly recalls her sex to her; and, to fulfil its function well, she needs a constitution which corresponds to it.[85]

While men are required to balance the general human vocation to perfect their natural capacities with their particular vocation as husband, father, and master of the house, they are not required to do so at every moment. Once they leave the household and enter the public sphere, they are free to set their own ends and enjoy the full rights afforded to the human being. In contrast, women are constantly constrained to the sphere of influence determined by their sexual nature and must subordinate their activities to those ends. It would be a contradiction—a violation of reason—for a woman to set her own ends; her rationality can be expressed as activity only through her husband.[86]

---

[85] Rousseau, *Emile, or On Education*, 361.

[86] Consider Fichte's logical determination of sexuality in the 1796 version of his *Wissenschaftslehre*: 'it is not at all contrary to reason for the first sex [the male] to have as an end the satisfaction of its sexual drive, for it can be satisfied through activity: but it is absolutely contrary to reason for the second sex to have as its end the satisfaction of its sexual drive as an end, for it would then have mere passivity as its end.' Sexuality for Fichte conditions the expression of rationality. For a woman to adopt an active stance in regard to her sexuality would be to forfeit the status of rationality, and thus of humanity. Fichte, *Grundlage des Naturrechts nach*

Carol Sotiropoulos argues that the proliferation of texts on the vocation of woman staged a 'conservative reaction' against the social upheaval of Europe in the late eighteenth century.[87] Yet it is vital to note that the assertion of complementarianism was not counter to the Enlightenment. Indeed, the texts 'by men alone' called on fundamental tenets of the Enlightenment—including vocation (*Bestimmung*), education (*Bildung*), and early education (*Erzeihung*)—to address a growing anxiety about the changing conditions of citizen society.[88] In *Fatherly Advice for My Daughter*, for instance, Campe's concern with the instability of sexual roles motivates his decision to include physiology in the curriculum for girls; they must learn that a woman's 'sickly constitution' renders her unfit for strenuous study or public office.[89] In *On Women*, Brandes's discomfort at the social change unfolding across Europe prompts his critique of the 'false culture' that causes women to become uncomfortable with their dependent status. His goal is to redirect culture back to nature's unchanging path via 'a detailed and rational account of the vocation and capacities of the female sex'.[90]

The influx of texts by men on the vocation of woman affirms Michel Foucault's observation that the power of discourse is established through performative repetition.[91] While this power was exercised through the publication of books, the growing popularity of journals in the late eighteenth century provided women with a forum in which to expose the fragility of that discourse.[92] A powerful example can be found in a two-part essay published anonymously in Christoph Wieland's journal *Teutscher Merkur* in 1791, entitled 'Some Characteristics and Principles Necessary for Happiness in Marriage' ('Ueber einige zum Glück der Ehre notwendige Eigenschaften und Grundsätze'). The essay consists of a letter from a married woman to her sister, soon to be married. While much of the advice is conventional, its

---

Prinzipien der Wissenschaftslehre, 394. I follow Michael Baur's translation in Fichte, *Foundations of Natural Right*, 266.

[87] Sotiropoulos, 'The Case of Amalia Holst', 113.

[88] For an analysis of the role of gender in practices of nation-building, see Yuval-Davis, *Gender and Nation*, 21–5.

[89] Campe, *Väterlicher Rath für meine Tochter*, 26.

[90] Brandes, *Ueber die Weiber*, 17–18. C.f. Holst's examination of 'false culture' on p. 105.

[91] Foucault, *The Order of Things*, 111.

[92] Of course, not all journals founded in the late eighteenth century made space for independent women writers. Journals such as F. J. Bertuch and G. M. Kraus's *Journal of Luxury and Fashion* (*Journal des Luxus und der Moden*) promoted luxurious living as a fundamental part of the economic and moral life of the German states, filling the educational vacuum left by a woman's discontinued education with ideas that shape her as a passive and decorative object. For a study of women's journals at the time, see Madland, 'Three Late-Eighteenth Century Women's Journals'.

author—later revealed to be the travel writer and poet Emilie von Berlepsch—includes an attack on male writers who seek to define the vocation of woman in reference to men.[93] Citing Brandes's *On Women*, Berlepsch contends that society's low esteem for women is a form of 'misogyny [*Misogynie*]'.[94] She declares that the 'negative consequences of this misogynist tone on society and morals in general cannot be doubted', and that its 'influence on the happiness of marriage, as unerring as it is, will perhaps be recognized by many'. Berlepsch seeks to alert her readers to the fact that misogyny contaminates the minds of husbands, making it impossible for women to take personal satisfaction in their traditional duties. To resist the growing constraints on a woman's happiness in marriage, she redeploys the prevailing Enlightenment discourse by calling for woman's 'independence [*Selbständigkeit*]'.[95] If the current social conditions are to be challenged, women must learn to 'stand alone' and develop a critical 'way of thinking' without reference to the opinions of their husbands.[96] While her solution is one of mitigation rather than reform, Berlepsch's argument nevertheless reveals the instability of gender relations at the close of the eighteenth century. If the present treatment of women is not a natural ordinance but a matter of social construction, then it can and even should be otherwise than what it is. Berlepsch contends that the power for change lies in the hands of woman, who is not a mere mother and housewife but, as the first teacher of her children, 'also an educator [*Erzieherin*]', responsible for shaping the future generation of citizens.[97]

2 The Text

2.1 Overview

While Holst refuses to confine her critique of misogyny to a journal for women, her argument in *On the Vocation of Woman* nevertheless shares the critical orientation of Berlepsch's essay. Like Berlepsch, Holst unveils the pernicious influence of male writers who seek to define the vocation of

---

[93] Berlepsch's essay anticipates several of the arguments presented in Holst's *On the Vocation of Woman*. For a study of Berlepsch's literary achievements, and the major themes in her essay, see Dawson, *The Contested Quill*, 258–62.
[94] [Berlepsch,] 'Ueber einige zum Glück', 83.
[95] [Berlepsch,] 'Ueber einige zum Glück', 89.
[96] [Berlepsch,] 'Ueber einige zum Glück', 90.
[97] [Berlepsch,] 'Ueber einige zum Glück', 100–1.

woman by reference to man and seeks to transform the normative definition of woman from within traditional roles. She begins the text by identifying two criticisms levelled against women's education. The first is that a woman's physical and intellectual capacities mean that she is unable to keep up with men in matters of higher learning. The second is that to aspire to do so would contradict her individual duties. She observes that if either criticism were true, then it would be pointless to try to refute them. The first would entail that a woman *could* not refute them, the second that she *should* not (p. 10). Holst dismisses the first charge fairly quickly: there is no substantive evidence that women are intellectually inferior to men (pp. 11–12). Indeed, there is extensive evidence in the sciences, arts, and letters that women have the capacity to keep pace with men, even exceed them in some areas. Yet *should* women do so? The structure of the book is shaped by her response to the second charge. The first chapter turns directly to the Philanthropinists' claim that higher education contradicts a woman's threefold calling and lays down her general response. The following chapters examine the three duties in turn, aiming 'to prove that a higher education of woman does not contradict her threefold calling [*Beruf*] but rather elevates and ennobles it' (p. 42). The final chapter considers the case of unmarried women and concludes with a call to women to cultivate their minds through what Holst terms 'higher intellectual education'.[98]

In the first chapter, 'Does Higher Education of the Mind Contradict the Proximate Calling of Woman as Wife, Mother, and Housewife?', Holst attacks the connection made by male writers between the present subordinate status of women and the natural order of things. The first step is to expose the error that permits male writers to deny women an equal share in the human vocation. This error is to claim that 'physical strength is proportionate to mental strength' (p. 11). Building on her argument in *Observations*, Holst singles out Rousseau, whose identification of mental and physical strength infected the Philanthropinists with a false anthropology that obliterates 'the line that separates the state of nature from civil society' (p. 14). By doing so, he 'proposed to drive humanity back into the state of nature, without understanding that remaining in this state was against nature's intention' (p. 13). Holst then turns to the evidence of history and

---

[98] What Holst means by 'higher intellectual education' is not immediately clear, much to the frustration of one her early reviewers (p. 120). Her most elaborate definition occurs towards the end of Chapter 1, where she outlines three principles of higher intellectual education. See Section 2.2.4.

catalogues an array of notable women who have had a significant influence—for good or for ill—on the course of human civilization. The point of her catalogue is not to vindicate the capabilities of women; she has already dismissed the idea that women are not capable of higher education. It is, rather, to demonstrate the inescapable co-dependence of men and women in the progress of civilization, especially through the education of children.

Holst concludes the first chapter by raising a possible objection that, given the extensive demands of the threefold calling, women will not have time to indulge in higher education. Her response begins in Chapter 2 with 'Woman Considered as Wife'. She interrogates a claim found in the writings of Campe, Brandes, Pockels, and Meiners that women exist for the sake of men. Here the impact of Theodor Gottlieb von Hippel on Holst's argument is particularly evident. In *On Marriage* (*Über die Ehe*), Hippel rejected the prevailing view that child-rearing is the end of marriage and argued instead that each marriage is singular, such that every couple must determine their own goals together. Holst develops a similar egalitarian formulation of the end of marriage: 'to form the highest ideal of humanity in the most beautiful union' (p. 43). Attacking the claim that a learned woman will lack femininity, she argues that a higher intellectual education in fact enables women to fulfil their wifely duties with decisive action.

In Chapter 3, 'The Educated Woman as Mother', Holst sets out to show that higher education does not contradict a woman's calling as mother, and, moreover, that it is in fact necessary for the fundamental task of motherhood: the education of her children. As 'first educator', the reach of the mother's sphere of influence cannot be overstated (p. 68). Thus, if mothers are not empowered to prepare their children to be citizens of the world, the Philanthropinists' efforts to reform the schools and establish institutes for rural workers will prove to be useless. Holst examines the state of the industry schools in and around Hamburg and concludes that the single most effective way to enhance the living conditions of the working class is to educate girls to become reflective teachers of their children.

In Chapter 4, 'The Educated Woman as Housewife', Holst upturns Rousseau's presentation of Sophie as a subservient creature who labours tirelessly to ensure Emile's happiness with a reformed conception of the domestic sphere in which husband and wife both find their own happiness in the happiness of the other. The sphere of influence assigned to the housewife extends far beyond the happiness of her husband and children, for it also concerns the neighbouring community. In all circumstances, the educated housewife is a model of composure (*Gelassenheit*)—the mark of Enlightened subjectivity—as she serenely adapts herself to the demands of any situation she encounters.[99] Holst's tone is, at times, overbearing, as she sketches in detail how the educated housewife condescends to care for the moral and spiritual well-being of her servants and neighbouring workers. Again, her aim is to demonstrate that the Philanthropinists' efforts to ameliorate the living conditions of the rural working class through the construction of industrial schools would be better served by empowering middle- and upper-class women to promote the moral and physical health of their communities by removing superstition and placing the right kind of incentives in place. Yet in doing so she betrays a belief that civilization requires a class system in which the workers must settle for subordinate purposes (p. 94).[100]

The final chapter of the text, 'On the Education of Woman in the Unmarried State', is more radical than it might seem at first glance. Many of the Philanthropinists inferred from the subordinate status of women that, to cite Campe, 'marriage is really the only...means [for a woman] to obtain a definite condition, sphere of influence, protection, reputation, and a higher level of freedom and independence'.[101] In contrast, Holst carves out a sphere of influence for unmarried women without reference to men. The modern conditions of the upper and middle classes, she notes, are such that some women will remain unmarried.[102] Of the various modes of employment available to such women, Holst recommends the role of educator as the one most befitting to her vocation as a human being. She argues that the unmarried woman must pursue an even higher intellectual education than her married peers, for the temptations and vices facing women who remain in such a state are greater than those facing married women. Yet the opportunities are also greater. Only the unmarried woman can dedicate her full attention to higher intellectual education and use her knowledge to benefit the future of humanity though her teaching and reflections on the sciences.

[99] For a study of the role of *Gelassenheit* in the construction of Enlightened femininity, see Menhennet, 'Heroic Femininity in the Popular Novel of the "Goethezeit"', 263.
[100] A similar tension between women's rights and the acceptance of class divisions can be found in the work of other middle-class feminists of Holst's time, including Staël, Genlis, and More. See Section 2.2.5.
[101] Campe, *Väterlicher Rath für meine Tochter*, 33.
[102] Basedow also acknowledged that some women 'will not be sought in marriage', and thus recommends that a girl's education might outstrip the demands of marriage. However, this is not to 'become an expert in this or that art' but simply to ensure that she can 'amuse herself and arouse no disgust in casual critics'. Basedow, *Ausgewählte Schriften*, 182.

Holst contends that it is not higher education (*höhere Bildung*) but miseducation (*Verbildung*) that leads to the vices that are often found in unmarried women and concludes by calling her women readers to strive for the ongoing education of their minds.

2.2 Reconstructing Holst's Arguments

2.2.1 Cataloguing Learned Women

To highlight the mutual dependence of the sexes in the progress and decline of civilization, Holst begins her first chapter with a catalogue of notable women who have influenced society for good or ill. Her concern with establishing a transcultural identity of women across time and place distinguishes Holst from several of her contemporary women writers, such as Staël, who seldom reference other women. The practice of listing prominent women throughout history was an established genre in German literature during the seventeenth and eighteenth centuries. Works such as Peter Paul Finauer's *General Historical Inventory of Learned Women* (*Allgemeines historisches Verzeichnis gelehrter Frauenzimmer*, 1761) and Christian August Wichmann's *History of Famous Women* (*Geschichte berühmter Frauenzimmer*, 1772) catalogue learned women—including women philosophers—to show that dedication to study does not disqualify a woman from fulfilling her threefold duty. Yet, as Ebbersmeyer notes, after the publication of Wichmann's *History of Famous Women* in 1772 there is a conspicuous absence of texts celebrating *gelehrte Frauen*—an absence that coincides with the explosion of texts that define the vocation of woman in such a way that learnedness contradicts the very nature of femininity.[103] Holst redeploys the suppressed genre to deconstruct the physiological determination of sex and to re-establish the interconnection between the sexes in all matters of civic life. In contrast to her contemporary male writers, who define gender roles according to a clean break between the public and private spheres, Holst avows that history tells a story in which the sexes are 'too closely connected, each has too powerful an influence on the other, not to have this certain effect' (p. 22). From her catalogue of notable women, she concludes that, 'since the influence of women intervenes

---

[103] Ebbersmeyer, 'From a "memorable place" to "drops in the ocean"', 445–8.

so powerfully in the driving forces of human happiness, much—infinitely much—depends on the education of women' (p. 28).

If the early reviews indicate the broader reception of her book, Holst's strategy failed to convince those committed to a normative conception of woman as the passive sex. The reviewer for *Hamburg und Altona* readily admits that her catalogue of learned women proves that women *can* grasp the higher sciences. Yet he denies that it proves that they *should*, for it fails to demonstrate 'for a single one that she has fulfilled her threefold calling in a humane way' (p. 123). This claim is not strictly true; Holst's discussion of Dorothea Erxleben, the first German woman to receive a doctorate and the first woman in Europe to be accredited as a medical doctor, includes testimony from Erxleben's son that, 'despite her exceptional calling, she was a good wife, mother, and housewife, and fulfilled all the obligations of these affairs' (p. 37). Details aside, it was never Holst's intention to provide model cases of female learnedness. Rather, her aim was to show that, given the interdependence of men and women in the progress of civilization, it is an insult to reason and a disaster for civilization if women are not permitted to freely develop their minds.

2.2.2 The Sexless Mind
While Holst pursues a diverse range of strategies in the text, her argument centres on a single claim that women are first and foremost members of humanity, and thus hold an equal share in the human vocation to perfect their natural capacities. This argument does not deny a meaningful difference between the sexes but aims to redefine how sex mediates the expression of humanity. Holst begins by affirming a fundamental tenet of the Enlightenment: as human, woman is 'a perfectible being fit for developing its faculties, both physical and moral' (p. 9). Yet she then notes that, as woman, she is also the bearer of a 'gentle, amiable, and often unrewarded...threefold calling' (p. 9). Here it is vital to note Holst's distinction between the human vocation (*Bestimmung*) and woman's threefold calling (*Beruf*): her aim is to replace Campe's claim that women are bearers of *two* vocations, one of which places a normative constraint on the other, with a single vocation that is expressed through the modalities of one's sex. As far as the mind is concerned, men and women are not complementary but equal.

If men and women bear an equal calling to perfect their capacities, why do women, at present, tend to be intellectually inferior? Holst diagnoses the present disparity between men and women as a fault on the part of men, specifically their 'failure to acknowledge the possibility of the same constitution of thinking in the female sex' (p. 16). Building on the argument she began in *Observations*, Holst pins the blame on Rousseau, who gave this failure a platform. By prioritizing the state of nature, Rousseau provided the Philanthropinists with philosophical grounds to take physical strength as a normative foundation of right. Holst contends that, by connecting right with strength, the Philanthropinists grossly miscalculate the advantages afforded by culture, which 'outweigh, by an indescribably great measure, everything we could say in favour of the state of nature' (p. 14). To assume that physical and mental strength are proportionate is baffling for anyone who claims to be educated, she asserts, for physical strength loses its value 'as soon as humanity passes from the state of nature to the state of culture' (p. 12). Through this transition we forfeit the right of violence and receive the immeasurably higher right of justice.

To counter Rousseau's influence on her male contemporaries, Holst presents an alternative account of the social contract in which the transition from the state of nature to the state of culture consists in a conception of right wherein the scale of physical strength is replaced by 'the judgment seat of sound reason' (p. 43). This transition was ordained by nature all along, she contends, which intended that human beings should not remain locked in violent contagion but rather 'develop all of their powers' (p. 15). Once human beings have made the transition from nature to culture, rights are no longer determined by physical strength but by reason alone. The Enlightenment project can thus only be completed when members of both sexes acknowledge the same constitution of thinking in the other. This argument was played out again and again in nineteenth-century feminist texts. In *The Subjection of Women* (1869), for instance, John Stuart Mill and Harriet Taylor argue that while men established their dominance in a time when nature held sway, we have now moved beyond nature in other respects and it is time to follow through by moving beyond male dominance.[104]

2.2.3 Exposing the Dynamics of Power

Having exposed the blatant error perpetuated by her male contemporaries, Holst dares to ask *why* it has been so readily made. Her answer delivers a penetrating insight into the dynamics of power: 'Only the human inclination that makes one unwilling to share rights that have been enjoyed

---

[104] Mill, *The Subjection of Women*, 127–31.

exclusively for so long' (p. 16). The standpoint Holst adopts as a woman anticipates the critical insights soon to be made by Hegel, Marx, and Nietzsche, who unearthed the ideological structure of Enlightenment self-fashioning. Applied to gender, however, it resonates more deeply with the feminist writings of Mill, Hedwig Dohm, and Simone de Beauvoir.[105] Those who continue to claim that women are naturally unsuited to play an equal role in the cultural sphere have received their positional power due to the contingency of strength rather than the necessity of reason, 'and men would not like to admit this' (p. 18). The pleasure men take in their happy state ensnares them in a state of self-deception, unable to realize the immeasurable advantages of culture and thus stifling the progress of Enlightenment.

Holst's critical diagnosis of the workings of power draws attention to the Philanthropinists' obsession with an imaginary learned woman and their disinterest in the many *actual* women who, due to vices that stem from their ignorance, genuinely overlook their duties. For Holst, this obsession betrays a particular male fear that a learned woman lacks femininity. No one complains when a man is educated beyond his particular calling. Indeed, an excess in learnedness is praised among men. Yet as soon as a woman gains knowledge that extends beyond the requirements of her threefold duty, men feel compelled to write long treatises to implore other men to see that a learned woman will be less pleasing, affectionate, and yielding. At one point, Holst pushes even further to claim that such writings betray the male fear that 'in the course of their higher education women may think of calling to account the many injustices they have had to endure' (p. 60). Yet this claim remains undeveloped.

Despite the radical implications of her critique, Holst does not advocate for women's participation in the public sphere. Every time she gets close to displaying the full implications of her critique, she seems to pull back, and her focus remains fixed on the advancement of women's education.[106] Any attempt to restrict the higher education of woman must fail, she argues, for

---

[105] In 'Nietzsche on Women', for instance, Dohm turns Nietzsche's critique of power back on his own work to show that his image of the overman is self-undermining: if his partner is reduced to a slave, the overman is not a true master but remains ensnared by the subservient relation. See Dohm, 'Nietzsche on Women', 131. In *The Second Sex*, Beauvoir presents a striking critique of the role of male power in the construction of truth: 'Representation of the world, like the world itself, is the work of men; they describe it from their own point of view, which they confuse with absolute truth'; Beauvoir, *The Second Sex*, 175.

[106] For just a few examples of Holst's hesitancy to follow through on her critique, see pp. 29, 60, and 90.

the level of education required to fulfil her threefold calling is without limit. Here Holst turns the discourse of the Philanthropinists on its head, advocating for women's study of physiology, anthropology, natural history, geography, the arts, and philosophy on their own terms. To instruct their children in such a way that does not simply skim the surface but offers 'deep knowledge [*tiefe Kenntnisse*]' (p. 35), women require far more than elementary books could provide. This is especially true for practical philosophy, which ties the disciplines together:

> But as far as practical philosophy is concerned, which reassures and strengthens one's convictions through the investigations of important truths about *how*, *where*, and *why*, I maintain that these investigations, as the highest duty of all thinking beings, cannot collide with their individual duties. Nature would have to contradict itself. (p. 41)

A contradiction between the human vocation (the highest duty of thinking beings) and woman's threefold calling (her individual duties) is impossible, Holst contends, for both are given by nature. Of course, one could claim that if a woman 'were to become a speculative philosopher'—if she were to dedicate her life entirely to higher knowledge—she might fail to 'fulfil her duties as a wife, mother, and housewife' (p. 41). Holst concedes that such a calling may interfere with a woman's duties, yet only if she were to 'rise so high as to create her own philosophical system' (p. 41). As we see in a Leibniz or a Kant, the creation of a philosophical system often requires an unmarried life. Yet even here Holst refuses to concede a limit on female learnedness. How much would society actually lose if a woman were to dedicate her life to philosophy? 'No more than they lost through the celibacy of Kant or Leibniz, who enriched the world merely through the immortal works they birthed as children of their minds' (p. 41). Even professional philosophy should not fall outside the remit of woman's possibilities. If we accept the learned dedication of Leibniz and Kant as a legitimate expression of the human vocation, it follows that the particular calling of one's sex can be suspended for non-reproductive social ends.

2.2.4 The Principles of Higher Intellectual Education

The exceptional circumstance of professional philosophy aside, Holst lays down three guiding principles for the higher intellectual education of women in general. The first is that 'the education of women must be entirely free' (p. 31). Here Holst builds on the theory of education she presented in

Observations, in which there can be no predetermined restriction on where a student's genius may lead. This principle completely rejects the idea that elementary books can form the basis of a woman's education. Even the ancient texts must be available to her, which requires the extensive learning of languages. And philosophy, 'the science that teaches us our true conditions in regard to the highest being, ourselves, and the external world', must be the soil from which all her knowledge grows (p. 31).

The second principle is that the higher intellectual education of women 'must flow from the only true source: humankind's duty to develop all its powers and to contribute to the well-being of the whole as an active member' (p. 31). Holst anticipated that her book would be criticized by her male interlocutors for displaying an inordinate desire to transcend her station. Once more she overturns this criticism by pointing to the present social conditions, which make it practically impossible for women to acquire a legitimate desire for higher learning. Inordinate desires arise when women are denied the true source of knowledge. If education does not spring 'from the duty of humankind, nothing could encourage us to develop our intellect other than the wretched desire to shine, and what a miserable purpose that would be!' (p. 32). Echoing Wobeser's lament in the Preface to *Elisa*, Holst contends that true 'knowledge makes us humble and self-effacing; half-baked and superficial knowledge makes us vain and proud' (p. 31).

The third principle places a constraint on women's higher intellectual education: it 'cannot be extended to all individuals of the female sex' (p. 32). Holst concedes that the higher intellectual education of women 'extends only to the upper and middle classes'. Here we see that her goal is not to present an unbridled defence of civic rights; the call for women's higher intellectual education already stands at the limits of acceptability.[107] It would be ridiculous to require the higher intellectual education of the wife of a day labourer or tradesman, Holst argues, for the sphere of influence associated with learned knowledge is beyond the practical remit of the lower classes. While she claims that 'the gifts of nature are and must be unequally distributed' (p. 32), Holst's defence of women's access to higher education clearly undermines any notion that women from the lower classes

---

[107] One of Holst's reviewers attacks her on this point, arguing that if humanity is conflated with learnedness, such that the vocation of *all* human beings is to perfect their powers through higher intellectual development, then higher education must be offered to every citizen of the German states. This is impossible, he argues, for humanity is perfected through taking up *one* calling. *Hamburg und Altona*, 357.

are less able. 'How many philosophical minds,' she muses, 'which lacked the opportunity for education but could have competed with a Kant or a Leibniz, slumber unnoticed and unused behind the plough!' (p. 40).

2.2.5 Holst's Prejudices

Nevertheless, the reader of *On the Vocation of Woman* is faced with the difficult task of discerning whether Holst's more unsavoury remarks are offered to reassure her readers that she is not a radical ('I do not want to be a preacher of revolution [*Revolutionspredigerin*]', p. 10) or whether they are genuine expressions of prejudice. There are two especially troubling cases. The first is Holst's scathing remarks about the Jewish origins of Christianity. At the start of the chapter on marriage (Chapter 2), Holst seeks to undermine the arguments of male writers who appeal to the Bible to justify the ongoing subordination of women. Brushing aside two millennia of scriptural interpretation, she places the Book of Genesis before the judgment seat of sound reason and finds nothing more than a 'collected fragments of the dark legends of human understanding in its infancy' (p. 46). She dismisses the Jews as an 'uncivilized people' (p. 45) among whom 'women have been despised and suppressed' (p. 46) and rejects the Hebrew scriptures as a legitimate foundation for a people who claim to be civilized. She then attempts to recover a non-Jewish Christ from the snares of Paul, who 'founded the Christian religion on Judaism completely against the intentions and spirit of its gentle founder' (p. 46).

Holst's critique of Christianity's Jewish origins arguably falls short of the anti-Semitism that was nascent in her time, for she shows no interest in secular arguments of Jewish usury and cunning that emerge in the nineteenth century. She seems more embedded within the religiously motivated anti-Judaism of the eighteenth century, which established the inferiority of the Jews from scriptural and cultural sources. Nevertheless, her anti-Judaism cannot be dismissed as a mere rhetorical move to establish solidarity with her readers. Far from gaining their rapport, her dismissive attitude to biblical criticism gave her reviewers grounds to dismiss her intellectual credibility (p. 119). Holst's strategy is all the more surprising when one considers that Hippel used the very passages of scripture she derides in order to defend women's rights. In *On Improving the Status of Women* (*Über die bürgerliche Verbesserung der Weiber*, 1792), which Holst commends in her Preface, Hippel critiques the ongoing subordination of women through a subversive reading of Genesis that prioritizes the equal creation of man and woman in the first creation account.[108] The narrative of the Fall is not a remonstration of feminine desire, he contends, but a vindication of *woman* as the first to take steps towards enlightenment. Ignoring Hippel's radical interpretation, Holst sides instead with the rationalist biblical criticism of Émilie du Châtelet's *Examinations of the Bible* and Jean-Baptiste-Claude Delisle de Sales's *Philosophy of Nature*, in which the scriptures are crudely evaluated against the ideals of the Enlightenment and found to be in want.[109]

The second case is Holst's acceptance of the current status of the working class. While she does not explicitly lay down her views on class relations, her argument seems to be that nature has ordained some level of inequality in the growth of civilization, such that inequality is and remains a driving force in the civilizing process. Similar views can be found in her contemporaries. In *Idea for a Universal History with a Cosmopolitan Aim* (1784), Kant proposed that the antagonism that arises from inequality can be seen as 'unsociable sociability', such that human affairs advance not according to the design of individual human beings but according to a plan of nature.[110] While we might *desire* equality, nature acts differently and yet always with our best interests in mind.[111] Clearly Holst does not think that the working class are less capable (recall her lamentation of the Kants and Leibnizes slumbering behind the plough). Her argument is rather that, given the hidden providence of nature, the working class 'must satisfy themselves with subordinate purposes' (p. 32).

Contemporary readers will feel the contradiction between Holst's defence of women's access to higher education and her classism, and perhaps conclude that her rejection of the working class from the scope of higher education cannot be genuine. On closer inspection, however, such a conclusion is difficult to maintain, for her acceptance of class-based society is thoroughly intertwined with her defence of women's education—a view found in other

---

[108] Hippel, *On Improving the Status of Women*, 65.
[109] See Du Châtelet, 'Examination of Exodus', in *Selected Philosophical and Scientific Writings*, 207–13; Sales, 'On Humanity in Relation to God', in *De la philosophie de la nature*, I 247–368.
[110] Kant, *Idea for a Universal History with a Cosmopolitan Aim*, 8:20.
[111] Kant's argument can assist us to understand Holst's broader reliance on nature's plan, which operates for the good of humanity *despite* human intentions: 'Here there is no other way out for the philosopher—who, regarding human beings and their play in the large, cannot at all presuppose any rational *aim of theirs*—than to try whether he can discover an *aim of nature* in this nonsensical course of things human; from which aim a history in accordance with a determinate plan of nature might nevertheless be possible even of creatures who do not behave in accordance with their own plan.' Kant, *Idea for a Universal History with a Cosmopolitan Aim*, 8:17.

conservative feminists such as Hannah More.[112] Holst attacks the Philanthropinists for restricting women's education to knowledge that is essential to their threefold calling, and yet she praises Friedrich Eberhard von Rochow's institutes for developing a standard curriculum tailored to the situation of working-class children (p. 94). She laments the fall of middle-class women into poverty, who must resort to handcraft to make a living ('But what a poor and intellectually depressing business it is to have to work for the vanity and luxury of others!', p. 74), and yet she argues that servants must align their labour to an end set by their masters. She contends that middle-class children must be offered reasons for every classroom rule, and yet she asserts that adult servants must be treated as children and instructed by means of incentives (p. 98). Even one of her reviewers, who vehemently opposes the idea that women should have access to higher education, criticizes Holst's paternalism. Never has one of noble birth, the reviewer laments, proven to be 'so aristocratic, so dismissive and dictatorial towards the most numerous class of people' (p. 124). This lament, however, is not so much directed against the idea of subordinate purposes as against Holst's instance that the middle and upper classes pursue higher purposes *exclusively*—a view she shares with Du Châtelet. While the rational nature of every human being must be directed towards higher purposes, the reviewer argues that the physical part of us must, from time to time, settle for subordinate purposes. Once again, Holst's view of the working class does little to advance her cause, so it seems unlikely that she simply intends to win the favour of her conservative readers. It is more probable that, despite her lifelong efforts to advance women's education, Holst retained a belief that class society had a necessary role to play in nature's plan, which reflects the specific character of her Protestant faith. The full implications of her radical argument to extend higher education to those unacknowledged by power thus remain unexplored.

2.2.6 The Public Status of Women
The tension between Holst's defence of woman's full participation in the human vocation and her desire to appear as a reformer rather than a revolutionary leaves the public status of women unresolved. This stands in

---

[112] Like Holst, More encouraged middle-class women to extend their activities and interests beyond the home, and to improve the living conditions of working-class men and women through piety and educational philanthropy, yet she retained a class-based politics. For instance, see More's critique of the supposedly emancipatory politics of the French Revolution in *Considerations on Religion and Public Education*, 18–21.

contrast to Hippel, who argued explicitly that women's sphere of influence must be extended such that they can enrol in a university, seek a profession, and take up positions of public office (see Section 3.2). Nevertheless, while she does not explicitly advocate a radical change in civic relations, Holst's critique of male prejudice and her appeal for the reform of women's education cannot leave the public status of women unaltered. Consider the following determination of the sexes, which is typical of Holst's ambiguity: 'As human beings, both are in completely equal relationship to humanity, even if as a consequence of our civic relations, as citizens of the state [*Staatsbürger*], the same cannot be said of both sexes' (p. 58). Does Holst accept civic inequality and yet affirm equality qua human being? Or does she implicitly critique the inequality of men and women as *Staatsbürger*, revealing such inequality to be unjustified when placed before the judgment seat of reason? Given her constant allusions to the fact that higher education will inevitably lead women to become conscious of their subordinate social status, Holst's underlying position seems to fall closer to the latter. At the very least, the contemporary reader *wants* her position to fall this way. And yet it is telling that, despite dedicating an entire chapter to historical evidence that displays women's civic abilities, Holst does not identify a legitimate place for women in the public sphere. Several passages indicate that she does not want to replace the 'invisible threads' of the state apparatus with open access to public office and business. She confines women's sphere of influence to the 'small inconspicuous roles', as long as they are permitted intellectual freedom (p. 29). It seems that the public sphere, for now at least, remains off limits.

For better or for worse, criticizing the present social conditions of women is not Holst's primary agenda. Her strategy is to present a sustained defence of women's higher education in faith that the dialectic of history will bend towards mutual acknowledgement. Through the higher education of women, Holst declares, 'the source of these investigations [i.e. philosophy] will refine, establish a principle for, and extend women's sphere of influence' (p. 41). As for the reluctance on the part of men to give women access to this source,

> One could easily conclude... that these men were afraid that in the course of their higher education women may think of calling to account the many injustices they have had to endure. For a creature who knows its duties according to their source and in their entirety will, of course, also acquire knowledge of its rights along the way, for the two cannot be separated from each other. (p. 60)

These are pregnant words. Holst anticipates the critique of Enlightenment that would shortly follow in the work of Hegel and Marx, who unearthed the fear behind the master's drive to maintain the servant's subordinate status. It is thus surprising that she does not grasp the radical implications of her argument, or, if she did, that they remain tangled with her defence of women's education.

3 Reception and Sources

3.1 Reception

The reception of *On the Vocation of Woman* provides a stark insight into the obstacles facing women philosophers in the German states at the turn of the nineteenth century. In Appendix 2 I have included three reviews that appeared in *Beilage des Hamburgischen Correspondenten*, *Kaiserlich-Privilegirte*, and *Hamburg und Altona*. To my knowledge, they constitute the only scholarly attention received by Holst's book following its initial publication.[113] What is striking about the reviews is that each gives more attention to Holst's moral standing than to the argument she presents. The reviewer for *Beilage des Hamburgischen Correspondenten*, who signs off as 'K – r.', evidently knew Holst personally. While he praises her defence of women's rights, and claims that her book surpasses Pockels, Meiners, Brandes, and others in thoroughness and rhetorical power, his aim is to reassure potential readers that her literary achievements did not take away from her duties as a loving mother and faithful educator of her children (praise ultimately goes to her husband, who is blessed with such a wife).

The anonymous review appearing in *Kaiserlich-Privilegirte* shows us why a reviewer seeking to promote Holst's book might include an endorsement of her moral standing as a woman. Dismissing her repeated claims that a higher education enables women to better fulfil their threefold

---

[113] There is much scope for further research on Holst's possible influence on later feminist writers who called for educational reform. For instance, Holst's vision for an intense programme of home education in *On the Vocation of Woman* shares several parallels with Wilhelmine Halberstadt's call for mother educators in *On the Dignity and Vocation of Women* (*Über Würde und Bestimmung der Frauen*, 1808) and Betty Gleim's call for collective schooling and advanced academic education in *Education and Instruction of the Female Sex* (*Erziehung und Unterricht des weiblichen Geschlechts*, 1810). While there may be indirect ways in which Holst's book had an enduring influence, its immediate reception, unlike *Observations*, was mostly negative.

calling with a single gesture ('The woman who wants to fulfil her manifold...duties...obviously lacks the leisure that is indispensable for the thorough and continued study of the sciences', p. 119), the reviewer launches a personal attack. While the author evidently *thinks* that her higher education places her among the great pedagogues of her time (Meiners, Pockels, Ewald, etc.), her 'scornful remarks' about the arguments of learned men reveal that 'it is impossible to consider that [the female sex] is destined to rise to the scientific culture of men'. Even if one were to concede that women have the capacity for higher intellectual education, the reviewer submits, it is 'obvious that the author was prevented from obtaining the necessary instruction in the subjects she is talking about by her domestic duties' (p. 119). The review concludes with a profoundly uncollegial piece of advice that excludes Holst from the growing community of literary pedagogues:

> The author, by the way, is to be advised to continue the praiseworthy business of developing her mind in such a way that her actual female vocation does not suffer from it; but also to guard herself, due to her desire to charm gallant men by showing off her immature intellect, from seeking flattery at the expense of pure truth.   (p. 119)

The reviewer's advice can help us to grasp Holst's tenuous position as a woman writer. Whatever contribution she might have to offer the reading public is weighed against her moral standing, and her motivations are held in suspicion until proven otherwise. This attitude affirms Staël's sober reflection on women writers: 'When a woman publishes a book, she makes herself entirely dependent on public opinion, and those who dispense this opinion make her profoundly aware of it.'[114]

In a lengthy piece published in *Hamburg und Altona*, an unnamed reviewer attacks Holst's argument that learnedness (*Gelehrsamkeit*) and education (*Bildung*) must go hand in hand if humans are to realize their vocation. Because she 'confuses the concepts of learnedness and humanity', the reviewer opines, 'she spends most of her time throughout the work attacking a straw man' (p. 122). Dismissing Holst's contention that a woman's education requires higher learning, the reviewer affirms the Philanthropinist trope that 'a learned woman, in the proper sense of the word, is in herself

---

[114] Staël, *De la literature consideree dans ses rapports avec les institutions sociales*, 296.

neither human, nor wise, nor amiable' (p. 121). Learnedness is not an essential part of the human vocation but, rather, 'a trade [*Gewerbe*] that nature seems to have ordained [*bestimmt*] for man' (p. 121). In contrast:

> woman, with the duties that nature and *femininity* have imposed upon her, is permitted no time for it. If the woman wants to be a scholar by profession, she must renounce the name of wife and mother, and even more of *housewife*. None can do this for her other than... nature. (p. 121)

The reviewer concludes that because a woman's charm lies in her natural humanity (rather than her acquired learnedness), 'the author must concede to me that *true learnedness*, which is often diametrically opposed to charm and grace, cannot be present in *charming women*, if she properly separates both concepts [i.e. learnedness and woman] from one another' (p. 125). The gendered constraint on learnedness places Holst back into the very bind she went to such lengths to untie. She must either accept that she is not learned, and thus plays at a game beyond her station, or that she no longer represents women, for she has departed from the vocation given to her by nature. There is simply no legitimate standpoint from which she, as a woman, can make her demand; a woman philosopher is a contradiction in terms. It seems that Holst's bold decision to 'hand this small work over to the public' was doomed to fail from the outset (p. 7). The reviewer clearly felt no need to deal with her argument that a woman's duties can be upheld while transforming the normative definition of woman within them.

3.2 Sources

While Holst celebrates the intellectual achievements of women throughout the book, and insists that women can and should cultivate their minds, she introduces the text in a way that hides the existence of other women writing in defence of female education.[115] The challenge of discerning Holst's sources is made difficult by the fact that, in comparison to the canonical texts of the German Enlightenment, we still have little understanding of the networks of women writers and the degree to which local, national, and

---

[115] For instance, Angelika Feurer attempted to redefine the 'vocation of woman' several years before Holst. See [Feurer,] *Die Bestimmung des Weibes zur Hausfrau, Mutter und Gattin*. Yet Feurer's book, like Berlepsch's essay, does not go as far as Holst's declaration that women are equal bearers of the human vocation.

1 INTRODUCTION

transnational networks interacted. What we do know, however, is that pedagogy in the late eighteenth century was a highly international field, and the writings of English, French, and German women educators would have been readily available in a cultural centre such as Hamburg.[116] Holst's aim in *On the Vocation of Woman* is not to throw off the duties traditionally bestowed on women but, rather, to extend woman's sphere of influence within them. This places her closer to conservative feminists such as Angelika Feurer and Wilhelmine Halberstadt than to the radical feminists we tend to celebrate today, who explicitly defended the public rights of woman.[117] For a point of contrast, consider Émilie du Châtelet's remarks in the Preface to her translation of Bernard Mandeville's *Fable of the Bees* (written between 1735 and 1738), which call for women's access to the sciences without reference to female duties:

> I feel the full weight of prejudice that excludes us [women] so universally from the sciences, this being one of the contradictions of this world, which has always astonished me, as there are great countries whose laws allow us to decide their destiny, but none where we are brought up to think.... Why do these creatures whose understanding appears in all things equal to that of men, seem, for all that, to be stopped by an invincible force on this side of a barrier; let someone give me some explanation, if there is one. I leave it to naturalists to find a physical explanation, but until that happens, women will be entitled to protest against their education. As for me, I confess that if I were king I would wish to make this scientific experiment. I would reform an abuse that cuts out, so to speak, half of humanity. I would allow all women to share in all the rights of humanity, and most of all those of the mind.... This new system of education that I propose would in all respects be beneficial to the human species. Women would be more valuable beings, men would thereby gain a new object of emulation, and our social interchanges which, in refining women's minds in the past, too often weakened and narrowed them, would now only serve to extend their knowledge.[118]

---

[116] For a study of the practices of translation and cultural transfer in the pedagogical community, see Mayer, 'Female Education and the Cultural Transfer of Pedagogical Knowledge in the Eighteenth Century'.

[117] In *Über Würde und Bestimmung der Frauen*, for instance, Halberstadt called for educator-mothers rather than women freed from household duties. For a discussion of conservative feminism in the British context, see Guest, 'Hannah More and Conservative Feminism', 158–9.

[118] Du Châtelet, 'Translator's Preface for *The Fable of the Bees*', 48–9.

Despite viewing the restrictions placed on female education as an 'abuse', and advocating for the public rights of women, Du Châtelet speaks in the conditional, and does not identify concrete means of change ('if I were king...'). In contrast to Du Châtelet, whose wealth and independence allowed her to move outside the constraints of social convention, Holst situates her critique within the prevailing social structures that restrict the opportunities available to women. Her primary concern is with interrogating and ultimately transforming the existing institutions that determine the course of a woman's life.

Two texts published in 1792 forged an explicit link between female duties and civic reform. Wollstonecraft's *A Vindication of the Rights of Woman* and Hippel's *On Improving the Status of Women* both issue a demand that men justify the elevated social position they have assumed, which blocks one half of humankind from receiving full access to education. Yet each takes the demand in a different direction. In *A Vindication of the Rights of Woman*, Wollstonecraft claims that women's rights cannot be vindicated without a radical restructuring of the social order, including the abolition of royal succession and the removal of class-based society. In *On Improving the Status of Women*, Hippel appeals to his fellow men to see the injustice they have meted out on one half of humanity and calls for a deep and yet incremental reform of civic institutions, beginning with marriage and continuing all the way to state governance. While scholars have argued that Wollstonecraft had a major influence on Holst, a close examination suggests that Hippel—and other reformers who sought to transform rather than transgress the traditional roles of women—had a greater impact.

The connection Holst forges between access to knowledge and women's rights has led several commentators to declare Holst as 'Germany's Mary Wollstonecraft'.[119] A decade before *On the Vocation of Woman*, Wollstonecraft lamented the 'neglected education of [her] fellow creatures' and dared to ask, who 'made man the exclusive judge, if woman partake with him the gift of reason?'[120] The first German translation of *A Vindication of the Rights of Woman* appeared in two volumes in 1793 and 1794, commissioned by the progressive schoolteacher and intellectual Christian Gotthilf Salzmann.[121] Like several of her contemporaries, including Gouges and

---

[119] Rahm, 'Nachwort', 153; Sotiropoulos, 'Scandal Writ Large', 107–8; Gerhardt, *Wenn die Frau Mensch wird*, 84.
[120] Wollstonecraft, *A Vindication of the Rights of Woman*, 1, 12.
[121] Salzmann worked for a brief period of time with Basedow at the Philanthropin but left on bad terms to found the Schnepfenthal Institution in Gotha. He commissioned the

Genlis, Wollstonecraft unapologetically presents her argument from a woman's standpoint. In words that resonate with Holst's opening demand in *On the Vocation of Woman*, she begins by noting that the prevailing assumption in books on education by men—that women are intellectually subordinate to men—left her unable to leave her pen untouched.[122] Refusing to adopt the supposedly non-gendered standpoint of her male interlocutors, which always ends up privileging the social status of men, she offers a distinct and yet impartial insight into the rational vocation of humanity:

> I shall first consider women in the grand light of human creatures, who, in common with men, are placed on this earth to unfold their faculties; and afterwards I shall more particularly point out their particular designation.[123]

Wollstonecraft seeks to refashion the order of dependence such that the circumstances of sex are second to matters of humanity. She attests that while women 'may have different duties to fulfil', they are nevertheless '*human* duties, and the principles that should regulate the discharge of them, I sturdily maintain, must be the same'.[124] The driving force of her argument is that the human vocation to unfold one's faculties is prior to the particularities of one's sex:

> I wish to show that elegance is inferior to virtue, that the first object of laudable ambition is to obtain a character as a human being, regardless of the distinction of sex, and that secondary views should be brought to this simple touchstone.[125]

While Holst adopts a similar standpoint in *On the Vocation of Woman*, she presents a different view of the role of education in social reform. Wollstonecraft freely criticizes the established structure of power, from which the wretched conditions of oppression have 'flowed from hereditary honours, riches, and monarchy' and enabled men to entrench the prevailing

---

translation to return the favour to Wollstonecraft, who had translated his *Moralisches Elementarbuch* into English in 1790.
   [122] Wollstonecraft, *A Vindication of the Rights of Woman*, 2.
   [123] Wollstonecraft, *A Vindication of the Rights of Woman*, 3.
   [124] Wollstonecraft, *A Vindication of the Rights of Woman*, 75.
   [125] Wollstonecraft, *A Vindication of the Rights of Woman*, 5.

formation of power as 'the dispensations of Providence'.[126] Yet her radical project was never wholeheartedly received in the German states.[127] In his Preface to the German translation, Salzmann distanced himself from Wollstonecraft's critique of hereditary succession and argued that the benevolent rule of the monarch should mirror the rule of man over his wife.[128] Christoph Meiners, a prominent Philanthropinist, claimed that *A Vindication of the Rights of Woman* was an insult to the rationality of the German people and dubbed Wollstonecraft an 'obstinate enemy to princes and nobility'.[129] Holst does not mention Wollstonecraft in *On the Vocation of Woman*, which has prompted several commentators to argue that she did not want to associate her work with the controversies attached to Wollstonecraft's name. For instance, Berta Rahm argues that Holst deliberately refrained from citing Wollstonecraft for the reason that 'she did not want to aggravate the gentry'.[130] Similarly, Sotiropoulos claims that the conservative reaction to Wollstonecraft 'would certainly have deterred Holst from encouraging readers' association with her'.[131] Yet there are other possible explanations for Wollstonecraft's absence in the text.[132] In contrast to Wollstonecraft's radical claim that the emancipation of women is tied to a broader social revolution that would abolish royalty and class, Holst retained a belief in monarchical institutions and the social systems they represent. In the context of early British feminism, her incremental approach to reform places her closer to Macaulay and More, whose texts were also translated into German in the 1790s. In the German context, it places her closer to Feurer and Hippel (and in the French context, to Genlis), who argued that the improvement of woman's status must be achieved gradually and within established institutions.[133]

Hippel studied theology at the University of Königsberg in the late 1750s, where he attended Kant's lectures on physical geography and metaphysics. After abandoning theology for a career as a private tutor, he returned to the university and graduated with a law degree in 1764. His sharp legal mind

---

[126] Wollstonecraft, *A Vindication of the Rights of Woman*, 19.
[127] For an examination of Wollstonecraft's reception in Germany, see Botting, 'Nineteenth-Century Critical Reception', 51; Botting, 'Wollstonecraft in Europe', 513–15.
[128] Salzmann, 'Vorrede', in Wollstonecraft, *Rettung der Rechte des Weibes*, I, xvii–xviii.
[129] Meiners, *Geschichte des weiblichen Geschlechts*, IV 243.
[130] Rahm, 'Nachwort', 158. [131] Sotiropoulos, 'Scandal Writ Large', 104–5.
[132] Recent scholarship has shown that several early feminists have been misunderstood through hasty comparisons with Wollstonecraft. For a study of this phenomenon, with potential connections with Holst's case, see Gardner, 'Catharine Macaulay's "Letters on Education"'.
[133] For a comparison between Hippel and Holst, see Greif, 'Theodor Gottlieb von Hippel und Amalia Holst'.

and considerable managerial skill were duly noted, and he quickly rose to the status of city counsellor. Following a series of extraordinary events, he was then appointed as the city's Governing Mayor (*Kriegsrath*) by Frederick the Great, who, becoming impatient with the incompetence of the established authorities and learning of Hippel's considerable capacity for administration, usurped convention by placing the young lawyer in the city's highest office.[134] While most of his contemporaries either ignored or sought to restrict women's rights, Hippel fought tirelessly to improve the civil status of women. In 1774, he anonymously published a witty treatise entitled *On Marriage* (*Über die Ehe*), arguably the first work in any language 'to advocate in a systematic way equal rights and treatment for women in the marriage relationship'.[135] By its third edition of 1793, Hippel had developed a flexible account of marriage that could encompass as many different privately defined ends as possible.[136] The 'ultimate purpose of marriage [*der Endzweck der Ehe*]', he argues, is not the propagation of humanity, nor can it be defined by any subordinate end. Following the Roman formulation *arctissimum vitae commercium* (the most intimate union of life), Hippel defines marriage as 'the closest possible unification of life [*die genaueste Lebensvereinigung*]'.[137]

Hippel did not challenge the established distinction between male and female sexuality. He simply claimed that sexual nature, and the marriage institution in which it is expressed, is irrelevant to the public reception of rights. In *On Improving the Status of Women*, which he also published anonymously, Hippel argues that humankind is set apart among animals by virtue of its perfectibility. The institutions it creates are to be tirelessly improved according to the precepts of God's will as revealed in the scriptures and natural law. With these foundations in place, he then argues that the state is falling far short of its perfection, for it leaves 'half of the resources of mankind unknown, unassessed, and unused'.[138] What makes Hippel's argument so radical—indeed, more radical than Justi's call for women's institutes—is that it unearths the role of *men* in the ongoing suppression of women:

---

[134] For an introductory biography of Hippel's fascinating life, see Sellner, 'A Paradoxical Life'.
[135] Sellner, 'A Paradoxical Life', 37.
[136] Hull, *Sexuality, State, and Civil Society in Germany, 1700–1815*, 324.
[137] [Hippel,] *Über die Ehe*, 93. Unless otherwise noted, citations to *Über die Ehe* are to the third edition.
[138] Hippel, *On Improving the Status of Women*, 62.

Wherever *it* [*reason*] is to be found, there resides humanity. And to undervalue this dignity in the other sex deliberately, amidst the radiance of her divinity, is equivalent to leaving no stone unturned in the determination of our own [i.e. men's] importance. Not a mere code of laws written on clay tablets would be shattered here; rather, we would be sinning against the divine spirit which resides within ourselves.[139]

Following Rousseau, Hippel undertakes an anthropological examination of the historical conditions that have led to the present state of domination. Yet he contends that Rousseau only uncovered half the story, for he failed to explain how it was that men came to dominate women. The 'obstacles to a moral reform of the human race', Hippel states, 'arise chiefly from the fact that we have desired to erect this temple of reform from our sex alone, while the fair sex has been left to lie in ruins'.[140] Rousseau's argument is all too convenient for the beneficiaries of this trajectory, for men 'would like to convince the other half of the human race that it is not *we* but *nature* who pushed them into the background and subjected their will to ours'.[141]

Hippel's anthropological analysis opens a profoundly different assessment of the state apparatus to that presented by Rousseau. The key to the state's perfection is not found in an imagined past, in which men (and not women) were truly free from coercion. It lies, rather, in an uncharted future in which the equality of the sexes becomes a fundamental precept of citizen society. Wollstonecraft made a similar argument in *A Vindication of the Rights of Woman*, claiming that 'Rousseau exerts himself to prove that all *was* right originally: a crowd of authors that all *is* right now: and I, that all will *be* right'.[142] For both Wollstonecraft and Hippel, the present subordination of women shows that the perfection of humanity requires the triumph of reason over the raw might of nature. Yet, in contrast to Wollstonecraft, Hippel contends that this future equality cannot be instantiated in a revolutionary flash of unmediated political will. If the established institutions were to grant women not privileges but rights, then women will come to the complete fulfilment of 'that great calling of nature [*den großen Beruf der Natur*]: to be the wife of her husband, the mother of her children, and, by

---

[139] Hippel, *On Improving the Status of Women*, 68.
[140] Hippel, *On Improving the Status of Women*, 62.
[141] Hippel, *On Improving the Status of Women*, 93–4.
[142] Wollstonecraft, *A Vindication of the Rights of Woman*, 22. For an early and more extensive insight into her critique of Rousseau, see [Wollstonecraft,] 'Review of translation of *Letters on the Works and Character of J. J. Rousseau*', 360–2.

virtue of these noble designations, a member, a citizen—and not merely a denizen—of the state'.[143] Here we see that Hippel does not reject the duties that were traditionally attached to the female sex. Rather, he refashions the Philanthropinists' notion of the female vocation (*Bestimmung*), in which a woman's duties stand in competition with her vocation as a human, as the female calling (*Beruf*), which is in fact the very means of her public status. Hippel's goal, in short, is not to dismantle but to extend woman's sphere of influence. While the means of reform are incremental, the result is no less radical. The civic equality of the sexes can only be achieved if 'the state opens to women its civil chambers, its courts, its lecture halls, commercial establishments, and its places of employment'.[144]

In the Preface to *On the Vocation of Woman*, Holst recommends Hippel's *On Marriage* and *On Improving the Status of Women* to her women readers, and laments the poor reception of the latter (pp. 7–8). In a footnote to Chapter 1, however, she distances her argument from Hippel's claim that women should take up state offices. She 'cannot agree' with Hippel on this point, for 'such a complete upheaval in civil relations would likely give rise to a lot of confusion' (p. 10). The sincerity of Holst's remark is disputable. She had reasons for keeping Hippel's radical claims at arm's length. Following his death in 1796, Hippel's enemies felt safe to speak out against him. Once it was revealed that the Governing Mayor was in fact the author of two of the most disputed texts of the decade, his name fell quickly into disrepute.[145] Yet there is also evidence to suggest that Holst may not have been alive to the tension introduced by her defence of women's higher intellectual education and her expressed acceptance of unequal access to the public sphere. The tension between higher education and public rights permeates the text and calls for further examination of the motivations and substantive views that underpin her rhetorical strategies.

4 Conclusion

There is much work to be done to unpack the philosophical importance of Holst's bold and yet incomplete text. The connections between Holst and

---

[143] Hippel, *On Improving the Status of Women*, 80.
[144] Hippel, *On Improving the Status of Women*, 165.
[145] Hippel's identity was revealed by Kant, who published an article on 5 January 1797 in the *Allgemeiner Litterarischer Anzeiger*, and a second on 21 January in the *Intelligenzblatt der allgemeiner Litteratur-Zeitung*, in which he declared the facts of the matter. Hippel had revealed his authorship to Kant on the condition that Kant preserved his anonymity. When rumours emerged in the years following Hippel's death that Kant himself was the author, Kant decided to publicly settle the case. For an extended account of the episode, see Sellner, 'A Paradoxical Life', 65.

other women writers of her time, and her potential influence on later works of philosophy, in the main part remain to be established. In contrast to the canonical texts that are conventionally taught and studied in the field of German philosophy, such as Kant's *Critique of Pure Reason* and Hegel's *Science of Logic*, *On the Vocation of Woman* is not a work of systematic philosophy. Indeed, Holst prefaces her book with a remark that presages Virginia Woolf's sobering analysis of the material conditions required for authorship in *A Room of One's Own*, declaring that her duties as a mother and teacher have denied her the time and resources required for such a project. Its philosophical significance lies, rather, in its critical orientation as Holst leverages her experience as a teacher to expose the contradictions within the pedagogical writings produced in the German Enlightenment. For her work to be accepted as philosophy, an enormous shift would have to occur via the celebrated critics of the Enlightenment, who, in the wake of Kant's critical method, expanded the task and scope of philosophical analysis to include genealogy and radical historical critique. *On the Vocation of Woman* was perhaps one step too far ahead of its time to have been fully appreciated for unearthing the workings of power and transforming the fundamental institutions of society from within. Throughout the text, Holst retrieves the significant influence that women have exerted in philosophy, statecraft, and the arts despite lacking the opportunities available to men. Yet she also laments the silence of what might have been, had men taken hold of the full implications of Enlightenment. For Holst, the gaps in the history of philosophy bear witness to a profound loss incurred by the failure of those in power to acknowledge the possibility of the same constitution of thinking in those who are subordinate to them. One of the challenges facing her contemporary readers is to fill those gaps where we can and to expand the range of voices—both past and present—in philosophy understood as a collective, critical, and unfinished project.

Note on Translation

On the Vocation of Woman is written in forceful prose that moves seamlessly between abrupt, single-sentence paragraphs and dense, complex sentences that can last an entire page in the original edition. In the Preface, Holst unapologetically states that the text was written in the few moments of leisure that presented themselves to her in the course of her tireless work as the mother of three children and headmistress of a progressive school for girls, and asks that readers judge her argument with such constraints in mind (unsurprisingly, her reviewers do not grant her that leniency). In contrast to Berta Rahm's 1983 edition, which combines Holst's shorter paragraphs and breaks up her longer ones for the sake of readability, I aimed to reflect the cadence of the original as closely as I could. Nevertheless, in several cases I judged that Holst's multi-clause sentences would be better understood if they were separated into manageable parts. I have added translator's notes where I felt that the reader's experience would be enhanced by a brief contextual remark. These are indicated by superscript numbers referring to the Notes section in the end matter of this volume, and should be differentiated from the footnotes that appear in the original. Where I have added a reference note to an original footnote, it appears in square brackets. On several occasions, Holst (or her printer) misspells a name mentioned in her catalogue of notable women; I have retained her misspellings and provided corresponding notes to alert the reader. The titles of texts mentioned by Holst are left untranslated so that the original language is apparent. Citations from the Bible, at least in the notes, are taken from the New King James Version. Holst never cites the Bible directly but paraphrases from memory. In such cases, I translate with the style and wording of the New King James Version in mind.

Several of Holst's key terms pose difficulties in translation, and readers should be mindful of the following principles I have followed. The most important pair of terms in the text, *Bestimmung* and *Beruf*, have no obvious equivalents in English. *Bestimmung* is most literately translated as 'determination', but can also be rendered as 'purpose', 'vocation', or 'destiny'. I have gone with 'vocation', both to highlight the practical implications of Holst's usage and to mirror the well-known translation of Fichte's *Die Bestimmung des Menschen* (1800) as *The Vocation of Man*.[1] While *Beruf* in contemporary German is primarily used to refer to one's profession or occupation, in the eighteenth century it still conveyed the elevated meaning carried by the English terms 'vocation' and 'calling'. Thus, to maintain the distinction between *Bestimmung* and *Beruf*, I have translated the latter as 'calling'. The entry in Zedler's *Universal-Lexicon* of 1733 captures the conceptual overlap between *berufen* and *bestimmen*:

> Calling [*Beruff*], to call [*berufen*] someone to something, means nothing other than to ordain [*bestimmen*] someone to something, or to oblige [*verpflichten*] him to do something in particular. Calling is therefore a duty according to which we are obliged to preform something in particular in human society.[2]

The connection between *Bestimmung* and *Beruf* was sufficiently close that many of Holst's interlocutors used them interchangeably. In *Fatherly Advice for My Daughter*, for instance, Campe states that young women are 'destined for and called to [*bestimmt und berufen zu*] everything that woman is to be to man, to humanity, and to civil society'.[3] Thus they have a 'twofold vocation [*zweifache Bestimmung*], one *general* and one *particular*, one as *human being* and one as *woman*'. In contrast, Holst separates the general human vocation from the particular female calling. As a human being, a woman has a single vocation: 'to develop [one's] faculties, both physical and moral, in beautiful harmony to an ever-higher perfection' (p. 9). As a woman, she bears a special calling as wife, mother, and housewife. Holst advances a philosophical anthropology in which the human vocation undergirds and is unqualified by the particular calling of one's sex. For the human vocation to conflict with one's particular calling, Holst declares, 'Nature would have to contradict itself' (p. 41).

---

[1] In her study of vocational education in the eighteenth century, Christine Mayer translates *Bestimmung* and *Beruf* as 'determination' and 'vocation' respectively. While this rendering maintains the higher sense of calling associated with *Beruf* in its eighteenth century use, I decided not to follow her pairing, as the English term 'determination' can be confused with 'focused effort' or 'working decisively towards a goal', which, in the title especially, is misleading. Moreover, it obscures the connection between Holst's book and Spalding's and Fichte's *Bestimmung* texts, which are conventionally translated as *The Vocation of Man*. See Mayer, 'The struggle for vocational education and employment possibilities for women in the second half of the nineteenth century in Germany', 85–6.
[2] Zedler, *Grosses vollständiges Universal-Lexicon aller Wissenschafften und Künste*, III 1449.
[3] Campe, *Väterlicher Rath für meine Tochter*, 5.

NOTE ON TRANSLATION lxi

Bildung, a pivotal concept in the German Enlightenment, poses special difficulties due to its polyvalence. Throughout her writings, Holst stresses the importance of *Erziehung* (upbringing, early education) for the general process of *Bildung* (formation, education, development) and the specific process of *Ausbildung* (institutional or formal practices of *Bildung*). Readers should remain sensitive to the fact that I move between various English terms for *Bildung* depending on context. I use 'education' for the description of a general process of formation as human beings (the most common use in the text, as in the book's title), 'formation' when it conveys a particular imbuing of form to the mind or person, and 'development' for instances that convey a teleological sense of completion or perfection. In each case, *Bildung* refers to a goal-directed movement that, when grasped in its true sense, works towards the ideal of humanity (my rendering of Holst's repeated phrase *ächte Bildung zur Humanität* as 'true education towards humanity' seeks to retain this sense of motion). In most cases I also translate *Erziehung* as 'education', though I use 'early education' in cases where the distinction between *Erziehung* and *Bildung* is important. The term *Geistesbildung* occurs only in the book's title. In most cases I render *Geist* and *geistig* as 'mind' and 'intellectual', accepting that the English terms carry more cerebral connotations than the German. In several cases, however, I use 'spirit' or 'spiritual', when the German terms are used to convey a more holistic meaning. After experimenting with several formulations, I decided on 'higher intellectual education' for *höhere Geistesbildung*. Yet it should be noted that 'higher education' does not refer to institutional settings of 'tertiary education', as it does in contemporary English, but to a more fundamental process of formation in keeping with the human vocation.

Gelehrsamkeit, which I have translated as 'learnedness', has the special meaning in eighteenth-century German as the marker of a scholarly trade. The connection between 'learned' (*gelehrt*) and 'scholar' (*Gelehrter/Gelehrte*) is unfortunately lost in English; when Holst plays with the connection, I translate *Gelehrter* as 'learned man'. While some of her contemporaries argued that women should be *geschult* or *gebildet*, few dared to claim that they could or should be *gelehrt*. That Holst's defence of the *gelehrte Frau*— the woman who dedicates herself to higher intellectual education—is one of the most controversial claims in the book is evident in the review published in *Hamburg und Altona* (see Appendix 2).

Ueber die

Bestimmung des Weibes

zur

höhern Geistesbildung

Von

Amalia Holst, geb. von Justi

Berlin, 1802

Bei Heinrich Frölich.

Most humbly dedicated to
Your majesty
The reigning
Queen of Prussia

When I considered the ideal of feminine greatness and perfection, your majesty came to mind as a lofty and sublime example. Guided by that ideal, I have tried to adapt it to and present it in the various circumstances of life.

As a child of the Prussian States, I observed with the deepest devotion the noble and humane actions of the great regent couple, who now fill Prussia's people with such joy. Though from a distance, I delighted in your grandeur and nobility.

Your gracious kindness gives me hope for forgiveness if I dare to dedicate these imperfect pages to you. My heart's desire, which is to fervently venerate your kind virtues, compelled me to express my feelings.

It will be a great encouragement for the future and a generous reward for my endeavours if your majesty will graciously condescend to accept them.

With the deepest admiration, I am,
Your majesty,
A most humble servant,
The author.

Preface

I do not hand this small work over to the public to put even more strain on the reading world, which is already overladen with books. No. It strikes me as a need of our times that a member of the other party, a woman, should take up this important matter about which men, almost exclusively, have already written so much.

Men, when they judge our sex, are constantly partial to their own and rarely allow justice to be done to ours. Or, if they want to be generous, they go too far indeed. Only a woman can properly judge the individual situation of woman in all its aspects and degrees.

But will she not be guilty of the same charge of partiality to her sex?

Certainly, if her preference pulls her more to one side than to the other. If she does not stand high enough on the level of culture to abstract from the love of her sex on a matter so important for humanity, and if she is unable to estimate her place in the series of beings simply as an active member of the whole.

I have endeavoured to treat men as fairly as I could. But my mind was also indignant due to the injustices of several men. If I might convince them, and if I might convince my sex of the importance and scope of their calling as human beings and as women, then my efforts would be sufficiently rewarded. For my part, to have contributed my own small piece in the improvement of humanity is the goal of my innermost striving.

As to the manner of presentation, I feel its imperfection to a far greater extent than any critic of this art could inform me. But if one considers that this work is merely the product of leisure, and that this leisure has been sparsely available to me, then I will be granted some leniency. I feel the imperfection of my work, which falls well short of the ideal that I had in mind. My highest purpose was to be useful. I will succeed in this aim if one is impartial enough to judge me according to my circumstances.

To my women readers, I especially recommend the works of the late von Hippel. What he has written in *Über die bürgerliche Verbesserung der Weiber* and *Über die Ehe* deserves our most serious consideration. I am amazed that his works have been so little read that his posthumous writings, which were intended to be included in the second edition of *Über die bürgerliche Verbesserung der Weiber*, had to be reprinted on their own. So many copies were still in stock that a second edition was not feasible.[1]

My women friends, read von Hippel with a fervent striving for ever greater education. He will bring you a bountiful return.

1

Does Higher Education of the Mind Contradict the Proximate Calling of Woman as Wife, Mother, and Housewife?

So much has been written about the female vocation in recent years. Men have dared to set a limit that our minds may not transgress in the field of knowledge. They deem that the higher education of our understanding stands in contradiction with our individual duties.

Until now, no woman has stood up and said aloud that she knows and discerns the standpoint she holds as a thinking being, as an active participant in society's best interests; that she knows, loves, and treasures the gentle, amiable, and often unrewarded female virtues of her threefold calling; that she is nevertheless deeply convinced that the fulfilment of these vocational duties to the highest degree is not hindered but indeed only dignified and perfected by higher education; that she knows that, as a thinking being, she must abstract from being a woman and consider herself first of all as a human, that is, as a perfectible being entitled to develop its faculties, both physical and moral, in beautiful harmony to an ever-higher perfection.

The silence so far is inexplicable to me.[1] Have women lacked knowledge, have they failed to gain a proper appreciation of their own standpoint? I dare not make such a claim. It would be refuted by the many excellent achievements made by women in almost all fields of knowledge. Or have they not felt how humiliating it is to be given one-sided instructions from men, and from men alone, on the standpoint we are allowed to take?

I would not claim this either. The high sense of many noble women, and the indignation often expressed in intimate conversation about the demands of men, would refute it.

Whence then this silence about a matter so close to our hearts? And why should it fall on me to publicly raise a question that is so deeply felt and taken to heart by us all? Indeed, I am content to think that there are many of us who could say it far better than I.

So be it! In the name of our sex, I challenge men to justify the right they have presumed for themselves, which holds back an entire half of humankind, barring them from the source of the sciences and allowing them at most to skim their surface.[2]

Can we allow this presumption? Will they justify it? Have they so far managed to do so?

These writers have given two main reasons for opposing the higher education of women: first, our physical and intellectual capacities render us incapable of soaring equally high as men in the lofty regions of knowledge; second, aspiring to participate in these high places of intellectual culture contradicts our individual duties.

It would be foolish to try to oppose these claims if either of them was justified. In the first case we could not, and in the second case we ought not, follow this higher drive of thinking. It would be a forbidden fruit we were not allowed to taste.

For I consider every occupation or enjoyment that causes us to neglect the obligations of our particular situation, even if it is permitted and noble, as the consequence of that half-culture, that pseudo-Enlightenment, which is more harmful than knowing nothing.

But I say this only in passing. Given that a discussion of the second question will be the main purpose of this work, I want to begin by answering the first.

Are we essentially subordinate to men in terms of physical and intellectual capacities?

In terms of physical power, the answer is a resounding yes! Although some esteemed writers have attempted to answer in the negative, I would not want to argue against general experience, and I am no friend of paradoxes.*

---

* Both the author of *Philosophie de la nature* [Jean-Baptiste-Claude Delisle de Sales] and von Hippel in his book *Über die bürgerliche Verbesserung der Weiber*, along with several others, have tried to make this claim. The ingenious von Hippel defends our rights with a great deal of subtlety, while others try to suppress them. He criticizes the oppression and neglect of women, and even goes further to argue that they ought to take part in various state offices. Yet as much as I recognize the notable zeal with which he takes up our cause, I cannot agree with him on this point. Rather, I believe that such a complete upheaval in civil relations would likely give rise to a lot of confusion. The general question of whether both sexes will ever rise to the level of education where this could be achieved without harm cannot yet be answered with certainty. And I do not want to be a preacher of revolution. Satisfaction with one's conditions is the first requirement of happiness. Let us be satisfied with our threefold calling and put all our honour into fulfilling its obligations. Only then can one acknowledge that we have fulfilled the human duties through the appropriate and harmonious development of our capacities, not under false pretences but by right. [See Sales, 'General Remarks on the Human Body', in *De la philosophie de la nature*, IV 77–88; Hippel, *On Improving the Status of Women*, 165.]

Exceptions do not make a rule. When a farmer who has only developed her physical powers is stronger than a learned man, it is simply a natural consequence of her different way of life. If she outperforms the weak and nervous squire with her strength, this proves nothing against general experience.

But if we have to admit that women are in general weaker than men in regard to physical strength, does it necessarily follow that they are intellectually weaker? Is one the consequence of the other?[3]

Are our brains constituted differently to those of men?

No anatomist has yet made such a claim. The only thing that physiology has shown is that our nerves are finer and more irritable and our tendons less taut than those of men. But does this have a negative impact on the operation of our thinking, by which I mean, on the power of thought itself? Does our physical weakness entirely exclude us from rigorous thinking?

Does our mind therefore think according to a different set of logical laws to those of men? Does it receive objects of the external world in a different way to men?

What man could possibly make such a claim?

To ask the question once more, who has properly examined this organization in its origin, development, and end, through all its modifications?

Surely no one could seriously claim that an organization more suited for thinking would depend on or require tauter muscles and stronger nerves, and that such would be the prerequisite for better thought! Countless experiences offer us examples to the contrary, for how often can it be noticed that thinkers are generally weaker in physical strength?

It would be mistaken to object to the idea that this higher level of thinking weakens the body, that the noblest humours are withheld from the animal body and fed to the brain as the finer substance. Also, from infancy great thinkers have been found to be smaller and less physically strong than other children, and just as irritable and weak as women. And it is only from the irritability of learned men that we can explain the sensitivity and outrage that arises when their writings are criticized, not to mention the vicious abuse they often hurl at one another.

The claim that physical strength is proportionate to mental strength cannot be proven, and nor can the reverse. Indeed, since there are countless examples of the opposite, I cannot understand how practically all the writers who have written about the vocation of woman can call upon this unproven claim and infer from it the inferiority of our intellectual power. Even less can I understand how educated men can attach such a high value to physical strength. For as soon as humanity passes from the state of nature to the state of culture, physical strength loses its value and can no longer serve as the basis of any law for cultured peoples.

When humanity still lay in the cradle of its childhood and the mind slumbered as an embryo, so to speak, physical strength alone determined the value of the individual. It took ceaseless effort, the experience of several millennia, before humanity could come to know, appreciate, and order the wonders and operations of nature that surrounded it, before it could ascend to the intelligible, achieve something in the field of abstractions, and connect these abstractions with practical reason. The human mind could only develop slowly at first. Gradually it came to grasp the various parts of the external world.

If we look back to antiquity, we find that in all nations, during the infancy of their minds, physical strength claimed the highest rank of all. Saul became king because he stood a head taller than his competitors. Nimrod was king due to his prowess as a hunter. Homer's heroes and gods are all marked by their physical strength. In the *Odyssey*, Pallas Athena tells Telemachus: 'Thou, too, friend, for I see thou art a comely man and tall, be thou valiant, that many an one among men yet to be born may praise thee.'[4] In Greek, as well as in most ancient and modern languages, the words 'power' and 'virtue' have the same meaning.[5] This is proof enough that back then people recognized no other virtue, no other value, than strength and bravery. Hercules became a god because of his power and virtue. Minerva was the goddess of both wisdom and bravery. The giants threatened the gods with war, and only Jupiter's greater strength was able to hold off their attack on Olympus. Power against power was the right of nature. Everything was settled with the sword or the fist.

Even love was only a matter of satisfying physical needs and the business of procreation. Love lacked a moral sanction, and there was still no sense of the fine and delicate bond between souls. Humanity was barely one step above the animals.

But should it always remain that way? While they were physically giants and morally children during this early stage, should not human beings, in the fullness of time, reach the mature age of understanding? If we can now enjoy this beautiful, flourishing intellectual age, why should those men, who have reached such a high level of culture, still assert these rights against *us*, rights that only befit primitive human beings and are no longer valid once humanity raises itself to the level of rational, thinking being?[6]

Nevertheless, all the writers who attempt to define the female vocation set out from this law of the strongest. They use it as the basis of their claim that women are subordinate to and dependent on men, and to establish that women have inferior mental powers.

Consult all of the writings that men have written about this matter and you will find that, with only a few exceptions, they all proceed from this principle.

Even the meritorious Mouvillon, who is so keen to protect us against the accusations of Herr Brandes,* considers our situation from this point of view.[7] Indeed, he describes the female condition in such a way that it must take a lot of courage to be a woman! But our situation is hardly so pitiful. While these men set out from primitive natural laws in their theorizing, in practice their behaviour towards us must, in cultured nations, be reckoned according to the laws of convention and morality. Although the laws that bind us still lie in chaos, we must create a level playing field and a secure standpoint by means of our minds and our moral behaviour.

Clearly the writers who have written so much about women take a misguided starting point only because they overlook the line that is so sharply drawn between nature and the moral law as the codex of cultured nations. J. J. Rousseau was the first to make this error. This fanatic confuses nature and culture throughout his work.[8] Due to his immeasurable ambition, he was not satisfied with the unmerited homage he received and showed himself to be completely egoistic in both his actions and his writings. Of course, Rousseau's ego had to suffer the scorn of other learned men such as Voltaire. Yet his wounded self-love could not bear it. He thus poured the proverbial baby out with the bathwater and rejected learnedness everywhere. He proposed to drive humanity back to the state of nature, without understanding that remaining in such a state was against nature's intention.[9] The only reason that nature bestowed so many capacities and powers upon us is that we might develop them, and desire to move from nature to culture. Rousseau's vivid imagination prevented him from seeing that while the state of culture certainly has its disadvantages if it proceeds along a crooked path, these disadvantages result solely from the limitations of human nature. He also failed to see that if we counted the

---

* Herr Brandes's bitter and satirical attacks on women do not in fact deserve such a serious rebuttal. His book should instead be satirized, an honour it rightly deserves. Surely a coquette must have teased him, or a pseudo-scholar misunderstood his merit, causing him to write the book in the raw indignation of wounded self-love. If he was lucky enough to find a faithful and kind woman afterwards, he has long since regretted this sin.

advantages of culture, they would outweigh, by an indescribably great measure, everything we could say in favour of the state of nature.

Rousseau may have had a similar experience with women during his sojourn in Paris. Although, as a fanatic, he was generally a favourite among our sex, he could well have found learned women among them whose learnedness was not always in harmony with true education towards humanity. Such was the case in France in those times, though it is seldom the case now. He could have found a few women whose pretentions and behaviour destroyed the beautiful proportion between feminine virtues and duties and made a hasty conclusion about all women who raise themselves above the ordinary. So he concluded just as hastily about the learnedness of women as he had previously done about learnedness in general, and thus limited their education to knowledge that would fulfil the duties of their threefold calling. He did not, however, consider that, to fulfil their duties, women would require the aid of a *higher* education.

It is always worth comparing the theoretical claims of such men with their own practice of these maxims. This Rousseau, who closely adhered to the estimable domestic virtues in his writings, did not manage to fulfil them in his actions. Indeed, he was a bad husband and an unnatural father. It is well known that he put his children in an orphanage, where he let them die. And he did not think to record this, the greatest of all sins, in his *Confessions*. He then married his housekeeper, who was the mother of these unfortunate children. She was completely uneducated in the manner he claims that women should be. Nevertheless, in her simplicity she understood the art of leading him about in any way she liked. To this end she made skilful use of his hypochondria, which enticed him to see enemies where there were none. She aroused this fear whenever he was not at her beck and call, as was often the case. As a highly esteemed and intelligent writer put it, 'It was not Rousseau the philosopher but Rousseau the eccentric who, with Therese as ever serving as his muse, declared man to be the natural despot of women. Although man is stronger than woman in terms of the body, is he also stronger in terms of the soul? When we speak of the right to rule, is not the soul more important than the body?' (*Über die Ehe*, p. 85).[10]

With his enthusiastic and abundant eloquence, Rousseau had the gift of bestowing upon his arguments the air of truth. Thus he swept many writers away with him. Following his error, these writers overlooked the line that separates the state of nature from civil society.

In the raw state of nature, only the right of the stronger, power against power, is decisive. It results in the right of retaliation: as you do to me, so

I do to you. Whoever does not exercise this one law of natural man and is thus ruled by his opponent, whoever is weaker, must either give in or take refuge in cunning to keep the scales in balance.

In this state of nature, it was a matter of necessity that women, weaker in physical strength, were assigned the second place, giving way and bowing to power.

But humans could not remain in this state of savagery for long without being destroyed. This is precisely what the author of nature intended, who determined that they develop all of their powers. Humans began to feel this and learned to see the advantages that the social contract would grant them. Yet to enjoy those advantages, and to preserve that right in its full force, they had to give over something that as primal humans they had considered as a natural right. So now there was even more confusion than before. Their powers were brought together as society and thus violence reached its peak.

If, with the formation of the social contract, humans had been able to transform themselves into philosophical minds as if by a stroke of magic, then the right of the stronger would have been instantly erased and the social contract based solely on the moral laws of equity and reason. Everyone could have their share in happiness, determined and attained by the appraisal of their worth and their benevolent contribution to the common good of the whole.

Yet this first attempt, like the subsequent development of the legal contract, was merely the work of need. Philosophers began to contemplate it only long afterwards. Humans thus kept as much of the state of nature as was compatible with their current needs, until new difficulties arose, advancing forward only one step at a time.[11]

Those who held the power took care of themselves first, and the weaker had no voice. And because the weaker had no voice, women always had to silently withdraw. They were not allowed to assert their rights as human beings.

But when the blossoming of the human mind has finally come to bear its fruit, when it has arrived at the beautiful moment when reasons must be given to explain why things are arranged as they are, and how they could have been better arranged, when the human mind has reached the conviction that reason is the only privilege that raises us above animals, the entire right of the strong disappears and physical strength is relegated to a subordinate rank, where it belongs. Of course, physical strength still holds rank among the lower, uncultured peoples. But those who have climbed to a higher level of culture know a better value. Its plumb line is equity, its scale understanding and reason.

If Rousseau and several other writers talk so much about the physical weakness of woman, and attempt to deduce from it her subordinate status, if they claim that nature has granted to her a lower position, they misinterpret this kind mother of all beings. They carry over the natural right of raw, uncultured human beings to the social contract of those who are morally cultured. Thus, they fall into error, upheld by a failure to acknowledge the possibility of the same constitution of thinking in the female sex.

What is the cause of the error that occurs when intelligent men philosophize about human rights and civil relations? Only the human inclination that makes one unwilling to share rights that have been enjoyed exclusively for so long.

We do not need to look far to find evidence of this. Just look at our violent rulers, whatever their names. To what Machiavellian sophisms did they not resort in order to assert their rights, which they gladly protect at any cost, over that which developed human reason called to account?[12]

If French women had been more educated, they would not have been so happy with the arbitrary and yet extensive privileges they enjoyed. However, they found more comfort in their idleness and self-satisfied vanity. Had they been more educated, this great matter of humankind would have been addressed in the Revolution. I only recall one woman who proposed it, but she did not receive any support from her sex.[13] Such will remain the case until the mature, perfected education of women lies behind us.

If physical strength should still claim the rank that it had before, the first porter could have chased Frederick the Great off his throne. The first cart-pusher would have contested the rank of our immortal Lichtenberg, and the labourer would have been preferred to many a philosopher.

Most rulers would not want to concede that human reason is the only true foundation of right. Unlike Frederick the Great, there are few who can prove their rights to the throne through intellectual ability. And no philosopher or scholar would come to their aid. Yet still they are unashamed to assert the stale right of the barbarians against us.

Whatever these men philosophize about the physically and intellectually subordinate powers of women, it remains undeniable that women have had and still have an extensive influence in all fields of knowledge, as well as in the various institutions and relations of civil constitution.

Since the influence of women cannot be established through concepts alone but requires experience, it will be fruitful to make a short historical tour to see how women throughout the world have participated and are still participating in either the good and the upright or the ill and the crooked, depending on whether they were benevolent and educated or malicious and uneducated. After doing so, we will be able to conclude that the whole of humanity can only win and never lose by a better and higher education for women.[14]

In the earliest recorded times we already see Semiramis, who fought against physical powers with cunning and sagacity to become victorious.[15] Her ambition drove her to use any available means, enabling her to assume the throne by murdering her husband and to preserve her rule by wilfully neglecting her son's education. We follow the history of the Babylonian Empire and see how much this woman's sagacity has done for salvation, and how much her ambition for disaster, in the succession of bad monarchs until the Empire's downfall.

Women also had a great influence in Phoenicia, as they did in Carthage, a colony of Tyre, the capital of the Phoenician Empire. Dido (or Elissa), founder of the city of Carthage, may have contributed a great deal to this influence.[16] Virgil depicts her story in his poem. Yet she did not die out of love of Aeneas, who lived 300 years earlier than she did. Livy tells her story in a very different way, and more to her honour. But it is too well known to recount here in detail. If my female readers are not familiar with the story, I recommend they read *Histoire des femmes*, translated from the English, in the first volume, pp. 159 ff.[17]

Elissa remains unique in the history of humankind as the founder of a great empire, famous and flourishing through its trade, shipping, and many discoveries.

Even among the Israelites, whose laws were so unjust in respect to women, where they were neglected and despised according to the customs of the East and the influence of ancient myths, a woman held the most important of all public offices.[18] Deborah had been a judge for a long time, and had a marked influence on her times.[19] There was also Judith, who single-handedly freed them from a menacing warrior, and Esther, who as queen shared the Assyrian throne and saved them from imminent destruction.[20] While I cannot present the actions of the first two as a pattern for morality, there can be no denial that they had an impact on matters of great and extensive importance within the state, even among a people who lacked any sense of the dignity of women.

It is a strange phenomenon that in both ancient history and the recent past, despite all their oppression and subordination, women are respected as worthy of the rank of rulers of states, and that many—very many—have shown in their government how much they deserve the confidence of nations. The often-repeated objection that where women sit on the throne, men in fact rule, does not even merit refutation. For let us turn this sentence around and say, where men sit on the throne, women rule through the influence that both sexes have always had on each other.[21] This would place the majority on our side, and men would not like to admit this.

Just list the great sequence of women rulers—Semiramis, both Artemises, Zenobia, Cleopatra, and those of recent history whom we will continue to examine—and you will find an extensive inventory.[22] How much did Cleopatra not do to ensure that the great struggle for the rule of the world did not fall in favour of Antony but Octavian? Was Antony not rendered inactive by his aroused sensuality, such that it bound him? What a different series of events would have occurred if victory had fallen in favour of Antony in the decisive Battle of Actium!

Women had more influence with the Romans than with the Greeks, especially in regard to the origins of the nascent Roman state. As is well known, Rome was founded by bandits and murderers (Romulus was the murderer of his brother). Its foundation was hardly based on laws of equity and integrity. But although the laws were not in favour of women, these chaotic origins nevertheless worked to their advantage. The total lack of women in Rome meant that the men had to abduct the Sabine women, who possessed a higher degree of culture than their captors. As peacemakers between the Roman and Sabine states, the abducted women attained a certain importance and a noticeable influence, which they continued to assert.[23] The Palladium of their city bore the image of Minerva, and women as well as men were deified by the Romans. Their statues were placed in the temples, and if they performed great acts of valour they were buried in the Field of Mars along with men who performed such acts.

What scholar of antiquity does not know of the sibyls, and what has been said of their prophetic and poetic spirit? The Sibylline Books of Rome were kept very carefully and consulted on important matters requiring decisive action.*

Some of the ancients even believed that Homer borrowed many of his verses from Daphne, one of the oldest sibyls and poets. I cannot vouch for the truth of this claim, and this is not the place to investigate how much of

---

* Plato said the following about the sibyls: 'If we wanted to say how much benefit they have brought to many through their knowledge of the future, time would fail us.' In *Pfylander*. [Holst is referring to *Phaedrus*, yet she misquotes, as Plato speaks only of one sibyl: 'We will not mention the sibyl or the others who foretell many things by means of god-inspired prophetic trances and give sound guidance to many people—that would take too much time for a point that is obvious to everyone' (244b).]

what was said of the Sibylline Books and their prophetic writings is true or false. I mention it merely as evidence that even among the ancients the influence of women was very significant.

Like all ancient peoples, the Romans had goddesses and priestesses. How highly they esteemed the Vestal Virgins, the keepers of the sacred fire! The lictors wore the insignia of administrative justice when they came before them, just as they did before the senators.

Lucretia's voluntary death ended the reign of Tarquinius Superbus, and led to the expulsion of the tyrant along with his criminal sons.[24] Her deed resulted in the founding of the Republic, causing a completely different series of events than would otherwise have occurred.

When Coriolanus stood before the walls of Rome with a victorious army, and threatened its imminent destruction out of revenge for the insult he received in his fatherland, the only person who could beg for mercy from the indignant victor was his mother.[25] She came in the wake of several matrons and did not cease from pleading until she had softened her son's heart. Her son finally gave in, although he knew that he was now heading for his downfall. Thus the mother sacrificed her son for the fatherland. When in the senate they asked her to choose a reward for her service to the state, she simply asked for permission to build a temple at her own expense for the salvation of women. A proof of her great and unselfish character, and of the right to property that the women of Rome could exercise.

Cornelia, the mother of the Gracchi, knew that she raised heroes of men.[26] She was proud of her sons, for she had given birth to them not only physically but morally. It is only a pity that these sons and their mother lived at a time when Rome was already in decline, and when they were almost the only pillars among the moral ruins of great Roman urbanity. The women of their time had no appreciation of Cornelia's greatness; her glory was splendour and abundance.

The Roman women had a benevolent influence during the flourishing times of the Republic, when the Romans were still men. Later, their influence became less benevolent, and finally, under the emperors, when Asiatic luxury had corrupted their moral fabric, they became a harmful force.

Livia understood the art of manipulating her husband, Augustus, absolute ruler of the world, and making his will into hers.[27]

Elagabalus wanted his mother to have a seat and to vote in the senate, and soon afterward he formed a senate over which she presided.[28]

But it will always remain a marvel to me that the Greeks, who were such a highly cultured people with a fine sensibility for everything beautiful and noble, could entirely neglect women, the beautiful half of humankind, even though women had such a great influence in heroic times. Had the women been educated to the same degree as the men, what would they not have accomplished under such an organization, and in such a beautiful climate?

Herr Meiners is similarly unable to explain the neglect of women among the Greeks, for they are of Celtic origin, and the people of this line generally did greater justice to women.[29] He attributes this neglect to the fact that the Greeks were initially educated in Asia, where, as is well known, women lived imprisoned in harems. Yet if this is really the case, it is to be regretted that the Greeks abandoned their Celtic mores so quickly. Although they did not completely imitate their Asian teachers, and did not imprison women in harems, they nevertheless relegated them to gynaecea, where their whole education consisted of learning feminine handicrafts. They even remained ignorant of the art of keeping a household with decency, dignity, and thrift. The men only felt the need to instruct them in this economy, which is so necessary to women, once they had become wives.

If the education of Greek women had not been so neglected, they would have kept pace with men, and the men would not have fallen to the disgraceful vice I am ashamed to mention. The men would have chosen women, lovers in a nobler sense, instead of their so-called male lovers, and they would have been spurred on by them to practise the great and sublime in a more beautiful way and in a more noble union. But since the men could find no enjoyment in the conversation of their uneducated wives, who were merely instructed for the procreation of their kind and for housekeeping, so they, longing for entertainment, joined more and more firmly with other men. This bond became mixed with sensuality, and they fell into the most unnatural of vices.

Furthermore, the neglect of women in Greece gave rise to a kind of polygamy through the great army of hetaerae, who were not denied intellectual education. Here the men found better entertainment, which they sought more often than with their wives. Even married men lived openly with them, despite the fact that polygamy was prohibited by law. By this degradation of women, men simply avoided the influence of those that were theirs by law, for what the wives were unable to do was done through the hetaerae.

Already in Greece's early history we find the hetaera Leaena, who participated in a conspiracy.[30] When she was tortured for information about her co-conspirators, she bit off her tongue so that she could not be forced by the pain to make a confession. Her valour was commemorated by a tongueless statue.

Phryne, Lais, and others had their part in state affairs through the influence they had over their lovers.[31] Who does not know the power that the great Aspasia had over Pericles, the absolute ruler of Athens?[32] Men will never be able to escape the influence of women. Even in Asia, where they are locked up in harems, women are often the primary driving force behind state revolutions through their cunning and intrigue.

Despite the disregard of women in Greece, they were nevertheless deified. There were goddesses, priestesses, and prophetesses. And what powerful influence did they not attain by virtue of these last two occupations, for their priestly duties served to divide the time of public events. Juno had her priestesses in the various places where she was worshipped, just like Minerva and Apollo at Delphi. In Athens there was both a queen and king of sacrifices.

Among the priestesses of the Cybele, who were called Galli, there was a high priestess named Laberia Felicia, who presided over the other priests and priestesses.[33]

At Dodona, in the woods, there was a fountain that bathed the foot of an old oak tree with a soft murmur. An old woman named Pelias interpreted the sound to divine the future.[34] When the fountain diminished, the oracle was given to her by means of a cauldron. If she was clever, she could put anything into the mouth of her god. And clever she must have been, otherwise she would not have played such an important role.

Pythia, who proclaimed the oracle of Apollo at Delphi, also held a very important office.[35] She was certainly no mere tool of the priests, and it was not due to her stupidity that she was chosen. The answer she gave to Alexander, when he forced her to speak on a day when the laws did not allow it, was far from stupid. My son, she said, who can resist you? She could not have been wiser in her lie, since she had to choose between a despot and the strictness of the laws.

What a profound influence women must have had by administering their priestly duties! For it is known that in antiquity the priests were in possession of all knowledge and kept it secret. It was the priests and priestesses who decided on behalf of their gods when they were consulted for advice on important matters, such as whether the undertaking would be successful or not. It is well known that in antiquity no city was built, no temple founded, no war started, no journey undertaken, and no marriage performed without asking the oracles for advice.

Not only the Greeks but all ancient peoples had their goddesses, priestesses, and female diviners. The Egyptians worshipped the goddess Isis, the

Syrians Astarte, the Danes Freya, the ancient Germans Hebe and Nehalennia. The ancient Gauls had both female and male Druids, the old Germanic people had the priestesses of Irminsul.

It is curious that almost all peoples attributed the powers of divination to women, and that this belief was preserved consistently through the Middle Ages.

The old Germans attributed something divine to their women. The Allrunen were consulted on all important events. We also find a belief in women's magic and the art of divination among the brutish native peoples of America. This belief in the divining powers of women undoubtedly had a great influence across the world. Such women were feared, though often unjustly persecuted.

Women were held in high esteem among the ancient Germanic tribes, and earned their high status through their virtues. They were especially distinguished by their chastity, domesticity, and bravery. In battles they even fought alongside the men, and had an effect on their husbands by encouraging them to be brave. When the men would not heed their encouragement but fled in the midst of a desperate fight, the women would board the wagons and make it difficult for the Romans to win. When they were finally overcome, they preferred death to slavery and disgrace. The men held them in high esteem, asked for their advice on all important events, and believed them to be capable of divine and holy matters. They usually worshipped one or more prophetic virgins, such as Valeda or Arminia, who were practically living deities. Women were placed as judges at the sides of lords and noblemen, and even chosen as arbitrators. One can read more about this in Herr Meiners's *Geschichte der Weiber*.[36]

The influence of women on the most important matters was extensive among our ancestors. And this influence endured in all its purity as long as they retained their old German customs. Everyone knows the influence of women on the primary virtue of bravery during the time of the knights, which was valued almost to the exclusion of all other virtues. They encouraged men to perform acts of bravery, distributed the prizes, and often gave their hand as a reward for uprightness and valour. Women asserted a similar influence throughout the entire Middle Ages, although not always in such a fine way. Later, when the courts of love no longer bore witness to their influence on nobility and uprightness, it nevertheless displayed their effect on the prevailing ideas of the time.[37]

The influence of women will reveal itself in fine and noble morality if they enjoy a free, noble education, and the men of their times will have a better appreciation of it. But as soon as one sex sinks to a low level of culture, so the other is pulled down with it. The sexes are too closely connected, each has too powerful an influence on the other, not to have this certain effect.

History has erected many a sad monument to the harmful, devastating influence of women, just as it has preserved for us examples of the great and noble contribution of women to the good of humanity and states.

One reads with sadness and horror of the atrocities and devastation that the two sisters Brunhilda and Fredegund incited in Germany's history during the sixth century.[38] How long did the peoples bleed through the devastating wars that they kindled!

The Christian religion also owes much of its spread to women, and there are almost as many female martyrs as there are male. Christianity was first brought to Russia by a sister of the Emperor Constantine, whom King Garislaus had married.[39] In Poland it was introduced by the wife of King Micelav, as well as in Bulgaria.[40] And in England, when Christianity had almost come to an end, it was revived by the wife of Edelbert, daughter of Gilbert, King of France.[41]

In his history of women, Herr Alexander claims that women did not receive the honour of deification in the Christian religion, and they were not included in the priesthood.* But was Hannah not a priestess, and is Mary not deified?[42] Among Catholics, the Holy Virgin is worshipped more than Christ, and they seldom talk of God the Father. The number of saints who are women is just as great as those who are men, and both are venerated.

Women enjoyed great honour among the ancient Gauls, and even attended the council. In no other country has the influence of women been so lasting and all-encompassing up to our times as in France.

Like Anne of Austria, Marie and Catherine de' Medici were regents, although Salic law excludes women from the French throne.[43] Who does not know of Catherine de' Medici's great and terrible influence in the history of France?[44] Who is not aware of the horrors of the so-called blood wedding, which were largely her work? In no other history does the influence of women have such a powerful influence on state revolutions than in the history of France, for both good and for ill.

France would have lost its long war with England if three women under the reign of Charles VI had not saved it from ruin.[45] Already the prince was quite

---

* In the French translation of this work, vol. 1, p. 227. [See Alexander, *The History of Women*, I 170.]

discouraged, and wanted to retreat to Languedoc, where he could defend himself. Yet his wife, aware of her husband's wayward heart, suppressed her jealousy and united with his beloved Agnès Sorel to prevent him from making this desperate decision. The beautiful Agnès said to him that it had been prophesied that she would possess the bravest king of Europe as her beloved. Now that she realized that this could not be Charles, she would have to go to England to fulfil the prophesy. This declaration aroused Charles's diminished valour, and he plucked up his courage and took up arms. The work was completed by the dramatic events concerning Joan of Arc.[46]

This low-born girl gave the matter a completely different twist. She believed that she was inspired by heaven, which instilled her and the credulous crowd with heroic courage, and France was victorious. This story is too well known to be recounted here in full. Those who do not know it can follow Hume's *History of England*, vol. 4, p. 183, where the best and most authoritative account of this strange event can be found. Voltaire distorted it in his famous poem, just as Virgil distorted the story of Dido.

Women had immense power over the only truly great king of France, Henry IV. The great and clever Sully had to spend more effort and art countering the corrupting influence of his mistresses in stately affairs than all the other affairs of the great state machine put together.[47]

Under Henry IV, there was a war called *La guerre des amoureux*, for it began only when the lovers of both parties incited the conflict.

The influence of women on the weaker kings that followed was even more potent. As much as the unjustly called Louis the Great, or Louis XIV, imagined himself to be self-governing, it was he who, chasing the woman he loved, was clever enough only to save his dunce cap. He let himself be more or less controlled by her, until finally Maintenon managed to make of him what she wanted.[48]

Things got worse under Louis XV. How much did Du Barry and Pompadour not contribute to the state's ruin?[49] Would the pendulum have swung to France's shame during the Seven Years War if this Pompadour had not thought of following Maintenon? She, who by no means left her mind and her modesty to command the helm of the state. If you read the history and letters of Pompadour, you will be astonished at the audacity with which she decided the most important matters of state. She dismissed the worthiest and most experienced generals and put unworthy and inexperienced fools in their place, thus contributing great harm to France.

It is impossible to calculate how greatly women influenced the last French Revolution, the consequences of which were important for the whole of

Europe. I will not give a lengthy account of the facts here, as the history of the Revolution is still too new and is written in everyone's memory. If the queen had sought to acquire the confidence of the French nation, the Revolution, however much it had been prepared for by the previous domineering and weak kings, either would not have taken place at all or, if it did, only under milder, more favourable circumstances. And then what other benefits would have arisen for humanity? Charlotte Corday, who stands so great and sublime among so many scheming and self-interested people, by consecrating herself to death out of pure enthusiasm for the nation caused a completely different course of events by punishing citizen Marat, even if we cannot be sure of the details.[50] She demonstrated once and for all that tyrants do not have to be tolerated, a fact that Robespierre discovered soon afterwards.

In the field of literature, the women of France have also displayed a drive for influence beyond that seen in any other nation. Especially in the field of *belles-lettres*, they are practically the sole judges of merit. They have their salons, where they criticize newly published works. An author who fails to impress them will rarely have any success. What a pity that these women often abuse that privilege, holding back the deserving writer and lifting up the shallow one who flatters them, thus leaving posterity to tend to the laurels of a worthy poet's grave. This is probably due to the fact that among the women of France scientific knowledge and genuine human education seldom go hand in hand. There is a lack of humility, the crown of true merit, wherever scientific knowledge and education are separated. But we must also look for the cause in the pervading personality of the nation: the one who dwells on the surface and is fond of boasting about his superficial knowledge. The noble virtue of humility is seldom present in him.

In England's golden era under Edward III, when nobility was developed alongside bravery, women distinguished themselves in ways that were no less impressive. They too competed with men in the noble and brave. Following the death of John III, Duke of Britain, a war of succession broke out between the Count of Montfort, his male heir, and Charles de Blois, husband of John's only female heir. The countesses, however, distinguished themselves favourably.[51] When both their husbands were imprisoned, they took over the governing responsibilities left to them. They placed themselves at the head of their troops and performed wonders of bravery when they heroically charged at the besiegers. France, whose rivalry with England never lapsed, became entangled in these disputes.

Some took the side of Charles de Blois, others that of Montfort. The result was a war that had a lasting influence on both nations.

Philippa, the wife of Edward III, followed the example of these brave countesses.[52] The Scots, cheered on by France, invaded northern England while Edward and his troops laid siege to Calais. Philippa organized their troops, handed over command to Lord Percy, rode through the ranks of their soldiers, and encouraged them to be brave. Heartened by her example, they achieved a complete victory over the Scots, and the king was captured along with many Scottish knights. After Philippa had brought the royal prisoner to safety, she hurried to her husband in Calais. But let us hear Hume himself on the subject, who on this occasion gives great praise to women:

> Phylippa, having secured her royal prisoner in the tower, crossed the sea at Dover; and was received in the English camp before Calais with all the triumph due to her merit, and her success. This age was the reign of chivalry and gallantry. Edward's court excelled in these accomplishments as much as in policy and arms, and if any thing could justify the obsequious devotion then professed to the fair sex, it must be the appearance of such extraordinary women as shone forth during that period. Hume, *History of England* vol. 3, p. 249 etc.

That Philippa did not lose her feminine softness and gentleness through these martial talents is testified by her subsequent conduct towards the six citizens of Calais, from whom Eustache de Saint Pierre gained immortal renown. By prostrating herself before her husband, it was she who persuaded him to save them from an ignominious death. After her request had been granted, she took these venerable citizens into her tent, entertained them, and sent them back, showered with gifts. At that moment Philippa was greater than Edward.

During the reign of Edward III, the spirit of chivalry flourished to the highest degree, and the influence of women was powerful. The Order of the Garter was established during this time, the history of which is well known.

Margaret of Anjou, wife of Henry VI of England, distinguished herself with personal bravery and skill in the art of warfare during the long and bloody civil wars between Lancashire and Yorkshire, known as the War of the Roses.[53] She achieved several victories while her frail husband was in captivity, and she saved him on more than one occasion. When she finally had to admit defeat in the last decisive battle, during which her husband was once more in captivity, she fled to a forest with her only son. There she was attacked by bandits and her jewellery was stolen. But while the bandits shared the spoils among themselves, she took the opportunity to escape, and hid in a thicket in the forest. She underwent hunger and hardship for several days. Suddenly another bandit appeared, who rushed at her with a sword, intent on murder. Yet quickly seizing this frightening moment, she took her son by the hand, who was only young, and stepped forward with courage to meet their attacker. Placing the hand of her son in his, she spoke to him: 'Here, my friend, I entrust to you the care of the only son of your king, the future heir of England!' The bandit was flattered by this trust, and took her and her son under his protection. He led her to the Scottish coast, where she was able to escape to France. She lived there in solitude for several years, and tried once more to free her husband, who remained imprisoned in the Tower, and to bring her son to the throne. When her plans had failed, she returned and died a commoner. What courage, what determination, what presence of mind lies in the quick decision she had to make in this desperate situation to call upon the bandit to protect her son, and still to believe in humanity despite his lowly, fallen state.

Elizabeth's name will shine forever in England's history; from her arose the greatest time of its flourishing.[54] It was she who rebuilt the navy, stimulated trade, and, with supreme wisdom, settled the disputes between Protestants and Catholics. She achieved infinitely great things for England, and, while there are several stains on her memory, she achieved too much for these to diminish her greatness.

The Russians have already become so accustomed to the rule of women that it is difficult for an emperor to keep the helm of the government for long. How extensive is the influence of women in Russia's history! The two Catherines, Anna and Elizabeth, claim a very important and undeniable contribution to Russia, both for good and for ill.[55] The wise government and legislation of Catherine the Great in particular will remain a celebrated memory for a long time to come. She was remarkable as a regent, even if her genius is soiled by her moral shortcomings.

But enough of this historical sketch. We have no need for anything more extensive. My work would have grown into a folio if I wanted to be any more detailed. The historian, who reads history with a keen and impartial eye, can come up with this on his own.

I now turn to the influence of women in the early education of both sexes, which we must consider as infinitely more important than their influence in state revolutions. For this influence must be considered as the basis of the future character of individuals, and thus also as an effect on the whole.

The early education of all young citizens of the world, high and low, male and female, is generally the business of women. This is where their influence is revealed in the most decisive and all-encompassing way.

In a time when so much has been written about education by deserving men, it does not require any further contestation on my part to show how much the first impressions decide the future character of a young citizen of the world; how much a skilful hand can achieve and a clumsy one lay to waste. The first impressions are the most vivid, and last our entire lives. They remain as dark ideas, so to speak, lying in the background of our soul and continuing to have an influence often unbeknown to us in the reasoning behind our actions. If we have to struggle with our disorderly inclinations and moods, it is they, not original sin, that complicate the matter.[56] Alternatively, if we have developed a skill in the practice of every good virtue, if the principle of duty has developed in us, and if we work for our improvement and for the good of humankind according to sound reasons, it is far less difficult for us. We must then seek out the source of education and look back with gratitude to what our mothers and early educators have done. I will strive to develop this material further in the study when I consider the educated woman as mother.

From my discussion thus far, it follows undeniably that, since the influence of women intervenes so powerfully in the driving forces of human happiness, much—infinitely much—depends on the education of women. In the higher noble education of women, the whole of humanity is also being educated, for their work not only intervenes in the early education of all people, and not only intervenes in the driving forces of the state machine, but also exerts a powerful influence on the tone of society. Look around in cities both large and small. Notice the tone that prevails among society. You will immediately be able to discern the degree to which the women are morally and spiritually educated. The realm of moral beauty is our territory.

If we awake in earnest, if we fiercely strive for higher education, I ask not to make our work more difficult but, rather, to make it lighter in every way, for men certainly have as much to gain from our education as we do.[57] Indeed, if we take on the burden of the improvement of our higher education we deserve their thanks, not their blame. We could, of course, make ourselves even more comfortable, leave things as they are, and satisfy ourselves with the lower spiritual position assigned to us by the writers who have written about the female vocation. And since, as the saying goes, the world is after all governed by women, who guide the higher roles of men behind the scenes, the female sex has not, all things considered, done too badly, given what men have written about our dependence.

But we no longer want to rule in this way; we have awakened from our slumber. We throw away the invisible threads with which we have so far directed the great spectacle of the world from behind the scenes, for it is beneath our dignity as humans to further disguise ourselves to achieve our purpose through cunning and intrigue. We would like to satisfy ourselves in the colourful hustle and bustle of the world theatre with the small inconspicuous roles that are no less important for the whole. We only want to be free to fulfil the first duty of humankind, which is to train all of one's powers in the most beautiful harmony to the highest perfection. We share this duty equally, and it is as much our responsibility as it is that of men. Before we are man or woman, male or female citizen, husband or wife, we are human. And what is it that gives humans a higher status than animals? Only our perfectibility. The beaver builds its dam, the bee constructs its hive, the bird shapes its nest, the badger digs its tunnels, the ant fills its storehouse according to the type that nature has impressed upon it with an unchanging script. The human being alone is merely a capacity, everything else must be developed, reason must complete the work, it must be its own moral creator and form itself into a humane being.

Are we excluded from this obligation by virtue of being women? And if not, who then wants to clip our spiritual wings? Who wants to keep us through some petty purpose from being human in the most fundamental sense of the word?

> Should I not also live in that life?
> Who will perform the miracle
> And impart to my mind Sappho's power of thought
> If here by pot and spindle I let it idly rest?
>
> O men, men! How you teach us!
> If nettles bloom among your violets
> Along the streams of life,
> Who shall weed them? Your wife? Alas.[58]

Should we not concern ourselves with the most important objects of human knowledge? Should we accept everything on pure faith, not investigate for ourselves, not think for ourselves, not abstract the principles of our own thought, and form sure maxims by which to stand firm in times of danger? Who could deny this with any reason? Should these writers succeed in robbing us of this beautiful privilege? Would humanity be any better for it?

As we have seen, the interest of mutual interaction is so intertwined that each sex is constantly dependent on the other. Just consider the countries in the East, where women are degraded as mere tools of sensual pleasure, and see what the culture of humankind looks like as a whole. It is infinitely far behind in comparison to our Europe, where women hold greater possession of their human rights.

As fiery as I feel, my aim is to present as accurately as possible just how intimately both sexes are connected with each other, how powerfully they affect each other, how they are destined to walk hand in hand on the path to perfection, and how the refinement of one depends on the refinement of the other. If I am successful, men will not seek to put obstacles in our way. Instead, they will kindly offer us a hand to climb the ladder with them. And we would spare no effort, despising the dross that has hitherto bound us and oppressed our minds. Though it may not be us, our offspring may realize this beautiful dream.

So it is only through the highest moral perfection of women that men can obtain their own. And we cannot strive for the highest moral perfection without insight and free action. The writers who want to curtail our right to higher education may have felt that men require morally perfected women for their own perfection. Yet they do not want to grant that women need free education in order to develop morally. In all their writings they portray us as beings that depend solely on men and determine our education only with respect to the relation between man and woman. Yet I consider this portrayal to be an indisputable contradiction.

For example, Herr Ewald declares that being virtuous is a power too great for us to bear.[59] Thus we should not come to feel the morally beautiful but merely smell it. And yet he still demands that we should educate ourselves in keeping with men. What a contradiction!

I could list countless such inconsistencies from the books written about the *female vocation* if it would not distract me too far from my present goal. I will keep this matter for another occasion. Suffice it to say that such contradictions are always the consequence of starting from the wrong principles when treating a matter of such importance.

But if I insist on the higher education of women, I must first communicate to my readers what I actually mean by this idea, from which principles it is derived, and to which individuals I wish it to spread.

First of all, the education of women must be entirely free. We must be able to explore any field of knowledge to which our genius leads us. The treasures of the ancients must therefore be available to us, just as they are to men, such that their wealth may enrich us too. In like manner, philosophy, the science that breathes spirit and order into all other sciences so that they might serve humanity, should not be denied to us. Philosophy is the science that teaches us our true conditions in regard to the highest being, ourselves, and the external world. And finally, it is the science that teaches us to value things only according to their inner and true content. This beautiful source, which sheds light on our duties, as well as the *how* and *where* and *why* of all that is right and possible, must not remain closed to us. Everything that could be of interest to one as a human being—our dwelling place, the earth with its many revolutions, and its great ladder of being, the whole of nature—must be our museum in which we study the Supreme Being and explore the limits and boundlessness of all finite things. No less must we study the history of humankind. From history we learn what the cultured human was, is, and can be. From it we gain knowledge not only of ourselves but of people in general.

This education must be thorough, and, like that of men, based on proper sources. It must not come from elementary books written for women, in which we are treated like overgrown children. Thorough knowledge makes us humble and self-effacing; half-baked and superficial knowledge makes us vain and proud.[60]

Second, the higher education of human beings, and consequently also of women, must flow from the only true source: humankind's duty to develop all its powers and to contribute to the well-being of the whole as an active member. Let our personal improvement and our participation in the great plan of nature's Creator be our purpose. Then scientific knowledge will keep pace with fine education and represent the true ideal of humankind. This pure source from which flows the highest human education will make us humble even though we have reached the outer limits of human knowledge, lifted high above all others and conscious of our educated understanding. We will always say to ourselves that we have done nothing but our duty, that we received a greater talent than others, and with this we could grow more than was possible for the one who received less. In the spiritual as well as the physical creation there is a series that rises from the lowest to the highest. Nothing is completely similar, everything ascends the great ladder, for it would not be good if the same powers, the same capacities, were everywhere. There could be no action and reaction, meaning that everything would remain inactive and dead.

If I could only recommend to my sex that it is the duty of humankind to develop all our powers, that we cannot defend the honour of humankind without this high education, we would go further than men in this fine matter. With us, so many of the selfish ambitions acquired by men in the course of their education fall away. Apart from the duty of humankind, nothing could encourage us to develop our intellect other than the wretched desire to shine, and what a miserable purpose that would be![61] In contrast, men have many more selfish purposes than we do. The sciences are their livelihood, and through them they attain glory and honours. We are denied such desires, and indeed for our good, for we are therefore far more likely to be human beings in the nobler sense of the term. We desire and demand nothing more; the honour of humanity is enough for us.

But as long as our education is only conditionally granted to us, as long as we are still given limits on how far we may go, as long as we must proceed by trickery and not by asserting our rights when we are driven by our genius to exceed this line, and as long as we are prescribed with subordinate purposes, so long will our education, and the education of humankind in general, remain extremely unstable.

Third, this highest education cannot, however, extend to all individuals of the female sex. It would be foolish to demand an equal degree of intellectual capabilities. The gifts of nature are and must be unequally distributed. It would be just as foolish to demand this higher education for the lower classes, who must satisfy themselves with subordinate purposes.[62] It would be ridiculous to demand this education for the wife of a day labourer or tradesman. My demand extends only to the upper and middle classes: they must be able to follow their genius freely and unconditionally. In the upper and middle classes, education is conditioned by the measure of talent that nature bestows on each one. To be a worthy member of humanity, each must go as far as her intellectual capacity allows her. Her education must flow from the true source alone; each must achieve only according to what she is able to accomplish with sincere zeal.

But the question arises: if physical weakness does not presuppose mental weakness, if our minds think according to the same rules as the male mind, and if our brains are not organized differently to those of men, have women proved this in the various branches of science, a posteriori as it were? Here again history may tell.

As a philologist we have the famous Dacier, who is too well known to mention her works here.[63] I only want to add that if she is accused of pedantry, this accusation is more in keeping with her age than with her femininity. We also have Reiske, who is known to have written the better part of her husband's work.[64] Not to mention Schurman, the Countess of Stolberg, the unhappy but amiable Johanna Gray, and many others.[65]

As poets of antiquity we have Sappho and Korinna, the latter of whom beat the famous Pindar several times in the Olympic Games.[66] Among the Germans, the author of *Schwestern von Lesbos*, then Rudolphi, Emilie von Berlepsch, Brun, Göckingk's first wife, the young lady of A, and many others.[67]

Among the French, Deshoulières shines exquisitely.[68] Voltaire praises her in his *Siècle de Louis XIV*: 'Of all the French women who have sown in the fields of poetry, she has reaped the most verses.'[69] This eulogy does not say enough. She is the only one in France who achieved anything significant as an idyllic poet, except in our times, when de l'Isle is her rival. We also have Scudéry as a novelist, and as the author of some light and pleasant poems.[70] Although her novels were long-winded and adventurous according to the taste of her times, even Herr Pockels says that she possessed a healthier logic than many a French philosopher.[71] Then we have Chenon, who is known as a poet, painter, and musician.[72] Not to mention Countess Coligny as an elegiac poet, and many more poets for whom we lack the space and leisure to mention here.[73]

Even though the number of female poets is very respectable, even though their poems often have a high energy and breathe morality and nature everywhere, Herr Pockels feels licensed to make the following harsh judgment against them in his *Versuch einer Charakteristik des weiblichen Geschlechts*:

> In the poems of women, which can no longer be counted, one finds that nature is imitated but almost always defaced. As simple and unaffected is nature in all her beautiful and greatest appearances, so polished is she depicted in the verses of women. Nature wears her finest jewellery as one must display one's finery at court or in the ballroom. It seems that female poets believe that one cannot honour the good muse better than to put on all the adornment borrowed from others. And thus everything is spoiled.[74]

How disparagingly and falsely Herr Pockels judges the talent of an entire sex! If we only had the author of *Schwestern von Lesbos*, if we only had Deshoulières, we would have enough to refute this harsh judgment. One would have to read the poems of women with a very unfavourable prejudice against them to find what Herr Pockels has found. In general, they are far less pompous and adorned than those of men, and embody a fullness of feeling that comes from and speaks to the heart.

To soften his harsh judgment somewhat, Herr Pockels adds:

> I do not want to conclude from these remarks that women have no sense at all, or at least no real sense of the great and sublime. Such a claim would suffer from too great a generality. All I dare to say is that, as a rule, every feeling is greater and more vivid in men than in women. By reading ancient poetry, by nurturing our capacity for thought, and by studying nature and art in depth, we get to know nature in itself and in its sublimity earlier than women. We certainly have more prior knowledge for the contemplation and depiction of nature than uninformed women tend to bring with them. Vol. 1, p. 384.

Herr Pockels makes up for nothing with this remark. First of all, a fine poem does not require thorough learnedness. More often than not, learnedness harms poetry. As the entire history of humankind gives evidence, the great poets come before the writers of history, orators, and philosophers. Indeed, Homer's poems still provide the model by which our poets are formed. He wrote his immortal works when Greece's culture was in its infancy, and at the time of Greece's highest flourishing there was no poet to equal him. This is the nature of the human mind and its powers: the imagination is formed earlier than the understanding. It flies highest and expresses itself more powerfully when learned and scientific knowledge has not yet reached the maturity that produces order and clarity. That is why the field of imagination and poetry belongs above all to the young. When education is complete, when the years progress, the highest momentum of the imagination diminishes. There are only rare exceptions. Few have such a beautiful and rich abundance of imagination as our Klopstock, Wieland, Goethe, and Schiller, which has not been weakened but rather cultivated and refined through a deep and thorough knowledge of the sciences and arts. But this high knowledge did not make them poets. Nature alone is able do this, for no one has ever become a poet through learning. The best-known philosophers—Thales, Zeno, Pythagoras, Aristotle, Plato, Seneca, Leibniz, Descartes, and Kant—were not poets. The great orator Cicero made himself look ridiculous when he tried his hand at the subject. We lack the knowledge of the ancients, says Herr Pockels. We have just mentioned the renowned philologists of our sex, and how many we have in Germany, France, Italy, and England who know the ancients. And if the fine poem *Schwestern von Lesbos* did not reveal any knowledge of the ancients, the author would be three times as great, for she would owe everything to her own genius.

Moreover, knowledge of the ancients cannot make a poet; it merely refines and develops his skill. We have as few great poets among our philologists as among the great philosophers. If nature has organized women's minds in such a way that her feelings pour out into the language of poetry, her poems will only gain in power and imagination. This should be no surprise, for the writers who deny us so much have just granted that we exceed in imagination and feeling. Many poems by women are living proof of this, such as the songs of Amaranthe and Nantchen.[75] Göckingk is a splendid poet, but Nantchen's poetry is stronger in its perceptions and imagination.

Herr Pockels continues: 'Men bring a deeper knowledge of nature to their poetic depiction of natural scenes than the more uninformed women.' Is it really necessary for a true, beautiful, and captivating depiction of natural phenomena to have deep knowledge of them? Do we have poems of this kind from Linnaeus, Buffon, Löwenhöck, Schwamerdam, Müschenbrök, Bonnet, Klein, and others? It was precisely this deep knowledge of nature that prevented them from extoling its beauty! But there is so much evidence that women are capable of sublime, strong feelings, and that they have a sense of the manifold phenomena of nature, that there is no need to refute his claim. Even Herr Pockels admits that nature in general bestows on women the beautiful gift of poetry when he says that the poems of women cannot be counted.

Women have also tried and proved their talents as novelists. This again is proof of their vivid imagination. I have neither the space nor leisure to mention them all here, since the number is considerable. But I will mention the Countess La Fayette, author of *La Princesse de Clèves* and *Zaïde*, who was the first to write a French novel full of moral feeling, nature, and grace.[76] *Agnes von Lilien* can be seen as the ideal of a fine novel in aesthetic and moral terms.[77] If this novel were properly valued, the author would be honoured for providing a model of the German novel. Her example might serve to clean up some of the excesses of an exaggerated and impure imagination that tend to shape its component parts, which often make the novel, the longest form of reading, more harmful than useful. She demonstrates that the novel can teach many fine virtues, spread enlightenment, reduce prejudice, and serve as preparation for more serious reading. Our better novelists of the male sex are also perfectly suited to this purpose, especially the novels of Müller and La Fontaine. Other great novelists seem to achieve the aesthetic ideal by means of disregarding morality. These great men of art like to think that humankind now suffers from too much irritability and morality.

Yet they would be more certain of receiving the applause of posterity if they combined aesthetics with morality in beautiful union. *Agnes von Lilien* combines them perfectly, and for this reason I wish that this novel would come into the hands of every young girl.

Our Sophie de la Roche also has a forget-me-not in her garland, which the grateful public arranges for esteemed writers as a reward for their efforts to ennoble humankind.[78] Generally speaking, it seems to me that women are excellently suited to writing novels. Their imaginations are equally strong as those of men, but far purer. Morality is their domain, knowledge of human nature their science, the gift of beautiful presentation their talent. As long as they are educated, women will always be a blessing to humanity in this field.

The author of *Julchen Grünthal*, a witty and useful novel, has also shown herself to be a natural scientist.[79] In her *Naturkalender* she manages to combine the practical aspects of agriculture and the sundry products of nature with the basic elements of natural science, and to present her insights to our youth in a pure and lively fashion.

In her many and varied works, Madame de Genlis has developed extensive knowledge of the human heart in its many passions and inclinations.[80] Her writings teach the purest morality in a beautiful, flourishing style of writing, and are of great value to the aesthetic and moral formation of the young. The cultured mind also finds great satisfaction in her later writings.

Among the English we have many novelists, as well as many female writers who are distinguished for their moral writings for young people.[81]

Even in the field of medicine we have a woman who has earned great honour. The stepmother of the late Professor Erxleben was a practical doctor, and, as is proper, wrote and defended her doctorate in Latin.[82] Her grateful son tells the story in the *Journal von und für Deutschland* as follows.[83] She was the daughter of a practising doctor, who had two children, a boy and a girl. He sought to train his son in the medical profession, and, during the lessons he gave, his daughter was present, working on her handcraft. One day, when the father became frustrated with the son's slow progress, he noticed that his daughter was whispering the answer to him, for he could not find it. The father questioned his daughter and was surprised to find that she, simply by listening, had grasped more of the subject than her brother. From that moment on he decided that his daughter should take the place of his son, who was unable to take up the profession. His decision was a success, so much so that she became a master of the art. After marrying, she did not make use of it until her husband became dangerously ill, and was unwilling to seek assistance from any other doctor. She gave in to his urgent requests, and succeeded in restoring him to complete health. The cure caused a great stir, and she began to be asked for assistance by acquaintances and strangers alike, such that her practice grew extensively. The local doctors were, of course, upset, for their business began to dwindle. They appealed to the government to forbid her to practise, for she did not have a doctorate. And so she was forbidden. But she had the courage to write a letter to the recently crowned King of Prussia, Frederick the Great, and asked for permission to undertake one. The great king, who rewarded merit wherever he found it, granted her permission. She did indeed receive a doctorate, and practised as a doctor until her death. She also wrote a work in Latin on the subject of women's education, yet Professor Erxleben reports that it no longer exists.[84] What most honours this learned woman, however, is the testimony of this, her good son, who reports that, despite her exceptional calling, she was a good wife, mother, and housewife, and fulfilled all the obligations of these affairs.

In the diplomatic field we also have the well-known Chevalier d'Éon, who earned great fame through her career.[85]

In France, under Louis XIV and Louis XV, there were many female memoirists who can be regarded as historians of their time, and who are still frequently cited.

Among the women of France, there are many letter writers who have distinguished themselves in the field. There is still a large gap in this field among us Germans, but is it not possible to fill it? Do we Germans not have minds that are lively enough to share our ideas in a light, flowing style of writing, and in a pleasant and playful hand? Or are we held back by our way of life, which is less communicable and sociable?* The letters of Sévigné contain a wealth of feeling expressed in the finest way, and although the subject of her letters lacks variety, and contain long-winded lamentations about the separation of her beloved daughter, she knows how to nuance her expressions so that they seem ever new to us.[86] The subjects considered in the letters of the woman de Maintenon are more comprehensive, and she

---

* If the letters from the woman from Courland, Sophie Schwarz, could awaken our desire to imitate her style, this gap would soon be filled. These letters breathe the purest feeling for the beauty of both natural scenes and human dignity, and contain many useful truths. I wish that they would become the favourite reading of my young women friends. Womankind can rightly be proud of Sophie and her friend Elisa. [See [Schwarz,] *Briefe einer Curländerinn*, which records the letters exchanged between Sophie Schwarz and Elisa von der Recke, published by Johann Ludwig Schwarz in 1791.]

too knows the art of surprising us with ever new turns in the most trivial things.[87] Ninon l'Enclos deals with the philosophy of love in her letters, and has brought the art of love into a much more consistent system than Ovid.[88] Babet's letters to Boursault are written with a delightful grace, naïvety, and wit.[89] Boursault is more concerned with cracking jokes in the exchange, and falls far short of her.

It was with pleasure and admiration that I read the recently published work of Madame de Staël-Holstein called *De la littérature considérée dans ses rapports avec les institutions sociales*.[90] The undertaking of this work alone is a great honour to the author and to her sex. If she has not captured the entirety of her subject matter, if in particular she has dealt with German literature far too briefly and does not seem fully aware of its great scope and the heights it has now reached, and if she does not do justice even to the German language, this is not the fault of her sex. It is a general fault of the nation from which she received her education and under which she studied the history of literature. If one reads all the scientific books in French on the subject, how briefly they treat the so-called *North*. Millot's *Universalgeschichte*, for example, would not be useful if Christiani had not included *Die Geschichte der zweiten Hälfte Europas* in his translation.[91]

But the enterprise is so large, so extensive, that the mere idea of de Staël's study already displays genius and power. In this truly classic work she develops varied and thorough knowledge in a style full of energy and delicacy, yet at the same time with humility. She offers many illuminating and subtle remarks that betray genius and originality, which will give the thinking person material for developing many new ideas.

Women have also distinguished themselves in the fine arts, especially in music and painting. In the meritorious late Senator Kirchhoff's small but tasteful collection, I saw floral still-life paintings from a woman's brush whose name escapes me. In her paintings, nature had been so admirably depicted that I thought that I saw dust on the auricles and dew drops on some of the flowers. Madame Debor received the major prize from the Academy of Painting in Copenhagen. The altarpiece in the chapel of our orphanage stands as proof of her skill. But above all, Angelika Kauffmann shines as a great genius in this art.[92] I will sing her praises in the words of our excellent Herder:

> In all of Angelika's compositions, an innate moral grace is the character of her subjects. Even the wild becomes gentle through her hand. Her young men float on the earth like geniuses. Never has her brush been able to depict an impudent gesture. Just as a blameless mind may think of human

characters, so has she pulled such characters out of their shells, and with a beautiful mind that captures the whole in the slightest thing, she allows each part to emerge like a flower, harmoniously and gently ordered. An angel gave to her its name, and the muse of humanity has become her sister.[93]

To such praise I have nothing to add, even though there is far more to be said about this great artistic genius.

In the art of music, the blind Paradis has distinguished herself.[94] She not only played the piano with particular skill, expression, and delicacy, but also received acclaim as a composer. There is also Strinasaccy, whose wonderous delicacy and expression on the violin has delighted every ear.[95] And Westenholz in Ludwigslust plays the accordion with such skill that she is even able to play the allegro.[96] We also have the late Brandes, who was a composer, not to mention the late Bause, the great artist's daughter, and many others.[97]

The examples I have mentioned so far provide definitive proof that women have, despite their neglected education, achieved something in every subject of knowledge. The only objection one could make is that they have not been able to rise to the region of higher knowledge, to critical philosophy and higher mathematics. From this one might infer that they possess subordinate mental faculties. Would such a conclusion be correct? Would such a proof have generally validity?

Among the many thousands of men who have devoted themselves to learning from their youth, how many of them are truly great in these fields? Only the original minds that have constructed new and fertile systems come into play here. If we stick to counting them, how infinitely small the number is! And if this accusation were really founded, does not the main reason for this lie in the subordinate status, education, and way of life granted to women? Surrounded by trivialities from youth onwards, tied up with trinkets, chastened by coercion, and held back by an idleness that feels like comfort, how can, how should, a woman's mind penetrate through this fourfold fog and find the light?

And if her mind succeeds nevertheless, if it soars to its own conviction in the field of higher knowledge, what proof of the intellectual powers of women can already be seen under these conditions!

Do not tell me that genius overcomes all obstacles, that it shines brightly though every fog. This may be true in all other fields of knowledge, but not in philosophy. The highest of all sciences demands in its great and important scope a good deal of prior knowledge, which nature lays before us, and which only a learned education and continued, uninterrupted study can bring to maturity. How many philosophical minds, which lacked the opportunity for education but could have competed with a Kant or a Leibniz, slumber unnoticed and unused behind the plough!

There are simply no grounds to claim that a woman's mind is not organized in such a way as to grasp the higher sciences.

Experience contradicts such a claim. Some women have shown that they had a sense and a mind for these difficult sciences. Euler wrote his letters on natural science and philosophy, in which one can find the most difficult propositions, to a German princess (to Princess Amalia, sister of Frederick the Great, whom he loved above all his sisters and brothers).[98] She must have had both the sense and capacity for these higher sciences.

Christina, the Queen of Sweden, daughter of Gustavus Adolphus the Great, took lessons on Descartes's philosophy.[99] If she did not share her thoughts on the subject, it may have been the pedantic nature of the public, which had not yet been filtered out, that frightened her away. This great woman was so enthusiastic about philosophy and art that it led her to spurn the crown, a triumph for both philosophy and art, becoming the only example of this kind in history.

Our great Herschel's sister also devoted herself to the higher sciences.[100] Together they discovered planets, observed fixed stars, and traced the course of comets. Her brother probably taught her these sciences: proof that women are capable of the higher sciences if they have instruction in them.

As a young girl, Baroness Knigge published a work of logic for women.[101] She was not only interested in the more serious sciences, but must have possessed them.

The Marquise du Châtelet expounded the philosophy of Leibniz and translated and commented on Newton.[102] Voltaire said the following about her: 'Deservedly useless to the court, but revered among all the nations enlivened by the pursuit of knowledge, who have admired the depth of her genius and eloquence. Of all the women who could illustrate France, it is she who has had the truest spirit and the most unaffected wit.'[103]

Voltaire's testimony to the Marquise du Châtelet, that she has employed her great intellect with the least pretention, is further proof of my claim that it is only one-sided half-knowledge that swells the mind, whereas solid and thorough knowledge makes it unpretentious and humble. With these qualities one does not find a showpiece. For the true thinker, the eager truth-seeker, it is enough to be, not to shine. Indeed, it takes almost the same degree of knowledge to distinguish such a person from the rest of humankind. The semi-informed person boasts, and puffs himself up with the little he knows. But he only deceives the ignorant one; the knowing one smiles and...remains silent.

And how many writings of women there are, which prove that they are not strangers to speculative philosophy and are fully engaged in practical and moral philosophy. To name but a few, the writings of Madame de Staël prove the former, and those of Genlis prove the latter.

Since women have achieved something with their neglected education despite being rejected from the source of wisdom, the question of whether they are really capable of achieving something fruitful in the field of speculative philosophy will not be decided until a considerable number of young girls have been educated in the same manner as boys, and with the same resources. Only then can experience determine the matter.[104]

Here one might raise an objection. If a woman is to be a speculative philosopher, and a great one at that, how will she fulfil her duties as a wife, mother, and housewife? The serious and deep science of philosophy occupies the whole life of a thinker, often demanding that he stays up late into the night. If a woman were to rise so high as to create her own philosophical system, she would have no time left to fulfil her taxing duties. I concede this point, but only in the case of real genius. But since such minds are extremely rare among men, and always will be, they would likewise be rare among women. If one of them were to give herself entirely to these serious sciences, if she were to find in these lofty regions the satisfaction for all her strivings for happiness and thereby become useful to the world, who could forbid her from remaining unmarried, as Kant is and Leibniz was? As human beings, are women to be regarded as less free than men to grow the talents entrusted to them, to go wherever their genius drives them? Would they not be as beneficial to the good of humankind as they would be through the reproduction of their kind? Would the population lose so much through this? No more than they lost through the celibacy of Kant and Leibniz, who enriched the world simply though the immortal works they birthed as children of their minds.[105] These exceptions would always be rare, and would not interfere with the fulfilment of female duties in general. But as far as practical philosophy is concerned, which reassures and strengthens one's convictions through the investigation of the most important truths about *how*, *where*, and *why*, I maintain that these investigations, as the highest duty of all thinking beings, and thus also of women, cannot collide with their individual duties. Nature would have to contradict itself. On the contrary, the source of these investigations will refine, establish a principle for, and extend women's sphere of influence.

But surely women will lack the time to do so. Let us consider this claim in the second part of this book, where I will examine the woman as wife, mother, and housewife, and attempt to prove that a higher education of woman does not contradict her threefold calling but rather elevates and ennobles it.

2

Woman Considered as Wife

Does the Higher Education of Her Mind Make Her Incapable of Fulfilling the Duties of This Position?

Do we exist just for the sake of men?[1] This question seems ridiculous when brought before the judgment seat of sound reason. Reason teaches us that both sexes are there to promote the happiness of one another, to form the highest ideal of humanity in the most beautiful union, and to work for the best of the whole.[2]

Nevertheless, with very few exceptions men seem to consider our sex from this erroneous perspective when talking about a wife's duties. And since their claims cannot be reinforced by a healthy philosophy, they take refuge in the Bible, which has often been used to warrant some nonsense or other.

Moses tells us that Adam was created first and on his own, so that it was only when he began to feel bored that the all-wise Creator recognized it was not good to leave man in such a state. The Creator realized that it would be better to make him a helper who would accompany him and help him pass the time.*[3]

Now I ask whether such a petty idea is worthy of the almighty Creator of nature? It was due entirely to the limited insights of humanity in its infancy, evident in the writers of this and other similar traditions, that such fables were invented. But if humanity continues to base the duties of its cultured nations on such a fable once its flowering mind has matured into fruit, it will remain a difficult task for the thinking person to explain this contradiction to themself.[4]

For if nature was responsible for producing such beings, it certainly also took care of their preservation with the same diligence that it displayed in their genesis. That it indeed did so is evident in the whole constitution of

---

* Rabbinism has embellished this fable with other remarks, which can be read in *Histoire des Femmes*. Feminine modesty forbids me from mentioning them here.

humankind, along with all other existing creatures. To prevent the obstinate creature from thwarting its purpose, nature combined its duty with the highest stimulus of pleasure. The animal has completely fulfilled its vocation by simply following this stimulus; yet the human being has not. The human being must learn to feel that it is not merely in possession of the senses but also of a heart and a mind. The sublime human was not intended to be a mere stopgap in nature who would blindly fulfil its purpose. Rather, marriage should be for him the purest source of harmonious feelings, the finest bond which leads him to the ideal of the highest perfection. Only in the union of this harmonious bond can and will humanity be what nature intended it to be: happy in striving for the highest development of its powers. Therefore, the duties and happiness of both sexes had to be completely mutual.

Thus woman does not exist for the sake of man, nor man for the sake of woman; they are created one for the sake of the other in completely equal relationship.

Yet even now, writers who are estimable in many respects praise Moses's creation fable as a story rich in meaning. Given the otherwise clear judgment of these men, it would be impossible to account for such a phenomenon if it did not expose the jagged edge of male pride and conceit. As soon as our investigations are accompanied by a lively interest or passion, we see what we want to see and not what is there. Our judgment is corrupted by passion.

Herr Pockels for instance makes his case by citing a long section from *Briefe über die wichtigsten Gegenstände der Menschheit*,[5] which calls on this oriental fable in the following manner:

> Moses' agreeable account of the origin of women, and how God came to the idea of creating the first woman, has always greatly pleased me and truly belongs here. It is not good for the human being to be alone; I want to make a helper for him, who will remain by his side!* Herein lies all that can be said about the vocation of the female sex, about its relation to ours, about its befitting education, etc., and other things we cannot deal with here.

---

* The author should have added: 'And I now want to transform this *human being* who was originally destined to be alone and make him into a *man*.'

The author continues:

> We men are and will remain the leading protagonists; our women are only our helpers. This is to say: *they exist for our sake.* Even the second chapter of Moses corrects the misunderstanding to which the first chapter might give rise. In the first chapter, God immediately creates a male and female together, but in the second, Adam is created alone and is led into the garden—and the garden is handed over to him, and all the beasts are presented for him to name them.[6] Since he finds no being among them that could be his helper, who would stand by him, he must (on the allegorical reading) give up a part of himself so that a woman may be made also for him. This remains a text that is bound to keep our women respecting us.[7]

In the author's defence, I would like to believe that this pronouncement is merely a joke. It would be quite unfortunate for men if they had to borrow the respect we owe them from this childish oriental fable. The author would have a very small view of his sex if he meant it seriously. The only respect that both sexes must have for one another is that which is based on sublime, enlightened attitudes and noble, humane actions. This is the only lasting and effective kind. All respect that is dictated by a positive command is despotism.[8] As such, it will only consist in external displays of servitude and remain alien to the heart and mind. It will thus be thrown aside at the first opportunity when there is nothing to fear or everything to gain.

It is altogether strange that men who claim to be educated still call on the books of Moses and the fables of creation they depict. It is more than probable that Moses did not write the books attributed to his name, and that they were written by several later authors who documented the tales of their fathers, as raw as they found them among an uncivilized people. If one looks into the sources of these traditions, one finds that they reflect the opinions that prevailed among the various peoples whom these nomads plagued with their presence, or where they were taken as slaves.[9]

The entire creation narrative of Moses reflects the coarseness of his people and his age.

About 6,000 years ago, the author tells us, it occurred to the Godhead to create something other than himself. Was this God from eternity? And if so, did he spend an uncountable number of years inactive or wrapped up in himself, sleeping through some long eternal winter only to come to life 6,000 years ago and begin to feel his agency? If this God was from eternity, were space and time coeternal with him? Moses, along with all the other ancient writers who have written about creation, have their God confront an unformed chaos. But the Creator who creates *ex nihilo* is an absurdity. The authors of the Books of Moses discovered the ancient philosophers' dispersed and dark notion of chaos; yet they failed to order it and illuminate its meaning.

The schedule according to which their God began and completed the business of creation is entirely human: one cannot do everything at once but must do one thing after the other. If the idea of creation points to a formative power of nature that God put into matter, which consists in a striving to take on shapes that can only develop slowly, then it is certainly beautiful. But this idea does not fit with God's command, let there be! As the author of *De la philosophie de la nature* puts it: Moses cut the Gordian knot by putting these words in the mouth of his God.[10] But all these partly great and partly parochial ideas of God are confused and exist only in embryonic form. Humanity's philosophical mind must first seek them out in the jumble of allegories and fables, in the hyperbolic language of the Orient, and interpret them correctly.

Indeed, the entire Old Testament is a mix of several handed-down grand ideas of the ancient philosophers, which contrast rather awkwardly with the notion of a national god that it depicts at every turn, who enforces his will whatever the cost and who rules like an oriental despot. Similarly, the beautiful, great idea of a unified God, which a translator probably inserted, stands wholly isolated; neither does it fit with the depiction of the deity as a merely national god, nor with the moral and ceremonial laws that developed in that nation. If the authors of the Books of Moses had correctly grasped this idea, they would not have taught about a national god but rather a God of the universe, and all the cruelties and persecutions of other nations would have been avoided.

It is therefore deplorable that the Old Testament is still considered from a misguided point of view, from which all kinds of nonsense are derived, and which cannot stand before the judgment seat of sound reason. If we consider it as the first document of humankind, as collected fragments of the dark legends of human understanding in its infancy, then it could and would be valuable and venerable to us. Yet in every other respect it is useless to us and even serves to our disadvantage.

From this very source also flows the idea of the supremacy of husbands over their wives. It comes to us from the Jewish people, where women have been despised and suppressed. For our priests have unfortunately founded the Christian religion on Judaism, even though it completely runs against the intentions and the spirit of its gentle founder.[11]

The author mentioned above also cites Paul as the authority on male domination and female oppression.[12] It is indeed sad that the great studies on the most important subjects of humankind in particular take refuge under the cover of such sources, when only the torch of philosophy and the judgment of sound reason can reveal the truth to us. Paul cannot be the authority here, and neither can Moses. It was he who, after having persecuted the Christian Church long enough, became a convert by a feigned miracle. He then poisoned the gentle and loving religion of Christ with a spirit of narrow-mindedness and intolerance, which the priests later expanded even more to the detriment of humankind, and which had been completely alien to the humane and tolerant founder of the faith. Let us only ever listen to Christ himself. Everything he says is so divine, so humane, so tolerant. He had both male and female students. And when two sisters, Martha and Mary, each tried to curry his favour in her own way—Martha by hustling and bustling about the house, and Mary by hanging onto the gentle, heavenly teachings of this great sage—he said to them: 'Martha, you are troubled about many things, but Mary has chosen the best part.'[13] With these words, did he not mean that women also have the right to educate their mind in the sublime truths of wisdom? And that we should not allow our mind to rest with pots and spindles?[14]

But our author does want to grant to us a measure of culture after all; namely, as much as we need to entertain witty men, but no more than that, and this is a consequence of the opinion that we exist only for the sake of men. Thus I say once more:

Woman does not exist for the sake of man, nor man for the sake of woman; they are created one for the sake of the other in completely equal relationship.

If I am right, it follows that the rights of men and women in marriage are completely equal. Marriage is a contract that two equally free beings make with each other to enjoy society in the most intimate and tender bond, and to give thanks to nature and society for this the sweetest pleasure by procreating their kind through wise and purposeful education.

In such a tender and intimate bond, any thought of authority based on positive laws falls away. Love does not prosper with authority and rule. I can respect and revere my master, but I cannot love him in the true sense of the word. Love makes everything equal.

But neither should the woman want to rule, as is the case among the people of the Mariana Islands. Marriage is such a delicate bond that at the slightest thought of domination from either side the relationship is broken.

Only the highest morality can ennoble this beautiful union, so that it does not sink to the mere animal business of reproduction or the convenience of self-interest.

One might object that in such a bond, which unifies two beings with different temperaments and occupations, it is extremely difficult in times of conflict to level out the scales when there is no authority to adjust them. To such an objection I reply that a bond maintained by authority is to be pitied. As the saying goes, it is the more reasonable one who is first to yield. Whoever is truly cognizant of the conditions of civil society knows and feels that if you want to enjoy the advantages of society, you have to take the inconveniences as well. It is a consequence of the imperfection of all human institutions that there is nothing under the sun that does not have its good and bad. The enlightened one weighs both on the scales of reason and finds that, in a good marriage, the good far outweighs the bad, and does not bicker over the little things.

It is natural that in such a close bond, such an intimate being-together as marriage is, weaknesses and struggles will develop alongside perfections. What mortal is free from this? But man and woman must carry both with gentle patience and strive to gradually get rid of them. This gentleness, this carrying cannot be one-sided. The woman cannot and should not be the only yielding party, for she would have to be either an angel or a slave. In either case there would be no happiness for her.[15] An angel cannot be in harmony with a frail person, and a slave who reflects on her condition cannot be happy. And whoever does not feel happy in the most intimate social bond cannot bring true happiness to the other.

But if the men who have written about the female vocation only allow us a certain level of education, only so much as is necessary for the diversion of witty men, for bringing up children, and for managing the household, and who curb our mind the moment it feels the power to move beyond these boundaries, so I ask: where is the judge's seat before which this must be decided? Where are the boundaries of the sciences that determine this (and only this) essential body of knowledge? There is only one science, just as there is only one truth and only one virtue.[16] So when will we stop making these miserable classifications and impoverished exclusions, which do not lead us along the shortest route to the final enlightenment and ennoblement of humankind? Once women have begun to educate their minds, once all the sciences come together at their margins—and as I said, there is only one science—who can, who may determine how far they can go? Do we want to settle for this classification? Should not, may not any one of us make as much with the sciences as he needs for his own particular calling? If women are born free and equal, surely they have the same right to restrict men to the sciences and knowledge that are required for the subject to which they devote themselves. They might claim that the doctor, the preacher, the lawyer, the merchant, the civil servant, the artist, and the craftsman can learn only as much as he needs for the fulfilment of his professional duties. The rest is detrimental to him, and only prevents him from performing his duties precisely and diligently. If women permitted themselves to make such claims, and so to limit men, would it be so bold? And is it less bold on the part of men to *want to limit us in this way*? Would the human mind not entirely wither away with such a miserable classification and petty exclusion? But men are not treated so severely. On the contrary, they are held in higher esteem if they have acquired many and varied skills in addition to the knowledge that belongs to the fulfilment of their actual professional duties. No one would think that they have neglected their duties. So why not let the same justice be granted to women? Why is there so much fuss about the learnedness of women? Why do the poets and essayists scoff at it with so much bitterness? Do men have a monopoly on learnedness?[17]

Let us once more hear from the above-mentioned author, whom Herr Pockels affirms in his *Versuch einer Charakteristik des weiblichen Geschlechts* as a refutation of the capacity of women for higher learning. Here is his account of a learned woman:[18]

> A learned woman is a woman who is only in possession of male knowledge, and looks down on feminine knowledge with distain and disgust. A learned woman is a woman who sits all day long to read, paint, or even write. A learned woman is a woman who speaks Latin, studies Greek authors, probably even understands Syrian and Arabic. A learned woman is a woman who solves algebraic problems, constructs synchronic tables, can cite Voltaire by heart, delves into the theories of philosophers, helps to settle their feuds, etc.*

---

* Note the way the author so strangely mixes everything up, moving immediately from synchronic tables to philosophical theories and then to Voltaire, as if it would require great erudition to read Voltaire. He who is fraudulent as a historian, superficial as a philosopher, whose greatest merit is a fine, flourishing style of writing and a rich source of gleaming wit, who possessed manifold yet superficial knowledge which he knew how to disperse and assert in all his writings with a boldness and grace that is unique to the French, he who did not prove or refute anything with satisfactory foundations, yet had a greater effect on his age than many a profound philosopher, and this for very understandable reasons, but as a completely singular genius deserves a completely singular appreciation.

But real learnedness lies as little in the sphere of women as does bravery. It is just as absurd to imagine a woman philosopher as it is to imagine a woman standing in rank as a soldier. The vocation of a woman is to become a wife, a mother, and a housewife, in fact, a pure wife, a perfect mother, and a prudent housewife. It is to this end that girls must study.* Everything that does not contribute to her vocation leads away from it, and makes her an unnatural sight. Now if one accepts that a girl can use her freedom to choose the life of a nun, this decision violates her vocation. A girl loses her essential merit when she, to play the scholarly game, becomes a nun. Nature destined her to be a helper. She should not be alone but alongside a man. To her, becoming a fertile mother should be a woman's crown of honour that cannot be replaced by a scholarly reputation. And what is all the fuss about the women we praise so highly? It seems to me that it is the same with them as with our great ones: if they do a mediocre good deed, the newspapers go mad about it.† The gallantry of some men elevates them to wonders of the world, for they may not even be noticed among their own sex. A learned woman may fudge her way into a foreign circle, but she will never achieve true manhood. The systematic is as little suited to the female addiction to change as it is to the heightened female irritability. Sustained and deep thinking does not agree with her weaker constitution—and, may I add, with her periodically sickly disposition and her physical vocation for the maternity room, to which her intellectual powers are directed. And to what end might a girl become learned? Should she also hold public offices in the state or the church? Let your women, says Paul, keep silent in the churches, they belong in the house!

But when such a learned maiden becomes a wife, how miserable is her husband, for she must keep his household in order and yet understands nothing about it. Or if she does understand it, she does not bother with the housework. What help is it to him that she solves algebraic equations if she does not keep track of expenses? What help is it to him that she constructs synchronic tables if she does not know what is going on in her

---

* So let the author also assume the responsibility to find men for all girls, which would be very difficult for him in present times.
† If we look to the mere flatterers who constantly surround our great ones and try to poison their hearts, if we look at the clouds of incense that threaten to muddle their minds, they deserve more praise than other sons and daughters of the earth if they manage to work their way through all of this and act humanely and nobly. Should not the learnedness of women deserve equal praise when we acknowledge the obstacles they have to overcome? And do not the men who encourage us deserve more of an applause than a reproach? We at least owe them a great deal of thanks.

house at the same time? What help is it to him that she translates foreign languages if he must plan the cooking schedule himself? What help is it to him that she knows how the Greeks and Romans dined if the food she prepares for him is inedible? What help is it to him that she has a sound judgment for the masterpieces of painting and sculpture if she does not mind if the tailors and linen weavers are cheating her? What help is it to him that she has perfect statistical knowledge and holds an economic map of Europe in her mind if she does not properly purchase and store her own supplies, darn her laundry, table linen, and garments, and allows everything to fall apart in the hands of the servants?

As it is with her as a housewife, so it is with her as a mother. Every aspect of motherhood is just as irritating to her as it is to the coquette. The cradle contrasts too much with the life of the scholar. It degrades her too deeply in the eyes of her affected dignity, and reminds her too loudly that she is a woman.* At most she brings children into the world, but one must ask, what kind of children? Born weak and ill, they bear the marks of their learned mother, who suffers incessantly from indigestion, vapours, and hysterical episodes. And then, having brought them into the world, she ceases to care about them any more. It is impossible for her to fulfil her maternal duties while continuing her studies.† Though they were formed within her, she strips the little creatures unnaturally from her breast and gives them away to venal harlots. She leaves them to her servants and is careful to keep at such a distance from the nursery that she cannot hear

---

* Is it a shame then to be a woman?
† I do not see the impossibility here. Or at least, I have found several examples of women who have made this impossibility possible. The doctor Erxleben mentioned in the first chapter, for example, and the second wife of the late Herr Dunker, a daughter of the late Pastor Zimmerman. I knew her for a long time, and discovered only a cheerful, funny woman who was simultaneously an excellent wife, mother, and housewife. It was only after her death that I learned from one of her trusted friends that she read her Greek and Latin authors with understanding and a sense of beauty. Here is another example from the letters of a woman from Courland [Sophie Schwarz], where the author expresses herself as follows: 'Among the many interesting acquaintances we have recently made is the poetess Bohlen. This woman was already known to us through several witty essays, especially the one entitled "Men and Winds" in *Der Deutsche Merkur*, which I enjoyed very much. What gives these products of her mind the greatest value is that they are crafted in moments of relaxation. This woman, with the most upright care for the upkeep and education of her large family, and with pressing cares in her home, knows how to set aside time for the exercise of her mental powers. Often in the throes of intensive housework she employs her mind to work out a fine song, and only when she has finished the work does she write it down. I am thrilled, dear Agnes, to be able to give such examples among our sex, so that you and the rest of my female readers will not find what I have said about the vocation of our sex impossible.' These and several other statements of the noble author of these witty letters convince me that she had the same opinion about the education of women. [The book referred to above is [Schwarz,] *Briefe einer Curländerinn*, 165–6.]

the crying of her little ones. How much the children eat, what they eat, whether they are kept clean, whether they see and hear good or evil—it is all the same to her. If they become ill, it does not occur to her to care for them herself, and if they die, she writes a dirge. In short, just as an uneducated woman spoils the children and brings them up incorrectly, so the learned woman takes no part in child-rearing.

Dealing with such a woman is true torture for a man. She thinks of nothing so petty as pleasing him but expects him to accommodate and pay homage to her at any time—and she reserves the right to accept or reject his words according to her mood. If he is weak enough to put up with it, she will soon become his ruler, and dictate to him his tastes, his lifestyle, the organization of his time, the selection of his friends, and the administration of his official duties. If he wants to claim his status as a man, he must either live as if divorced from her or have trouble and frustration at every encounter. Proud of her erudition, she breathes contradiction and domination, knows everything better than he, and does not let him do anything right, and even less accepts instruction. She is quick to flare up at him, and quick to sneer at him. She is always absent-minded and preoccupied. Unresponsive to warmth and disparaged by naïve cheerfulness, she entertains him with complaints about her poor health and demands that he should be an eternal reader at her bedside. But if he himself is ill, she has no time to attend to him in his need. She discharges her duties by making one uncharitable visit per day and by making three equally uncharitable inquiries about his condition. And, never does it come to the point that she should find pleasure in gathering her children around him and rewarding him with the greatest happiness life can afford, a quiet family happiness.

When I read this section to my husband, he was of the opinion that its author was only joking. He could not believe that the author was serious, nor that Herr Pockels could share his opinion. He probably only wanted to reproduce it as a caricature. But there is clear evidence that Herr Pockels had the same opinion as this author, as we see in the following note:[19]

> Some of the strokes in this portrait may be a little too strong, but it is taken from real life, and would remain true even if its colours were painted even more brightly.* It would remain true if it were drawn by the brush of the

---

* This is contradictory. First the colours are applied too brightly, and then it would remain true even if they were painted more brightly.

worst misogynist (the worst misogynist cannot draw impartially and thus cannot draw truly, for passion corrupts his pen). The author has only described one learned woman—what a horrible image he could have created if he wanted to condense the trifles and characteristics of several learned women into a whole.*

But let us return to our crude author. He continues as follows:

O the poor men who are punished with such women, they indeed deserve one of the first places in the litany. But—is it not they who do the punishing? Did not their pride of wanting to have an extraordinary wife entice them to the folly of offering their hand to a woman who has absolutely no capacity to make them happy? Of course, the wisest path they can take after this folly is to close their grief within themselves, as our K. is said to have done. But should not a single such example warn all men against similar choices?† I consider this to be the most effective means of healing the female sex of the craving for and partiality to learnedness—that our German strumpets become convinced that nothing is more capable of disparaging them in the eyes, minds, and hearts of men than these ailments. It is indeed one of the crooked parts of our age that girls now want to flaunt the male sciences. What else could they mean by this than domination over their future husbands?§ Now if they saw that not only this but even the search for a husband failed them, then would not every one of them about-turn, step back onto the tracks of their sex, and educate themselves according to their actual vocation?

I also wish that those of our writers who are now acting as stewards of the female world would align their arguments to the proper measure and purpose. They are the ones who actually shape the minds of our daughters, and yet they clearly write against experience and generalize from individual cases to the whole. They write against nature and against the order of things. They misjudge the difference between the sexes and their vocations. And they would upset the world if they succeeded in implanting their high view of women as public opinion. This is indeed no small matter, for all

---

* Whichever pseudo-learned women the author may have come across by some unlucky star, I have never encountered the likes of them.
† And an honest man could likewise experience the same misfortune with a fool enamoured by finery as with the pseudo-learned woman described here.
§ I do not see why this should be the reason why women develop their inclination towards the sciences. And is the superiority of men so fickle so that it cannot be maintained alongside the culture of women?

domestic happiness hangs upon it. Even for scholars, philosophers, and men in public offices, as for any man, this is the only happiness on God's earth. Should the men who give their lives over to thought, and thereby have to do without a thousand sensual pleasures, not even enjoy domestic happiness, thus have nothing at all on this earth! May God save for every man of our kind an uneducated woman. But I say this again: a so-called learned woman is and remains either a laughable or an adverse creature. Either her learnedness is not right, or, even if it were, then she is not right as a woman. If the latter, then as a woman she is a non-woman, something monstrous, and if this is how she is found in her natural state, she deserves merely to be gaped at and certainly never admired.

The author cited here seems to have formed a strange concept of learnedness. His manner of writing demonstrates that he takes learnedness and education to be two very different things. In the sense that I use them, they are one.

If learnedness produces these terrible effects, if it teaches us to despise all of our social duties, let us go back to the forest with Rousseau's woodsman. Let us strike down the one who draws the first border and says, this spot is mine!* Then we may destroy the beginnings of culture as it first emerged.[20] Let us eat acorns and roots, and never remember that we have a thinking mind, which through its education can rise to the divine.

Of course, if some learned men adopt a certain tone in their feuds with one another (a tone! I do not like to call it that), then one must certainly conclude that for them learnedness and education are quite different things. But to honour the past century, which has already supplied us with so many stunning blossoms of culture, and to give even greater honour to the new century we have just stepped into, let us hope that we will soon come to the beautiful moment when these men express themselves and act in such a way as to save the honour of learnedness and show that it is in step with the highest education towards humanity.

But to further unpack the author's concept of learnedness, let us apply it to men in a parody and see if a better image comes out of it. Then we might see who has best hit the mark. Of course, I cannot do it with such a crude and nervous style of writing; that would not become our sex at all.

---

* Rousseau claims that this should have happened to the first one who sought property, to protect us from tiresome culture and learnedness. See his book *Sur l'inegalité parmi les hommes et si elle est fondée sur la nature*. [Rousseau, *The Social Contract and the First and Second Discourses*, 113–14.]

A learned man is one who reads or writes books all day long. He believes that all the wisdom of life lies hidden in Greek, Latin, Hebrew, Chaldean, Syrian, and Arabic. As a philologist, he looks down with contempt on philosophers, mathematicians, natural scientists, historians, and the whole army of beautiful minds. He quarrels with other philologists about the pronunciation of a Greek word or the meaning of a mark in Hebrew. And since he has no time for reasoning, he gets by with grumbling instead.

The dogmatist proves what cannot be proven. His reasons are sufficient for him, and if someone finds them lacking, he takes this person to be an ignoramus, an idiot. According to the right of retaliation, he looks down on the philologist with the same contempt as the philologist looks down on him.

Now the mathematician completely believes that he possesses the philosopher's stone of learnedness. He smiles at all the arguments of the two previous learned men, for they fish in troubled waters. He alone can measure and calculate everything. His lines, circles, and calculations are the most evident; they speak to the senses and to the mind at once.

The theologian blesses himself and says to the whole world: your salvation depends on me alone! I care for the immortal spirit and eternal blessedness! I am the interpreter who proclaims God's will on earth. Believe! For he who does not believe will be damned.

The lawyer is proud of the care he takes in defending our laws. He thinks he possesses the spirit of the laws when he recites the *corpus juris* and the Pandects, when he guides the judge through the labyrinth of Roman laws, which are not in any respect appropriate for our constitution or our age, to confuse his sound judgment. He possesses the art of prolonging the proceedings indefinitely, and of helping his client to enjoy their rights only after he has seized their assets as legal costs.

The doctor claims that his science is the *non plus ultra* of all the rest, for he cures the human body of all its diseases. He either restores it to health or ends its suffering though a methodical death. To either end he studies the systems of the most renowned physicians. He always treats his patients according to the latest fad, so that they have the comfort of knowing that they died according to the newest method as they depart.

The historian says, I possess the documentation of humankind. I must tell you about the existence of Moses, Christ, Mohammed, Confucius, Lycurgus, Solon, Demosthenes, Cicero, Antisthenes, Pythagoras, Aristotle, Miltiades, Pericles, Homer, and Virgil, and acquaint you with the genealogies and the deeds of the great and minor kings. From me you will learn where the monuments of science and art are to be found. The philosopher, the orator, the lawgiver, the theologian, and the poet must draw from my source. The honour is due to me, to me!

Absolutely not, says the natural philosopher. It belongs to me. I draw the curtain behind which nature produces its forms. I know the laws by which it operates. By means of chemistry I dissolve bodies into their smallest parts and put them back together again. I can even produce gold, the most precious metal. I count and classify all created beings, from elephant to mouse, from ostrich to hummingbird, from whale to barnacle, from giant clams to cheese mites. My science even extends beyond the earth, for I know what is solid rock and what is water on the moon. The entire book of nature is open to me, I read anything I want, and with the help of the recently resurrected mysticism I penetrate into nature's most unfathomable depths and know their mysterious influence on bodies and minds.

The poet leaps onto his Pegasus and flies high into the ethereal realms of the sky where no mortal eye can reach him. Deep below his feet he sees the fiery ball, which the rabble call the sun. In seraphic tones he sings to us that which his imagination has created, so sublime and ornate, and pities us poor earth dwellers when we do not understand him. We are formed from clay too coarse to be able to fuse the highly sensual with the highly spiritual.

The merchant laughs and says, what do you all want? I alone have money. I alone possess the art of bringing coins from the farthest places into my coffers. For my hard cash, all the sciences must serve me. I can obtain for myself every enjoyment of which you can only dream. By the most refined luxury I let my collected wealth circulate through the manifold channels back to the state. Through my decency, even those who do not possess these goldmines may benefit.

But if a dutiful woman unites with one of the selfish men depicted here, what will be her fate? What good will it do her that her husband is praised in all the learned journals as a wonder of learnedness if he lacks genuine humanity, if he is always grumpy and glum in his home, if he forgets all the duties of a husband, father, and master of the house?

If she wants to discuss this or that important incident with him, because she thinks that four eyes are better than two, he snaps at her and says that she is disturbing his critical investigations. She can go and see how she might help herself. If one of her children displays a character trait that requires the most careful treatment so that it does not lead to ruin, even more she desires his insightful advice. But when she begs for his aid, he is hardly aware that he has children. He is acquainted with antiquity, and with worldly affairs, not with his own house. She lays out the dishes, but he is engrossed in his profound speculations. It is only when they are cold that he finally emerges. The wife begins an amusing, happy conversation, for cheerfulness and a serene mood during the meal contribute a great deal to better digestion. But even here he continues to spin the thread of his scholarly investigations, and all is condemned to a dark silence. The little ones must suppress their innocent cheerfulness and get up to mischief under the table. The mother notices but does not dare to scold them, for it would break the silence necessary for this polymath. One of their children becomes dangerously ill, so the mother seeks comfort and advice from her husband. While he vowed to her on the day of their wedding to share all joy and sorrow, she finds no support. He is busy with his scholarly investigations: was the poor woman who suckled Romulus really a wolf, or was she merely the wife of a man called 'Wolf'? She must carry her sad fate alone.

His wife, who until now has had to take charge of the whole household and the upbringing of the children alone, finally falls dangerously ill herself. He barely notices, provides no care, no experienced doctor. She dies, and when he receives news of her death he is taken aback. And if he belongs to the class of *beaux esprits*, he publishes her biography embellished with much praise.

In the meantime, until it is appropriate for him to take a second wife, he must take over the helm of the domestic administration and educate the children himself. Yet he is ill-equipped for the task. He can recognize the coins of the ancient Romans and Greeks, but those in use are foreign to him. He knows how the Persians and the Spartans raised their children, but how his own should be raised, given that some cultural progress has been made, is unknown to him. He has never been a husband, father, and citizen of this world. His highest goal was to gain immortality through his writings. He never worried about his duties. His learnedness only ever had this one-sided, selfish purpose.

His house catches fire. Yet he only saves his manuscripts, the means of his fame. He does not care how his children are saved. Let them perish in the flames, for he has saved the immortal children of his mind.

He is in his garden, and the smallest of his children approaches the bank of a pond and falls in. The others cry out for help, and finally he comes running. But he had developed his power of thinking one-sidedly; he had not developed the full spectrum of the powers of his mind in coordination with the powers of his body. Learnedness was only a means for him to gain renown, not to serve humankind. He does not know how to use his physical strength, and the child dies. The labourer or farmer could easily have saved it. If he is a poet, he seizes this opportunity to show his sublime feelings to the world in an elegy.

But enough of this! I could extend this parody much further and show that the sad consequences of the learnedness that the author had in mind can also be seen in my rendition of the learned man. True learnedness, which always keeps pace with the highest education towards humanity, is the only kind that is far from producing such excesses and deformities that are harmful to human and civil relations. Be it in man or woman, true learnedness honours all duties.

I am far from having the same opinion of our present learned man as I have expressed here. I merely wanted to parody the author's caricature of a learned woman, which portrays an original that certainly no longer exists, to show that if we draw such spiteful conclusions from the learnedness of women, then they must also follow for men. As human beings, both are in completely equal relationship to humanity, even if, as a consequence of our civic relations, as citizens of the state, the same cannot be said of both sexes.[21]

In general (thanks to fortune!) we are on a level of culture that makes the learned men and women we have depicted for evermore a complete nonsense. Pedant and learned are no longer synonymous. And as long as mysticism does not gain the upper hand, we will soon (soon!) arrive at the beautiful moment when our culture reaches its zenith, when learnedness and humanity will always and everywhere be one. Since men have made it this far, is it not then time that the dawn of this beautiful day should rise for us? Is it not time everywhere, once and for all, that all of these impoverished segregations cease? That both sexes, not separated by rivalry but joined by love and harmony, strive to climb the ladder of perfection together?

If marriage is a contract forged between two equally free beings to enjoy the benefits of companionship in the fullest sense of the word, and through the careful education of children to rear members who are an honour to humanity and useful to the state, we must first try to present the duties that the spouses have to each other. Here everything must be reciprocal; the duties of one are also duties of the other. The insignificant details of the more or less, the when or how, will not be considered here.

If any union, any association among human beings is to exist for the happiness of the contracting parts, they must first strive for a purpose, they must be united. For this to be so, they must be mutually just in the estimation of their value, forgiving and tolerant of their shortcomings and weaknesses, helpful and supporting in times of danger and suffering, obliging and thoughtful in their daily needs, and gladly participating together in life's joys.

Marriage, as the most intimate and permanent union, since it is bound for a lifetime, requires the fulfilment of these duties more strictly than in any other bond. It also demands of both spouses a common aspiration for ever improving education and perfection, so that by their example they may reinforce to their children the doctrines of morality.

Now, is it possible that learnedness or higher education will disorient women from the perspective from which they understand their duties? Would and must it not rather enlighten and correct their perspective? The educated woman will not simply feel but also understand with conviction that only by fulfilling all her duties, only by making the husband with whom she is so intimately connected happy, can she herself lay claim to happiness. No selfishness, no exaggerated demands will blind her and disturb the happiness of this beautiful union. True and genuine education or learnedness makes her humble and tolerant. But she is right to expect the same understanding of this relationship from her husband, for, I repeat once more, there can be no happiness here for one without the other.

It is here that I strongly recommend to men that they have everything to gain and nothing to lose in this intimate union through the highest education of woman.

In general, I cannot agree with the strict teaching and way of philosophizing found in Mr Schulz's *Sittenbüchlein für alle Stände*.[22] But he has one idea that I find to be rather beautiful. He claims that thinking beings form a line that goes up in gradual order from the lowest to the highest according to the power of thought. Every thinking mind has another on each side along the line, standing only a little above or below, and is thus its neighbour in the true sense of the word.

Now, in the course of their lives a man and a woman meet each other somewhere on the line and give to the other their hand to form their own bond. This meeting is not so difficult, for good minds easily recognize each other and happily join together. A mutual feeling of beauty and nobility in two like-minded beings is like iron on a stone; they strike each other, the sparks fly off and form a single blaze. What a joy for two such beings! This highest, most intimate bond will last a lifetime, so united and striking in its various forms.

From a single perspective they explore the most important and interesting subjects for humankind. Together they strive for the highest education, enjoying the purest blessedness this world can offer. Through their example and teaching, they implant this high ideal of humanity in their educated children.

The husband finds in his wife the most intimate friend, his most experienced advisor in every difficult situation. He discusses all his business with her, all the thoughts of his mind, and knows that he will be understood and appreciated. And she likewise with him.

They both look at the most important things of this life—religion, the understanding of nature, the constitution, the education of children—from the same perspective and meet together in their judgment. What a source of pure joy for them both! Monotony will not and cannot reign here; nature has kindly seen to this. It is not a union between man and man, or woman and woman. Even when they agree at this highest level, the rougher and gentler ones are so varied in their nuances that monotony simply cannot enter.

The major accusation made against the higher education of women, and why a learned woman will make such a bad wife, is that learned women are more pretentious. They are no longer gentle, pleasing, affectionate, yielding creatures. They feel their own powers more vividly (and the men theirs less). In short, they lose their femininity, as one often hears said.

One could easily conclude from this kind of talk that these men were afraid that in the course of their higher education women may think of calling to account the many injustices they have had to endure. For a creature who knows its duties according to their source and in their entirety will, of course, also acquire knowledge of its rights along the way, for the two cannot be separated from each other.

But even then, these men have nothing to fear from a truly enlightened woman. She knows only too well that in such a close and intimate union defying the rights of another is not the means to attain them for oneself. In general, one can only demand one's rights before a court, particularly when it depends on mine or yours, for it is concerning such claims that human beings have been most eager to make the laws precise. The rest of human rights, however, nearly all remain in a state of chaos.

It would be a great shame if in such a beautiful union as marriage the rights of either side were to be disputed! The tender and intimate bond of the soul would disappear.

I say also in this respect that the husbands of truly enlightened women have nothing to fear. True enlightenment and tolerance always go together. The woman who looks at the conditions of human society with a keen eye, who knows that as soon as the human being enters the social contract it must sacrifice something of its rights as a natural being for the advantages it receives, has calculated that this sacrifice will truly be a gain and that she cannot enjoy these advantages without making it. She applies the same principle to the narrower contract of marriage and is strongly convinced that she cannot enjoy the great, beautiful, and sacred benefits of this covenant without some sacrifice of her personal freedom.

She rightly expects her husband to show her equal understanding and equal fairness if she happens to come to a contrasting decision. And should her husband let himself be governed by passion alone, should he then act capriciously against her, she tolerates it. She yields, even if she is completely in the right, for her keen eyes tell her that by yielding she can only win. Her husband, inspired by the same spirit, levels the account. He is inclined to grant equal leniency in cases when she, too, is seized by a human weakness. So the union is never disturbed.

Moreover, an enlightened woman is far from that spirit of trifles which plagues reasonable men through their wives, and which is the cause of dispute in marriage ninety-nine cases out of a hundred.

As for the accusation of pretension, it is completely unfounded here. The educated wife certainly enters marriage with fewer demands than the uneducated one. Instructed by a proper knowledge of the human heart in its inclinations and passions, she does not expect that her lover's wooing will continue to flow throughout their marriage. She knows that the man who energetically strives for the possession of a desired good is in a state of ecstasy, which, once he possesses it, returns to its usual course. So she is not surprised when the passionate lover, now husband, becomes a warm, tender, respectful friend. In fact, she wins in this exchange. The honeymoon deceives her just as little. She knows the great attraction that novelty claims on us weak mortals, and how habit often diminishes the value of the greatest good, or at least does not allow us to feel it at all times. These insights ensure that she is not vulnerable to the natural events which are so understandable to the wise, but which the inexperienced often cannot explain, and which cloud the joyful days of both spouses.

I have already explained in general that, in my view, pretension and thorough knowledge are true opposites. No one is more modest in their judgments, in their demands, and in their whole behaviour than the thinker who has come so far in human knowledge that he can see that all things have two sides, and that we inhabitants of the earth, no matter how high we stand, no matter how much we can contemplate with our divine spirit, are still subject to error. He knows, feels, and heeds this human limitation, and is certainly modest and unpretentious in his judgment as well as his conduct.

In my view, the one who is pretentious, even if he knew everything and had mastered all the arts, is neither truly enlightened, wise, nor educated. He lacks the greatest, highest gift of God: a measured power of judgment, the ability to put together and order the various conditions of life, the subjects of human knowledge as a whole, and to appreciate them according to their value.

As for true femininity, that loving, gentle sense that finds its delight only in the happiness of others, I ask: would higher education drive it away once it had already been formed in the character of the individual? If it were not this loving sense that lay originally in the character of the individual, but, on the contrary, a certain hardness and selfishness, then a purified concept of the social duties, the conviction based on knowledge that we are not merely here to establish our own happiness but to promote the welfare of the whole, would perhaps awaken but never diminish it.

This higher education will then intensively weaken the loving sense and yet extensively strengthen it. And who wins, the individual or society? Without a doubt, both will win. The sacrifice of the one is replaced with the happiness of the other and both enjoy their share. Nothing is lost.

The multitude of writers who have written about the female vocation are so zealous about the higher education of women that they cannot abstain from base expressions.* Others who do not even want to concede to us that we are virtuous, for virtue requires strength, want us to be so very soft and delicate that we should not feel the beautiful, the noble, and the good, but merely catch their scent.†[23]

It is worth considering how much harm is caused by women recoiling from higher education, how inconsistent it would be to demand that women should be so very delicate and sensitive, and what is actually to be done with such ethereal creatures, given that their threefold calling depends on swift, certain, and sacrificial action. A woman must be in possession of both insight and strength to make these sacrifices at the right time. To merely

---

* Herr Pockels in his *Versuch einer Charakteristik des weiblichen Geschlechts*, who by the way has said some good and true things. [For an example of Pockels's 'base expressions', consider the above-cited passage in which he affirms Sintenis's claim that a learned woman is a monstrous, 'unnatural sight' merely to be 'gaped at.' Pockels, *Versuch einer Charakteristik des weiblichen Geschlechts*, II 343–4.]

† Herr Ewald in his book *Die Kunst, ein gutes Mädchen, eine gute Gattin, Mutter und Hausfrau zu werden.*

smell the beautiful, the noble, and the good would not make us advising wives, active housewives, and careful educators of our children. It would certainly do nothing good for men and for the whole of society.

In the rich experiences of my life, I have often noticed that nothing leads us more astray than feeling, and the faculty of imagination, which is the source of feeling. If we are to be at all suitable for practical life, then understanding must be the master of imagination, reason must be the sun of feeling, and the power of judgment, purified by experience, must be the pilot of both. The most important thing to realize about human value is that it is determined by our actions alone.

Why is it that some men get more agitated about learned women than about vain women, since there are infinitely more of the latter than the former? Why are there more men against strong characters rather than weak? Are they scared that if our strength were supported by our intellectual powers, it would be superior to theirs? If that were the case, they do not do justice to themselves. But rivalry cannot take place between the sexes. They are determined by the loving author of nature to produce and establish the happiness of each other.

> Man and wife, and wife and man
> Climb the heights of the divine.[24]

Of course, vanity and affectation are still dangerous diseases among our sex. But they would be less so if our education were based more on true human dignity and the human vocation; if we were granted the full possession of our rights as thinking and perfectible beings; if men themselves required that to gain their respect we must train all of our powers; if both sexes made it a mutual duty and a condition of their respect for each other to be thinking, human beings in the truest sense of the term.

Then all of that obsession with inferiority would disappear. Human beings would only want to distinguish themselves by a sense of duty, by virtue and high sense, which would provide a rich source of enjoyment. Boredom would no longer chase the wife out of the house to gossip about commonplaces in expensive, uninteresting, and large societies. Vanity and the desire for conquest would no longer drive her to plays and night performances that are harmful to health and morality. She would no longer darken her sisters with the wretched profits of shimmering finery, and would find no interest in attracting the attention of men.

The enlightened woman, completely steeped in her duty, also loves joy and sociability. But she forms a community of intelligent and honest friends with her husband. Serious conversation alternates with witty jokes, laughter, and cheerfulness, which are the spice of sociability.

As her husband's most intimate and trusted friend, she knows his financial situation well, and follows the same standard in her domestic life and with her clothes. Cleanliness and civility have equal rank. She has no interest in shining with the comfort of luxury and fashion.[25] She knows a higher value.

And who would win with this change? Would it not be the men? But we too—believe me, my women friends—we too will certainly win by this exchange! For nothing gives greater peace and more inner serenity than the heart-rending, sweet feeling of having fulfilled one's duty.

Consider for a moment the other side of the coin, the majority of marriages, especially in large cities where luxury and dalliance more commonly attract weak mortals.

Instead of the beautiful union, the intimately linked interest, we find two beings who live together in one house. They greet each other with habitual politeness, which in the wide world so often takes the place of real urbanity and warmth. Yet husband and wife act as if their interests were entirely separated from each other. The one has his girlfriends and lovers whom he courts, the other her admirers and intimates. They tolerate these people and chase after exotic delights. They are not familiar with the quiet domestic pleasures.

Since they are not true and intimate friends, the wife is unfamiliar with the husband's actual wealth. She often inspects it through the lens of luxury, and he foolishly surrenders himself to her whims. He needs her clemency because of his debauchery, and she requires his to the same extent, and thus vice sometimes begets tolerance. He is glad that his wife chooses other diversions and pleasures and lets him enjoy his own undisturbed. One tries to deceive and mislead the other. True domestic pleasures are replaced by intoxicating delights. Both want to please, but not at home. Both want to shine with finery. Vanity, affectation, and the love of fashion fill the wife's empty soul. And if the husband wants to assert his authority for once and to raise his voice to say no, and to refuse the ever-increasing expenditure of costs, the weaker woman takes refuge in begging, crying, cramping, fainting, and defiance. If the husband remains immovable, she makes use of her cunning and, I blush to say it, deception. To continue her expenditure, she withdraws what is necessary from the education of her children, from the maintenance of her staff, from giving to the needy. For luxurious women are usually the most meagre to all those who do not indulge in this idol of theirs.

One could not say that I paint with colours that are too bright. The wide world offers to me more than one original for this portrait. Yes, I have even had the unhappy experience of an affected woman who, when all the strategies she used against her husband to satisfy her enormous expenditure did not succeed, would sell herself. This aficionado would somehow have to get what her husband did not want to give, or could not give.

Indeed, vanity has produced more unfaithful women than any other passion. Woe to the heart of which vanity and unfaithfulness have together become masters! Their consequences cannot be counted.

Many a girl has lost her good reputation purely from vanity, from the lust for pleasure. If one could look into the motivations of her actions, she would not deserve such harsh judgment from the public. Vanity tempted her to accept gifts from men, which can only happen in very few exceptional circumstances. *Fille qui prend, se vend*, says the proverb.[26] The lust for pleasure blinded her, and, without considering whether it was becoming to her feminine tenderness, she let herself be driven to comedies, masquerades, and balls. She did not consider whether her actions were appropriate under the circumstances. Sometimes she managed to pull back when her good spirit warned her to leave the slippery slope on which she had stepped. Though she saved her innocence, her good reputation was gone! Others, however, fell, for their aroused sensuality got the better of them. Vanity and affection were the source of their unfortunate case.

The woman of knowledge, the woman educated towards humanity, will never succumb to the lures of luxury, vanity, and chic, or, rather, she does not need to enter into a struggle with her desire. Her noble soul and cultured mind lift her above this state. She strives for no other renown than the praise of the noble and reasonable. Her satisfaction flows from the sweet inner consciousness of having fulfilled her duties. The active interest she takes in all matters that are important to humankind fills her hours of leisure. She would have no understanding of boredom if her connections did not sometimes force her to go to large gatherings where head and heart often find so little entertainment. Fortunate is the man whose wife feels boredom here alone, for his gain is immeasurable. Boredom is the result of the most foolish things that make weak mortals ill.

But even in marriages that are not so bad the beautiful union is disturbed if the husband does not put complete trust in his wife. And for him to be able to do this, his wife must be educated, reasonable, and on the same level of culture as he. This requires that she has completely equal rights regarding income and expenditure, so that she might secure everything she needs as a rational woman. For she is not his housekeeper but his most intimate friend, a helper in the true sense of the word. If she is not, if her husband wants to assert his authority and dominance over her, then of course his wife knows how to settle for her fate, since physical forces, laws, and old habits are on her husband's side. But then the beautiful union is immediately destroyed. They are no longer two friends who have vowed to bear life's burden together unto the grave, to enjoy the beautiful flowers of happiness together. From now on her interests are desultory, and consist merely of the coarser pleasures.

When the stronger husband asserts his authority, the weaker wife responds by taking refuge in cunning and deception. This has always been the character of weakness when it collides with domination. I boldly call upon the experience of those who observe humankind.

Now, who would gain the most from this struggle? Certainly not the husband. But not the wife either. By boasting about a dominion that he does not possess, he becomes a marionette in her hands. He does not notice the threads with which she leads him, though often to her, her husband's, and her children's ruin. She will use this invisible superiority for the good or ill of the family, depending on whether she is reasonable or unreasonable.

But if she must stoop to pretence, she sinks from her dignity as an open, trusting creature that lives only for him, for she must lower herself to cunning and scheming to assert her will. And there is always a will in a woman; otherwise she would not be a free, self-determining being.

Oh the lords of creation are very easy to outwit! It does not take much for a clever, devious woman to draw them along wherever she wants. The more a husband boasts about power, the less he possesses it. But what a feeling this must evoke in the woman who sees through his imaginary power! How pitiful this so-called lord must seem to her!

From this moment on they are no longer friends, but act as enemies to each other!

But here too the difference between the enlightened and the uneducated woman will be easy to see. Both feel their secret supremacy. Yet the enlightened woman uses it only as a stopgap, for the good of her pitiable husband who misjudges his true interest, and especially for the welfare of her children and the maintenance of the household. In trifling matters she willingly yields, for the sacrifice of her human dignity is not worth the cost. Yet the uneducated woman, who has more pressing wishes and demands, needs her power for all her small purposes. She does not know true human dignity but tries to assert her will whatever the cost.

Oh you men! When will you learn to see that you can only win, and never lose, through the purposeful education of our understanding. I have often thought that marriage is the greatest masterpiece in nature. It takes an infinite amount of effort to merge two beings into one, each with its own personality to maintain, in such a way that a beautiful whole is formed. Marriage must be the true dual unity.[27] Only intimate friendship, true respect, unbreakable trust, and unfeigned openness can bring about the greatest and most natural of wonders.

Happy is the man who is of one mind with his wife! Happy is the wife who finds a husband on the same level of culture as her! And the higher both of them stand, the greater the happiness. They reach the summit of earthly delight.

But what if convention or some deception brings the educated woman together with a man of inferior culture? Even then her husband does not lose. On the contrary, he gains a great deal. The higher the woman's understanding is educated, the less she will take pride in this unhappy privilege. She will feel compelled to take the helm in domestic matters, and humbly hide this privilege from the world. For humility always goes with true merit. This is the most evident of all truths. She will miss the most beautiful of all joys, of being united with an equally tempered being, and not let her husband feel it. She will suffer the lack; he will not.

If I ever wished for Raphael's brush or Demosthenes' words, it is when I want to show men in the most vivid way how they can gain everything from our highest education and lose nothing, nothing at all.

And to women, I would like to engrave on their hearts with flaming letters that we can only claim respect from cultured men if we strive to rise and become noble human beings through the harmonious and purposeful training of all our powers. It is the deepest wish of my heart that idleness, delusion, and conceit no longer keep any of us from achieving this goal.

If my women friends were to get a clear view of their relation to humanity in general and to civil society in particular, and take its importance to heart, then many things would improve. For it is certain that much, if not everything, depends on our conduct. If women were everywhere and always what they could and should be, they would be better treated by men. Love is a matter of taste, and cannot be forced. But respect and friendship, which are more necessary than passionate love for a good marriage, cannot be denied to the one who truly deserves them.

3
The Educated Woman as Mother

Nothing in nature offers a more joyful and uplifting sight than the image of a loving, tender mother. If this mother at the same time becomes an educator, if she becomes a model for her beloved little ones through her high sense, through her noble, humane actions and her purposeful activity, she fulfils her sacred duties in their entirety. This lovely image inspires both reverence and admiration.

In an earlier section on the influence of women I discussed in extensive detail how wide-reaching our contribution is to the good or ill of humankind as the first educator of the young.

But can one nonetheless ask: does a higher education contradict the calling of mother? Or even more, does not the venerable calling of educating, caring for, and setting an example for her children in fact require knowledge, indeed, broad and thorough knowledge?

The gardener must have an intimate knowledge of the plant that he would like to cultivate, including its sex, its characteristics, and the time and duration of its flowering and ripening. He must know what mixture of the soil and what temperature of the air is beneficial for it. Should not the one who wants to educate the masterpiece of creation, the high, noble human being, be familiar with human beings in all their faculties, their drives, their passions, their perfection and potential? Should he not know the sensible and moral world for which he wants to educate this young citizen of the world in all its past and present events, and in all its consequences for him and his individuality?

What a high degree of one's own education this requires! Whoever wants to educate someone as a human being in the noblest sense of the term must feel and possess this dignity themselves. It is an undoubted truth that one cannot share what one does not have.

In the education of human beings, it is essential that the young world citizen is taught how to look at things from the right point of view, how to separate the essential, necessary, and useful from the insignificant, trifling, and useless, and how to sort them correctly. But if we are not able to do this ourselves, if we do not know how to sort and appreciate things according to their true value, how again can we share what we do not possess?

And what a rich store of knowledge, what a trained eye, what tested experience is required to do this! What a contrast there is between educator and mere teacher! And the mother is always an educator; it must be so.[1] The child absorbs its first concepts with its mother's milk. Without realizing it, the mother places objects before the child's eyes, and the child comes to value them exactly as she does. The value she gives to or withholds from things is so deeply interwoven with these nascent ideas that no later educator will be able to erase them. They subsequently determine the character of this human being.

One should observe a range of families, and pay attention to whether intellect, nobility, and morality are not cultivated more by the mother than the father, and, just as often, stupidity, baseness, and immorality. And this is very naturally the case. The mother morally and physically provides more material for the children's education than the father.

I read an epigram somewhere; the exact words have slipped my mind, but the meaning was this. A very ugly but extremely clever man married a very beautiful but incredibly stupid woman. When asked how it was possible for such a clever man to marry such a stupid woman, he replied: it was done in order to have children who would be as beautiful as the mother and as clever as the father. But through an entirely unsurprising *quid pro quo*, his children became ugly like the father and stupid like the mother.

In my shorter work *Über die Fehler unserer modernen Erziehung*, I already remarked how much I wished that the young world citizen, from early youth onwards, had only *one* educator and teacher united in the same person, who educated, taught, and guided him through life to the point where he became an active member of humanity and civil society.[2]

This *one* educator and teacher then knows the creature he wants to educate completely. He has followed his pupil's gradual development, which he has guided and organized from the beginning. He knows precisely all his powers and capacities, and wisely discerns how much of his teaching and education is beneficial for his comprehension at the time and for his future vocation. The pupil becomes fully accustomed to his method and his lessons; he comes to see their sense and is completely comfortable with them. At the same time, he comes to have the deepest trust in his educator and realizes that he owes everything to him.

But who is more adept to be the child's first teacher and educator than a loving and educated mother? She, who knows and understands the young plant from its first sprouting and growth. For this noble business, however, we ourselves require a high degree of education, and we require knowledge that is both plentiful and wide-ranging. The mere and often blind tenderness that nature has placed in the heart of all mothers is insufficient by a long shot.

But even more effective than teaching and moral instruction is setting an example. Its effect is always decisive, since without it the former are often quite fruitless.

But what a difference in behaviour there is between an educated and understanding woman and an uneducated one who lacks understanding. Her speech alone is enough to distinguish the former from the latter. The way she treats things and the value she attaches to them is planted early and unnoticed in the child's soul. The child hears entirely different things discussed, which quickly become familiar to it, things of which the child of the uneducated mother has no idea at all. If the mother's individual situation does not permit her to complete the business of education herself, the child's later teacher can only continue to build on the good foundation already laid. There are no weeds that were sown early in the young soul that need to be pulled out, which even the greatest care can seldom eradicate.

Despite everything that has been written about education—the most important of all human affairs—until now, no essential and fruitful improvement will be possible until mothers are in general more educated and thinking women, whose power of judgment is formed through knowledge. The later teacher will always be able to notice the mother's influence in this arduous business, not only in the good or bad foundation he finds to work on but also in the ongoing effect she will always have on her children, both sons and daughters, to a greater degree than their father. Tutors and teachers, as well as all others who have ever contemplated the matter of education, are certain to have often felt this truth.*

Only the power of the earliest impressions can explain how the same school, where all pupils receive the same careful education and the same illuminating lessons, can produce excellent boys and girls but also those who are no honour to humanity. The earlier example set by the parents, and especially by the mother, established either a proper or a warped point of view from which they learned to perceive things in the world, and which even the greatest master in the art of education is unable to shift.

---

* Even Herr Campe, who has made the improvement of education his business, gets worked up about the higher education of women in his *Väterlicher Rath*. Yet this experienced, knowledgeable man entirely overlooked the fact that he could expect the safest and most active help in this great business though the noble education of women.

In my view, it remains an eternally fixed principle that human beings are not born good or evil. They are born only with capacities that can be trained for good or for evil; groundwork decides everything here.[3]

The mother certainly has greater influence on this initial groundwork than the father. Whether or not she fulfils the first of her duties and breastfeeds the child herself, the child receives its initial impressions from her. In their early youth, children are in the mother's company far more than the father's. From her they learn to stammer their first sounds. From her hand all their manifold needs are met. She is their nurse, the comforter of their little hurts, the participant in and creator of their joys. Let the father be the nourisher and provider for the family. The child is not in a position to recognize its source. It recognizes no other hand than the dispenser of its joys and its necessities.

Hence the greater attachment of children to their mothers. Nature owed us this exchange for all the hardships, pains, and sorrows that only love can provide and make worthwhile. The greater attachment of children to their mothers ensures that we have the greater influence on their hearts.

The one who makes themselves the master of our love has our heart in their hands. Such a one guides it where and for what purpose they want. We are inclined by nature to bestow all perfections on the image of a beloved person. Their teachings, their example, thus creep gently and unnoticed into our hearts; their character becomes the pattern of ours, the ideal we emulate.*

But why then do not all good mothers have good sons and daughters? Because without an educated mind, mere goodness of heart is not enough as a model for a pupil who is not yet perfected. Because mere goodness of heart often degenerates into softness. Because crooked judgment, a skewed view of things, and a false evaluation of their worth can very happily exist alongside mere goodness of heart. Only when the heart's goodness is beautifully combined with a lucid, educated mind do we find the high ideal of humanity that is worthy as a model for instruction.

How many times has an education failed due to the mother's lack of insight and turned out badly despite her best intentions! Consider a man of understanding and intelligence, who is also a loving father and cares for the

---

* 'The mother's image is also the daughter as a whole, / As Thais is now, so will her child once be', says our immortalized and too soon forgotten Gottsched in her weekly magazine *Die Tadlerinnen*. [Luise Adelgunde Victorie Gottsched (1713–62) was a poet, playwright, essayist, and translator. She was married to the philosopher and critic Johann Christoph Gottsched, and helped him edit the weekly journals *Die vernünftigen Tadlerinnen* and *Der Biedermann*.]

welfare of his children. This man takes the great importance of an early and purposeful education to heart, and yet with regret he finds that his wife is not able to draw up a plan with wisdom and to follow it through with firmness. Now suppose that he draws up an appropriate plan for them both, and shares it with her. She approves of it, and genuinely intends to carry it out. But can she do it? In this case the will is not sufficient for the deed! The father cannot possibly go into sufficient detail to prescribe the rules of conduct for every case that occurs, for every clash, for the various dispositions of the children. Even if he could, which would in all likelihood be claiming too much, the way in which a matter is carried out is infinitely important. Woe to the one who takes on any business without having the necessary insight and power of judgment, who must seek advice from others who are familiar with its nuances! But three times woe to the educator if he finds himself in this unhappy position! Like an experienced captain, he must always know how to steer with knowledge and judgment. He must always have his eyes on the province of education and the true character of the student to be educated, and act according to his own insight and heartfelt, considered reasons.

If some mothers, who generally direct the early education, had not lacked a proper, mature power of judgment, the modern method of education would never have been driven to the terrible nonsense from which we have now retreated once more.[4] The proofs of this nonsense unfortunately walk right in front of our eyes, as an embarrassment to themselves and as a sad example to the world. Education is not like every other art. It is not possible to throw away a failed attempt and create a better one.

As our great Lichtenberg says, medical reason lays its failures in the grave, but to its shame the failures of pedagogical reason strut on two legs for all the world to see.*

Just look around you. If you are a philanthropist who feels the dignity of humankind, you will be saddened to see how stunted most of the products of the nonsense of the initial enthusiasm of modern education are becoming.[5] Their bodies are exasperated by sensory stimulation. Superficial knowledge has inflated their souls with arrogance. They have not been brought closer to the ideal of true humanity but pushed away from it.

---

* In a small but witty and spirited text, *Beweis, dass der Doktor Bahrt schuld an dem Erdbeben zu Kalabrien sey*. [*Proof That Doctor Bahrt Was To Blame For The Earthquake in Calabria* was anonymously published in 1785. Scholars now concur that it was not written by Lichtenberg but by Ernst Christian Trapp (1745–1818), who visited the Philanthropin in 1777 and became the first to hold a chair in pedagogy in Germany at the University of Halle.]

There is nothing in the world that does not have its strengths and weaknesses. So it is with both the old and new education. If our mothers, who were so busy introducing the new education to their children simply because it was new, had weighed with shrewd judgment the old against the new and chosen from each what is best, they would not have blindly followed the trumpet call of some of our modern educators. They would have found the golden mean and then provided us with sensible people.

One could easily have taken this road, for the old education provided us with so many excellent men and women that it should not have been rejected so quickly. How much embarrassment, and how much harm, could the next generation have been spared!

If it is a well-established truth that women have the greatest share in the education of humankind, then a high degree of education does not contradict their calling as mothers. In fact, this sacred calling demands it, and a great deal of knowledge, if women wish to fulfil their duties in the strictest sense of the word.

By giving our children existence, by enduring the pains of birth, we do nothing but what we must; to this extent our will is not free. By acquiring the sum of knowledge with restless zeal, by overcoming our idleness and the many difficulties that stand in the way of women's higher education, we enter into the rights of humankind, we act purposefully and of our own free choice. And then we have truly earned something for our children; we are not content to give them mere physical existence but also endeavour to give them moral existence through a higher education towards humanity.

The first thing that the young, helpless citizen of the world demands from us is to maintain its health. Very few children come into the world crippled, and even if they have inherited a weak constitution from their parents, a sensible diet can restore a great deal. Nature's reproductive power never slumbers, and we can assist it in many ways.

But the capacity to prescribe a sensible diet first of all requires knowledge of the human body, its inner and outer components, and the influence and effect of food on the body. That is, it requires knowledge of nature. Without this, the mother will always have to seek advice from a doctor. Without her own conviction based on knowledge, she can only follow this advice imperfectly. How many illnesses can be prevented by this knowledge, how many can be nipped in the bud, and how many costs can be saved!

It is one of the most evident truths that the soul is not able to do anything without the well-being of the body. A sickly child is held back in its moral progress and the formation of its understanding. It lacks the serenity and strength required for the acquisition of useful knowledge, and the soul ails like the body.

Now that the insightful mother has fulfilled her first obligation—she has preserved her child's health and given it a strong body—it is no less her duty to care for the health of its soul. But this consists in knowledge that is properly learned and purposefully applied. In short, it consists in the proportionate formation of all its powers.

What a wide field of knowledge is now open before her! If she considers it with understanding and a sense of duty, she strives to make all the required knowledge her own.

History, geography, natural history, natural science, and philosophy. Without philosophy, no single science can be appreciated and taught. It is the basis of all the others. It breathes spirit, life, and a sense of the common good into them all.

The knowledge of languages in addition to the mother tongue also belongs to this field.

Herr Campe, who in his *Väterlicher Rath* denies us so many sources for the education of our minds, also chides the learning of foreign languages. He claims that it is not only useless but even harmful.[6] I confess that I cannot see either vice. On the contrary, the learning of foreign languages can be very useful to our sex. Things being as they are in the world, there is no more honourable and profitable business for a young woman without means than to hold a position as a teacher in a rich and noble house, and for this, knowledge of foreign languages is absolutely necessary. If she combines her knowledge of foreign languages with an enlightened mind and genuine education towards humanity, she will find in this great sphere of influence opportunities opening before her to contest many prejudices held by the nobility and aristocrats and have a beneficial impact that will reach even distant generations. I think that this business is far more honourable than to provide for oneself through handicraft, the occupation Herr Campe advises us to acquire in case of need.[7] Anyone with some knowledge of the world knows that if the business of handicraft is to be enough to support oneself, it must be in fashion or laundry. But what a poor and spiritually depressing business it is to have to work for the vanity and luxury of others!

Once the question has been decided that we must develop our minds alongside men, the learning of foreign languages will be a fundamental part of a woman's education. There is a great difference between reading a book in the original and in translation, especially when it comes to poetry. One can also trace the course of ideas in different nations through the formation and construction of their words, and discern their level of education and character. And all other considerations aside, in the venerable function of being a mother alone the learning of foreign languages is necessary for us. We can teach our daughters ourselves, and judge the teachers of our sons. We can encourage and prepare them for their lessons and observe their progress. This will certainly be a great benefit to them. As for the objection that this would rob us of time that could be better spent elsewhere, I am of the exact opposite opinion. In our early youth we have a lot of spare time and nothing better to do than to fill it up with memory training.[8] One of the basic rules of education is to always keep the pupil occupied. By doing so we prevent many bad habits and vices, which in most cases are merely a consequence of youthful languor. Memory is certainly the first mental capacity that can be trained; the power of judgment slowly follows the path of wisely used experience.

If her situation should make it impossible for her to complete their education, how much can an educated mother prepare for the future teacher of her sons, and also of her daughters! But this will seldom be the case for a mother who is firmly imbued with a sense of duty and who possesses the ability to do so. For it is so beautiful and rewarding for mother and child if she is able to see the task of education to its completion. The lessons of a tender mother cannot be replaced by any teacher.

But the sacred business of education cannot be achieved with the mere surface knowledge that is still being handed out to us. No, we must have penetrated the sciences to their very core if we are to be able to communicate them properly.

Anyone who wants to teach a science must have learned it in its entirety, lest his teaching be constantly imperfect. Even the student will soon notice his ineptitude.

Our modern pedagogues have tried to replace the lack of knowledge among mothers with elementary books. Herr Basedow explicitly recommends such a solution.[9]

But what a waste to base teaching solely on elementary books. They can, of course, be used as a guideline for the pupils' introductory lessons. And yet a teacher must know and understand the science that he or she wants to teach. Otherwise the lessons will always remain imperfect. Elementary books can provide a mere skeleton of the sciences. Only the teacher whose mind is imbued with the sciences can offer an inspiring presentation, a true perspective, a beautiful form, and apply them to the education of minds and hearts.

For example, to thoroughly and usefully teach our children history for their education as human beings, we must know how to abstract the philosophy of history. Without doubt, this is the most important view of history, at least for us women, who are, even more than men, permitted to be human in the true sense. I like to leave the dry register of names of the greater and lesser kings, the true heroes, and the cruel villains, as well as the dates of the battles that took place, to men, who often have to study history from a self-serving regard. The lawyer and the theologian must, of course, learn history in a different way to the philosopher, to the teacher, and to women as first educators of humankind. The lawyer is particularly interested in the Roman and Saxon laws, the theologian in the tangled mess of myths and Church history, and in this study the mind surely begins to rust rather than acquire the advantages of a fine and moral education.

But the philosophy of history, in my view, consists above all in tracing the course that human inclinations and passions have taken through time, with various nuances. It then strives to investigate the causes for the rise and fall of the great nations; but especially to follow the course of the gradual development of the predispositions and capacities of the human mind from the first stage of culture to its zenith, to discover which advances in the sciences and arts, as well as in industry, have especially contributed to and continue to contribute to this development, and accordingly to organize, determine, and feel their value from a philosophical perspective. But to let history infuse the mind in this way, one must know it completely. One must have studied history in connection with the other sciences, so that one can survey it as a whole.

Only he who studies history in this way will find therein a secure and rich reward. It teaches him to know himself, to know people in general and the individual in particular. It is a trusted advisor to him in his dealings with others, teaching him how his actions affect them. And if their actions go against his desire, which he has formed from the highest ideal of humanity, he takes it with forbearance. He knows that there is a series of stages in the whole of nature, in the moral world as well as the physical, such that all humans cannot act from equally high motives, for not all can stand on an equal level of culture. Moreover, he knows the extent to which education, situation, and circumstances excuse many seemingly immoral actions. He investigates these cases and is tolerant. History has taught him this noblest, most humane of all virtues.

Only he who can survey history with such scope and from a philosophical perspective may dare to teach it to young people. Only he is able to assess the age and abilities of a young world citizen to determine whether he or she is sufficiently prepared through other knowledge for this teaching, and whether his or her power of judgment has reached the proper maturity to be allowed to look behind the curtain of history. And only he is able to judge how much he ought to share at each stage. When history is given too early, without a refined power of judgment and philosophical retrospection, it is certainly more harmful to young people than useful.

If this is so, will one still want to claim that women need only learn the sciences, and thus also history, superficially?* That we should receive only as much knowledge as is necessary to prevent us from being complete strangers to science? That our only motive for studying history should be capable of holding the odd conversation about historical matters in society? What a petty motive! It would be better if we cared nothing for what people did in the past and what they do now. Then at least we would be modest, and refrain from talking about things the importance of which we do not feel. For it is precisely this superficial knowledge that causes our sex to be often and rightly accused of adopting an overconfident tone and praising ourselves for trifling achievements.[10]

Half-knowing is worse than knowing nothing at all. It generates arrogant and impertinent speech, or at least causes us to remain silent. But thorough knowledge makes us truly humble. All knowledge must be gained only to the extent that it develops us into human beings in the most fundamental sense of the term. And it should be passed on to young people only with this aim in mind.

In her sublime calling as mother, as the first educator of her children's minds and hearts, should it be sufficient for a woman to have a poor grasp of history, as Herr Campe and several other writers have prescribed? I am convinced that she must possess the philosophy of history for this great and noble purpose.

Of course, I am in complete agreement with Herr Campe that we should not burden our memories with the useless nomenclature of unimportant people and facts. Only the people and actions that had a true and lasting influence on the progress or delay of the predisposition of human beings to

---

* Herr Campe, for example, says the following about learning history to his daughter in *Väterlicher Rath*: 'I wish you and the other young ladies of your standing a general overview of history and geography sufficient to orient you when there is talk of old and new world events, that is, to be able to determine the time and place when these events occurred, if not with complete historical and geographical accuracy (for this should hardly be a need for you) but in the main.' [Campe, *Väterlicher Rath für meine Tochter*, 103.]

culture belong to the philosophy of history. Only these are of interest to us as humans.

We should gain a grasp of natural history and natural science to exactly the same extent. Everything that surrounds us becomes so interesting when we have a proper view of nature! Apathy and boredom fall away and we come to enjoy the charm of life in its fullness, for it ennobles our hearts and minds. We ascend from nature to its great Creator, whom we consider in the most beautiful light. All miracles that run against the course of nature, all apparitions that do not agree with its laws, and all superstition that arises from ignorance disappear with this knowledge of nature. And even if we are not able to lift the veil behind which nature develops all its forms, even if we do not know how to define the matter or material behind it, we nevertheless learn that it acts according to eternal, unchangeable laws, and that neither it nor its author ever deviates from them, for they are designed with the highest wisdom and goodness and therefore can never contradict each other.[11] How much does the unity and diversity of nature, to which it remains faithful in all its works, occupy and refine our minds when we are able to follow the great chain of its productions!

A being who is familiar with nature will never depart from its laws, for acting against them will destroy our physical and moral existence.

A proper view of nature makes our whole life harmonious with its wise and gentle laws. It makes us gentle and friendly to all beings. It elevates us above the finery and tinsel of vanity. Like nature, our food, our garments, our whole life are simple.

Should not a mother, imbued with this purified feeling, be a better role model for her children by her mere example than those whose lives stand in contradiction to nature?

But just as the mere example of her knowledge will give her children a taste for nature's simple pleasures, so she will strive to inform them even more deeply in her conversations and her lessons.[12] She will know how to explain a thousand things to them, how to answer a thousand questions that the curious little ones so want to know regarding how, why, and whence. Asking questions is a characteristic of bright children, and to answer them properly is harder than one might think. An infinite amount of knowledge and judgment is needed. And yet how much does the manner in which such questions are answered contribute to the education of their minds and hearts.

The woman who understands nature directs the attention of her children first of all to the things that surround them. She teaches them the origin, the use, and the purpose of those things. How many occasions for interesting conversations, how much entertainment and occupation for the young ones, about which the teacher is so infinitely concerned! How delightful and entertaining does the knowledge of botany make our walks! We are able to combine several tasks together. We do not merely walk to strengthen our bodies by breathing in the fresh air and enjoying mild exercise. The knowledge of nature, and intimate friendship with all natural things, both uplift and refine our mind at the same time.[13]

For us, the sky does not simply appear to be blue; we know why it takes on this lovely colour. The west winds do not just fan us with their cool breeze, for we know the origin and function of these lovely feelings. Thunder, earthquakes, and storms are not tribunals, rainbows are not signs of God's favour, for we know the cause of their origin, effect, and use. We share this with our children when the opportunity arises, and thus keep their minds free from prejudice, superstition, and fear.

To the connoisseur of nature, the stars of the great and magnificent heavenly vault are not only points of light; she regards them from an infinitely more sublime point of view. The suns and planets attract each other according to the law of gravity and thus move in their eternally unaltered course and constantly maintain their trajectory. Great Newton, how much light you have kindled through this important discovery of natural science, by which you fortuitously discovered the law of gravity and ingeniously knew how to apply it! The epitaph does not overstate the case when it says:

> All nature and her laws laid hidden still in night,
> God said: let Newton be, and it all was light.[14]

What a sublime thought, when we look up into the clear evening sky, see the great vault above us, and think about the myriads of worlds, all populated with intelligent and sentient beings! How small does the earth, this little dot that we inhabit, appear to us within the universe. Like a drop in a bucket, as our great Klopstock calls it in his sublime and evocative ode *Die Frühlingsfeier*.[15] How great and divine does the Creator of this great universe appear to us! Our knees buckle beneath us and we fall down in prayer! We feel our nothingness and our greatness!

As the author of *Philosophie de la nature* says, 'If it is possible to be an atheist, you will give it up as soon as you study astronomy.'[16]

But let us cease this digression and return to our walks, moving on to the benefits and the conveniences that the knowledge of botany gives to us.

Grass, trees, and herbage do not merely appear as a vibrant carpet to our eyes. Even the small area we survey reveals so many wonders to us. In the class of grass alone we find such diversity and unity. The grasses provide such a great benefit to our nourishment and health. The smallest, most inconspicuous field flower, often unknowingly trampled underfoot, restores our diminished health. We draw them to our children's attention and teach them how the small and inconspicuous things are often far more useful than those that boast and enchant their eyes. We teach them to be wary of poisonous herbs and flowers, and thus prevent many unfortunate accidents.*

The manifold colours of the flowers, which stand in a single area and feed on the same mixture of the earth and temperature of the air, invite us to investigate the cause of this phenomenon. We can find the reason for such diversity only in the circulation of the humours; the way in which one plant absorbs certain components of earth and air, while another absorbs others, so that the sun's rays are refracted differently and one flower appears red to our eyes, another blue, this one yellow, that one white, etc.

To investigate all this is a noble and pleasant occupation for our minds and a source of sublime and pleasant feelings for our hearts. By inspiring us, we despise the pageantry with which so many of our sisters still squander their noble time.

> Happy the one who has the town escaped!
> To him the whistling trees, the murmuring brooks,
> > The shining pebbles, preach
> > Virtue's and wisdom's lore.
>
> The whispering grove a holy temple is
> To him, where God draws nigher to his soul;
> > Each verdant sod a shrine,
> > Whereby he kneels to Heaven.[17]

Thus sings our lyrical poet of noble love and nature, our Hölty, who unfortunately died too young. When we understand nature, we feel with him.

---

* A mother who had not warned her son about the berries of nightshade, because she did not know of their harmful effects, experienced this misfortune, and his whole body became swollen after eating some. The doctor's swift work saved him in good time. Another had eaten from the thorn apple, and died through an inflammation in his throat. I could list many more similar examples if space allowed.

If we are able to explain the cause and effect of things through our knowledge of nature, we will no longer indulge in the superstition that still dominates so many in our midst. I have known women who, when faced with a dangerous and protracted illness, entrusted their lives and those of their children to a charlatan rather than to a prudent doctor, expecting the help of miracles and quackery. And these were not women from the lower classes! They were women who had enjoyed a so-called education, and in other things judged very well. But how many dangers have already been caused to humankind by these miracle doctors. Belief in this will only cease with the higher education of women. Due to their particular situation, they have a far greater effect on young people and the lower classes. True and genuine enlightenment, which is still too concentrated in the minds of a few great men, can be spread and made useful to the public in practical life by women alone. The writings of enlightened men, which strive to combat superstition and delusion, cannot have this broad use. If they are to have an effect, the mind must be made receptive to written ideas in early youth (the business of women alone), and they can have no effect on the lower classes. But an enlightened woman has the opportunity every day, every hour, to establish better concepts such that the false ones fall away of their own accord.

I have known women of the upper classes who refused to have their children vaccinated, preferring to deprive them of their life, health, and well-formed physiognomy through natural smallpox. Since they had no proper understanding of the development and use of human capabilities, they feared that God would punish them if they interfered with his providential office.

I have known women from high society who imagined that things could happen to their children, or, as they say, that their children could be cursed. Fearing that this might be happening when a child became unwell, they took refuge in counter-magic rather than going to a skilled doctor. Others imagined that if a dead person in their coffin is dressed in the clothes of a living relative, the living person will wither away as the corpse decomposes. I knew a very wealthy lady who had all the perfectly good, discarded clothes of her children burned out of fear that if she gave them to the needy, something might happen to her beloved little ones. What a loss for the needy, and what a great disservice to the children to whom this superstition was passed on! I have known ladies who preferred to leave a company than sit down at a table of thirteen, for they believed that one of them would have to die in the coming year, and that this fate could meet them, their spouse, or their children. Yes, I have known some who believed in ghosts and nightmares in the vulgar sense.

From my own experience, I could write a whole book about the sad effects of the superstition of women. But this is not the place. Perhaps I will dedicate some of my hours of leisure to this material.

But it is sad for the philanthropist, the observer of humanity, when he finds that these opinions, which are contrary to all true enlightenment, still exist, even in the higher classes. They will disappear as soon as women rise to a higher culture, as soon as they have a true and thorough knowledge of nature.[18]

As I have mentioned, there is only one science. Every branch is always connected to another. Just consider the relation of entomology to botany: every plant nourishes and houses one or more insects. What nourishment and occupation this gives back to the thinking mind and the feeling heart! With awe and love we marvel at the works of nature. The Creator is manifest to us in sublime light, for he has placed life and sensibility everywhere.

The Hobbesian law of nature, the war of all against all, disappears. Nature could not give such hostile laws to her children. No, she could do no other. If she wanted to create the most diverse array of life and movement possible in a small space, each kind had to depend on the other, so that all of them, even if only the mayfly, would enjoy and rejoice. And even the mayfly will one day become happier in a different form of life; it will rise from level to level and finally enjoy the most perfect existence. For nature does not throw anything away, not even the smallest piece of dust. Only a perpetual changing of forms in an ascending line is its sweet and wise business; nothing here is lost.

Even the idea of weeds and vermin disappears with this proper knowledge of nature. Selfish people like to eradicate everything that stands in their way or is not precisely where they want it to be. If the thinker looks more deeply into nature's intentions, he will pull out the grasses that deprive the useful plant of strength and nourishment, remove the insects that consume it, but he will not slander nature. Rather, he will honour her motherly intentions everywhere.

Nature is a single chain; every link interlocks with another. From inert, dead metal and stone to sublime thinking and sensation, the masterpiece of earthly creation, there is no leap. Everything ascends the great ladder through an imperceptible gradation of steps, such that all is connected. The mind is enraptured by following this great series of steps, it worships and adores the immeasurable Creator of nature, and feels sublime and great at the thought that it has been placed at the highest level. It strives to live up to this dignity and to share it with others.

Should women remain excluded from this most sublime feeling simply because we are women? Because our bones are not so strong and our muscles not so firm? This would be a true crime against nature and against humanity. Far more shocking than a slight against the Crown, which is punished so severely.

Geography goes hand in hand with the study of nature and history. We naturally want to know where things originated and flourished, where the great ones lived and played their sublime and deeply influential role. So we research the character of our own place of residence. Who wants to be a stranger in his own home? And is not the earth, in the broadest sense of the term, our home?

And so we seize this kind of knowledge also, for we find it upon the path that we have already taken. Here too we see the diversity and economy of nature. For a sun may give light and warmth to our planet and the others, and the planetary spheres must go through their daily and annual revolutions. Through geography we discover the influence that climate, diet, politics, and religion have on human actions and the human power of thought.

We admire the pliability of the most perfect creature, the human being, who can live, think, and act everywhere, from the cold poles to the tropical regions. Nature has denied this attribute to animals, its less perfect creatures. Here too we honour nature's wise and loving intentions. By furnishing the perfectible human being with adaptability, nature wanted to reveal the vocation to develop its powers, and to know and teach about natural phenomena.

How much has been discovered due to this capacity of human beings to live in all climates? What do we owe to the men who made the journey to faraway places, who, to satisfy their thirst for knowledge, to enrich the world with a new appreciation and awareness, did not shrink from danger or complain! How much has been corrected through their efforts in natural history, ethnology, and geography! How many superstitions and delusions have disappeared through their labours! It certainly is a very important aptitude for humanity.

Rousseau may claim that human beings have descended from the orangutan, and that their vocation, like the orangutan's, is simply to satiate their hunger and reproduce their species. Yet nature and human dispositions disprove his delusion. As in many other cases, Rousseau's overexcited imagination took hold of his talents and led him astray. Why would nature have endowed us with so many powers and dispositions other than to develop them? Of course, we must not also become muddled here. We must always remain true to nature's wise rule, to *nothing in excess*. The sciences, like sensual desires, have their skeletons. Nature sets us boundaries everywhere; as soon as we cross them, our machine is destroyed. Excess always does harm. The fine and best humours, which rigorous thinking diverts from the machine's digestion and growth, must be balanced in wise economy with all our furnishings and functions and only be dispensed according to this proportion.

But that is precisely why we must study nature: to stay in its tracks. Mind and body must always be kept in harmony, for they are inseparable. And when we have learned to carefully map out the limits of our nature, we will never move away from its beneficent laws, never indulge in any matter. True and right knowledge will never mislead us.

When all of this knowledge has been fully and intimately formed in our minds, it will flow into our actions, into our way of thinking and speaking, and we will be able to communicate it to our children through everything we do and make it worthy of their esteem. In consequence, they will not have to overcome the difficulties in their education that we have had to overcome in ours. The wise mother imperceptibly leads her children by the hand of love up to the highest level of humanity. Constantly recalling the duty to develop all our powers, they are able to claim a more beautiful humanity in the most fundamental sense.

And if knowledge and the consummate education it brings are viewed and presented from this point of view, it can never bloat or bolster superficial know-it-alls; even if we reach the highest level of culture, we have merely fulfilled our part of the duty of humankind.

The mother who has reached this high level of education surveys the field of knowledge with fine judgment. She has the measure of her children's powers and knows the right moment and the perfect amount to share with them. She does not want to pick the fruit at the time of blossom, to make wonders out of them so that she will shine, for she will harm her child's health by a premature and overly strenuous education. Her own high education protects her from this petty vanity. Since she is familiar with the economy of the human body, she will never exploit or exhaust its powers. How many children become the victims of this parental vanity! How many have to suffer from strenuous knowledge that comes too early with weak nerves and an ailing body! It is a sacred duty of parents to provide the state—or better, humankind—with members of healthy mind and body.

Imbued with a feeling for this duty, the educated mother will never want to put her children on show to display her art of education. She knows that it is only when the work is completed, when the child has become a human being and a citizen in the most fundamental sense, that her child's thinking and actions may praise her work.

Furthermore, the educated mother will always model constant and purposeful activity to her little ones. When we reflect on the history of peoples, from the first, lowest level to completed education, we notice a common characteristic: the uneducated human being finds its highest happiness in idleness. This explains the idea of a paradise in which people enjoy their lives in leisure, where everything offers itself for their enjoyment. They regarded work and the exertion of powers as a curse from God, in the sweat of your face you shall eat bread, etc.[19] Work must have appeared to them as God's punishment. The paradise they would inhabit after regaining their blessedness places them once again in this comfortable state of rest, idleness, and the effortless enjoyment of sensual pleasures.

Even now among uneducated people one encounters the same notions of happiness. They work only out of necessity to earn their living, and their leisure is nothing but idleness.

The educated human being, however, knows no idleness. Purposeful occupation is for him a need, and relaxation is merely one variety of activity. He does everything with purpose and understanding, without pretention or entitlement. To be active has become his second nature.

How rewarding is this example to the young! The imitative instinct lies deep in the nature of human beings, who model themselves on this example without compulsion and further incentives until they are able to grasp the higher motives.

The more varied the perspectives from which we view the things in the world, the livelier our drive to activity becomes, the more fully we develop our measure of capabilities, and the more harmonious our whole life becomes.

One has gained everything in education if one has instilled a lively interest in activity and diligence in the student. Sensuality and luxury, the two faults of a cultured humanity refined in a one-sided and purposeless manner, lose their power over a mind that regards higher education as a matter of humanity.

The woman who is completely and intimately imbued with her duties will not flaunt her knowledge, nor will she ever put it on display. She always wants to be, and never to shine. The applause of her noble husband, and the applause of all that is noble, are her sweet reward. But praise is never the motive for a completed, even higher, education. This is and remains for her the only duty of humankind: to develop all of one's powers and to use them purposefully.

We live in an age and a condition where luxury is a necessary evil, if it cannot be described as such everywhere. Luxury is the refined enjoyment of life and is only harmful if it no longer balances our spiritual, physical, and economic powers. To eradicate it from the earth would be impossible, and even if it were possible, it would not be advisable. It is the consequence of culture, and employs a thousand hands and minds by indirectly sharpening the powers of invention. It thus contributes to the development of our human powers, and brings money, the great mover of human beings, into circulation, which would otherwise pile up into a dead mass in the coffers of the rich.

If luxury cannot and should not be eradicated, then we must educate our children to endeavour to calculate their powers with a measured eye so that they can weigh them against the limits and purpose of a refined enjoyment of life.

Luxury will never have a harmful influence on a fine, educated mind. Such a person knows a higher enjoyment and the purpose of his existence. His mind governs the senses; his goal is to achieve the ideal of humanity.

An educated mother will also introduce her children to the arts. They refine, ennoble, and elevate the enjoyment of life, and are moreover in perfect harmony with the sciences.

To sense and communicate the harmony of tones and colours with a refined feeling, along with the proportion and agreement of parts and the whole, is a gift that the Creator has also given to our sex and belongs indisputably to the consummate education towards humanity. Above all, they give the social joys of life an ever new, never ageing, charm.

Angelika Kauffmann, Therese Bantettimi, and several great practitioners in the visual and musical arts prove that nature has also shared the talent for art with women.[20] To develop each of our gifts is the duty of humankind.

Herr Campe in his *Väterlicher Rath* warns women against the education of their artistic capacities.[21] Along with several other writers who have written about the female vocation, he fears that the finer sense that comes with cultivating one's artistic capacities will make us reluctant to take on the often petty and unpleasant business that a mother, as the first provider and guardian of her children, must do. This is one of the main objections made not only against the education of our artistic capacities but against the higher education of women in general.

They first of all imagine that a higher education makes us averse to these detailed and often arduous maternal duties, for once our minds have been moved with such high momentum, they will no longer be able to lower themselves to these small matters. Second, they say that we will have insufficient time to fulfil these sacred duties in their entirety. The educated woman must refute both of these objections with her actions; otherwise, she is not educated but miseducated. If a woman has followed her sweet instincts, if she has become a mother, she has taken over the most important, the most sacred, obligations, and her entire, most intimate efforts must be directed towards fulfilling them all.

Will a woman who peruses a true and purposeful education lack time to fulfil her duties? Will some of the things that her duties demand of her seem too small or insignificant?

First of all, everything we call great or small in the world is highly relative. What is small in one relation becomes great in another, and vice versa. The hired maid who is responsible for the cleanliness and care of the children does a little, and usually only a half. The mother who is motivated by a high sense of duty excels in these very matters. The nobler source enhances her actions.

How could anything that lies within her individual sphere of duty seem too small to a noble, educated woman? How could a loving, tender mother who is well aware of all her duties recoil from anything that would concern the health and well-being of her beloved child? The higher she stands on the level of true culture the more vividly she feels the weight of her beautiful calling as a mother. How could something be too small, too unimportant, too burdensome and unpleasant for her? Only a mother can judge and sense the powers given by her maternal feeling and the sacrifices it makes possible.

There are probably examples of mothers who, through one-sided pseudo-education in this or that science or art, took a wrong turn and made themselves unworthy of the sweet name of mother. But there are still many more, endlessly more of us, who have neglected their motherly duties out of *vanity*, out of *love of attention*, out of *idleness*, or out of *ignorance*.

There is an infinite number of women whose empty souls find no entertainment at home in the sacred fulfilment of their motherly duties. Seeking something more, they rush from social engagement to social engagement while their children languish under their servants, where their minds are under an exclusively harmful influence while their health is irretrievably lost though the imperfect care and diligence of hired hands. If graves could speak, what ghastly tales of neglected children would one not hear? Such children are not neglected out of learnedness but out of ignorance, out of lack of a proper grasp of all the sacred motherly duties, out of neglect through the passions and foolishness to which an uneducated mind puts up little resistance, such that one becomes deaf to the motherly feelings that nature has imprinted so deeply on our hearts.

Here are some examples of motherly duties that have been neglected due to vanity, fashion, and indulgence, all of which are drawn from my own experience and are entirely true.[22]

I knew a woman, the mother of a large family, who could not spend a single evening alone without hosting or going out into society. When her daughter became dangerously ill, she could not make the sacrifice of staying home for a night. She went out into society and had messages sent every quarter of an hour so that she could stay abreast of what was going on. Finally, at the card table, she received a message informing her that her daughter had died. She did not interrupt the jovial company with her sadness, but only gave way to her motherly feelings later that night, when she saw the body of her child at home.

Another mother had invited guests to a ballet in her house. In the meantime, her child became dangerously ill, and was close to death on the evening when the merrymaking was supposed to take place. But the social engagement could not be cancelled. The child died while the mother was dancing. She kept the news of its death from both her husband and her guests so that nobody's pleasure would be disturbed, and announced it the following day.

Another fashionable woman finally became pregnant after a long wait for an heir. Her husband, who had so intensely desired the joy of becoming a father, begged that she take care of her health during this important time. She promised, but her chic and vanity triumphed over her promise. Fashion dictated that people should walk around dressed as lightly as if they lived in the tropics. In the middle of the harsh winter of 1799, she appeared at a social engagement in this fragment of a dress. The room was not properly heated, so everyone was wrapped in furs. She was in no position to triumph over her vain wish to show off her beautiful figure in society, and she caught such a cold that she miscarried a few days later, sinking her and her husband's hopes. In this case, vanity and chic became the murderers of a nascent member of human society. Oh how many horrible sacrifices have been brought about by vanity and chic! Driven to the extreme, they become the most evil of devils by which a woman can be possessed; whoever can exorcize them deserves great honour.

Another woman possessed by fashion became a mother. Fashion, her first god, dictated that mothers should breastfeed their own children.[23] Compelled to follow, she decided to nurse the child herself. Yet to sacrifice her late evening feasts or her night absences, which are fashionable in large cities, did not fall within the set of ideas she held in regard to maternal duties. This set was so limited that she thought the child would accustom itself to going a whole night without feeding. So she slept carefree in other houses. When she was at home, she always left the child with a servant in a room far away from her own, so that her peace and quiet would not be disturbed. The servant fed the child, which was crying out of hunger, with food that was too heavy for it to digest. It died, a victim of indulgence, comfort, and the ignorance of its mother.

If these four horrifying examples were insufficient, I could produce many more cases of the vanity, chic, and pleasure that accompany the uneducated women's ignorance of her duties. Compared to the thousands of victims of chic and vanity, female learnedness, even of the one-sided and misguided kind, has hardly cost even a single member of humankind. There is not a single example of a woman who, having risen to the highest level of humanity through her education, neglected these sweet and dear motherly duties.

If we add to this the infinite number of mothers who, even with the best of intentions, due to a lack of knowledge of the human body and dietetics, sacrifice the lives and health of their children in times of both wellness and sickness, the need for female education will certainly seem very urgent to us.

Why is it that far more children die in the lower than the higher classes? In particular, why is it that smallpox causes far more devastation there? First, because prejudices still hold them back from the smallpox vaccine, and second, because their care and treatment of disease remains imperfect and inappropriate. Let us suppose that an educated, knowledgeable woman is the wife of a landowner, a country parson, or a tenant; how broad would her sphere of influence then be! How beneficial to humankind can she then become!

If in her conversations with the countryfolk she gradually imparts better ideas, such that false ones begin to fall away by themselves. If she encourages them to take the smallpox vaccine, and prods them in the right direction. If she gives them wise advice on how to care for and treat the sick, and, from her own means, gives them food that is easier to digest, which they cannot always obtain. If she, having some knowledge in medicine, which always comes with a thorough insight into the nature of the human being, and which is so beneficial in the country where a doctor is not readily available, gives them medicine for their ailments, which can often prevent serious illnesses. How beneficial is she then to the preservation of their health and their bodies! And the health of their souls will be promoted by the educated woman if she, free of prejudice, eradicates the superstition that is so often prevalent among countryfolk. This will not be so difficult for her once she has gained their trust. If she, as a landowner, can see to it that a humane and educated man is employed as the schoolmaster, and if she shares with him her ideas about the education of the countryfolk, and collaborates with him and with the parson. If she, as an educated woman who duly appreciates the value of time and always lives her life in purposeful activity encourages the young people in the village in this useful virtue by rewarding them, by rural merrymaking, by supporting them and reprimanding them in the case of idleness. How deeply does the praise or reproach of an educated and esteemed landowner have its effect!

Nothing I have described here is an ideal. I saw it realized in the late Countess Botmer. Her husband was the senior civil servant at Traventhal in Holstein. They were both inspired by the same mind, and their memory will long be celebrated with grateful remembrance of the humanity they made joyous.

Now, if the advantage that the higher education of woman brings to her calling as a mother, as the first educator of the young, is so widespread and beneficent, and if the disadvantage that follows in the footsteps of ignorance and all the passions is so damaging and far-reaching, and if both are so strikingly obvious to the keen observer of humanity, how is it possible that the writers who have written about the female vocation should get so much more worked up about the rare exception of a pseudo-learned woman who is unfaithful to her vocation, who neglects her duties as a mother, than about the thousands who are unfaithful to their vocation because ignorance and unbridled passions, as in the above cases? Where might this obsession with female learnedness come from? These writers would not be so eager to look into the inner recess of their own hearts and admit with honesty the cause for this to themselves. They might be forced to blush; I will spare them this and not investigate the matter any further.

As far as the second objection is concerned, namely that, with a thorough knowledge of science and art, we would not have the time to conscientiously and punctually fulfil our motherly duties, this too is mere appearance. In the case of an impartial investigation it will be entirely dismissed.

The human being can accomplish infinitely much if he knows how to be frugal with time. Whoever is truly serious about the proper use of his powers and the useful application of his time can make things possible of which the idler, the waster of noble time, can hardly dream. And should the sciences and arts, which beautify our lives and bring them into harmony with nature, require any more time than large and extravagant society, games and parties, balls, masquerades, and the wretched task of dressing one's body according to fashion for these vain pastimes? Anyone familiar with that chameleon, fashion, will feel that a woman who wants to follow all the rules of this foolish goddess, all trends without letting one pass by, either has to have a very large fortune to pay other hands or, if she wants to and must observe economy and make this tinsel herself, then her hands are so busy that she neglects her husband, children, and household.

I know several women who greatly credit their husbands by sparing the tailor and the seamstress and doing these things themselves. If this occupation is only a secondary matter, and does not overstep the boundaries of reason, then it is praiseworthy to know how to care for your own practical needs. But if these women often go out into society, and place a high value on appearing each time in fashionable finery, then this petty occupation takes more time than the pursuit of knowledge and skill. And how unworthy of a rational being is this preoccupation to give the same dress always a new cut according to the obstinate ideas of fashion, to appear each time with a different headdress (or whatever it is called), and thus to waste noble time which should in the most part be spent educating our minds, improving our hearts, and fulfilling our sacred duties. Then the respectable but unnecessarily new-fashioned adornment of our bodies may accompany our actions as a secondary matter. But to treat fashion as the purpose of our existence is such a poor, miserable occupation that it makes us unworthy of being called rational beings. Nevertheless, many women spend their whole lives doing this, and fail to fulfil the duties of their threefold calling. And the above-mentioned writers do not get nearly as worked up about this evil, for only the higher education of women arouses their anger. One could almost believe that there is a scientific envy, just as there is a professional envy.

So, the eager striving after the purposeful education of our minds cannot lead to a lack of time to fulfil our duties.

In her play *La Bonne Mère*, Madame de Genlis offers a beautiful answer in the words of the good mother.[24] After wondering how she could find the time to continue working on her own scientific education so as to teach her children better than the ordinary teachers, and how she could still free up her time for friendship and the joy of social interaction, she found the answer: one always finds time to fulfil the duties that one values.

This simple and yet beautiful answer says everything in just a few words. There is always time enough to fulfil duties that have become dear to us.

But our duties only become dear to us if we are able to see their whole extent, if our motives are drawn from the only honest source: namely, if the fulfilment of our duties is the activity of humankind, the purpose of existence.

Why then should our individual duties be of such a nature and scope that we would be forbidden from the duty of humankind, the purposeful training of all our powers, when we find so many examples in men who, in addition to the professional duties they have chosen, are able to do so?

Oh one can do infinitely much if one acts with clear judgment, with a sense of order, and from principles!

Nature would have been very stepmotherly to us if it had denied only our sex the gift of this higher activity.

No, my women friends. This wise and benevolent mother could not deal with us so harshly. On the contrary, she demands that we develop all our powers in the most beautiful harmony. If we follow her beckoning, we will only then fulfil all our duties in their entirety.

Let all of us offer our hands in friendship. Let all of us work on our education with zeal and earnestness. It does not end with the complete education of our young ones. We must educate ourselves. We must constantly strive for our continued education, and remain awake and alert so that we are always stepping forward and never backward.

The sweet consciousness of having fulfilled our duties as human beings, as wives and mothers, to the greatest extent will give us happiness and serenity. We will share this joy with others. We will be appreciated and loved by our husbands and children, and at the same time we will be a high example for the latter. We will finally be able to enjoy a happy, honourable, and peaceful old age.

And then, if we pursue this great business of ours with sincerity, always with respect for our individual duties, we will finally come to the point where we will not fear our higher education but eagerly desire and promote it. Both sexes, which are determined by nature to have an effect on the other, will urge each other on in this beautiful matter of humankind in an ever-higher education. That this is not a beautiful dream will depend solely on you, my women friends.

4
The Educated Woman as Housewife

A higher education will also be useful to women in this aspect of her calling, and never disadvantageous. If we abstract from the duties of wife and mother discussed above, then it is a woman's duty as a housewife to maintain order and cleanliness in the home, to organize the servants and instruct each of them in their business, and to encourage them to order, diligence, and morality. She must also balance income with expenses, and arrange them in proportion to ensure that a small surplus is left for emergencies.

But here too there is enormous variation in a woman's sphere of influence. If she is rich and of noble standing, a woman will have a large number of servants to oversee. The profession or rank of her husband may require numerous extravagant feasts and rich banquets to be arranged. While she does not need to participate in their preparation herself, the success of such events depends on how she selects the servants to whom she entrusts the execution of her commands. It depends on her gift of discerning their abilities in this or that task with a perceptive eye, of directing them in accordance with their standing, and knowing how to keep them on task with authority and human kindness. And this indeed is no small feat in our luxurious times, especially in large cities, where good and loyal servants are rare.

The fact that this indispensable class of people is often so corrupted is due largely to the rulers themselves, especially to their lack of religiosity. The decline in religiosity has several causes. For one, public worship is probably no longer appropriate to the needs of the times. The thinking person rarely finds satisfaction there, and so withdraws. The pure idea of the deity dwells in him, its presence surrounds him everywhere, and his actions have high motives. Such motives can no longer be taught to him, he can no longer be admonished by them, for they are intimately interwoven into his being and are always present with him. But he would gladly fulfil his social duty and, in a place of assembly with his brethren, raise his soul to the deity if, as we have said, he found satisfaction in doing so.

So much for the thinking person. It is a different matter for one who carelessly worships the prevailing trends. Religiosity is no longer fashionable; he throws it away without having anything better, without morality. He recklessly rejects everything and conducts his actions without a plan or high motives. He has nothing but what passion and sensuality dictate at any moment.

The many witty writings we have received from France, and which we now also no longer lack in Germany, have mocked not only the propositions and interpretations of the theologians but also the basis of religion. Most people have read them, but few have considered them carefully. They repeat the sentiments, but neither the readers nor the writers know what they are doing.

These mockeries, veiled with ambiguity, are often the subject of discussion at table. The attending servants listen, hear, and retain some of it, and repeat it downstairs so that they might also have the air of nobility and wit. And thus religiosity, the only motive that this class of people is capable of, is lost.

Further, they see that while engaging in these mockeries, their masters bathe in affluence and rush from one pleasure to the next. What will the servants do? They will also seek to achieve this radiant happiness and revel in their own part of it. And to do so they will betray their guileless masters. For religiosity, which has so far kept them in line, is missing.

The number of domestic servants that luxury has introduced into our so-called great and wealthy houses is also a source of their corruption. The devil finds work for idle hands, as our good ancestors put it in the proverb. Next to religiosity, work—strenuous and plentiful work—is certainly a mighty bridle that keeps this subordinate class of people on the moral path. Failing to consider this, our rich sacrifice the good of this numerous class of people to their love of finery.[1]

In the end and above all, the moral corruption of common folk is due to the lack of a purposeful education for the lower classes, and to the schools, which are, to some extent at least, supposed to remedy this lack.

It is true that in many places it was felt that the existing free or charity schools were not suitable to remedy this lack of education, and so they were converted into more suitable industrial schools. Our much-deserving Rochow has written a great deal about this important matter, and his efforts for the benefit of rural people have already had a great effect.[2] Our thinking fellow citizens have followed this example by converting the old orphanage into a similar industrial school.

But this single industrial school will not remedy the lack of education as long as our church and charity schools, where the children of the poor are taught free of charge, are no longer adequate for the needs of the times.

Whoever has the chance to visit these schools cannot overlook their unsuitability.

In the morning, when the pupils rush into the classroom on their way to school fighting and grumbling, they begin a morning song in praise of the Creator. Still in this unruly mood, they shout it so loudly that he cannot miss it. Then the Bible is read, and passages from the epistles and gospels are recited from memory. Yet without a proper explanation they do not understand the language, rich in parables, and it has no use for their hearts. Then the catechism, which is not at all appropriate for the needs of our times, is recited and expounded with passages from the Bible. When all is done, they shout a song to their Lord God, once more at the top of their lungs, and stomp out with the final verse still on their lips. Their behaviour is just as unruly as it was when they entered. Even those who have prepared for the first communion exhibit the same unruly behaviour.

Then in the so-called evening school they are taught to calculate and to write.

During the rest of the day they are left to their parents at home, where in general they do not receive the most praiseworthy example.

The lower classes are more corrupt in Hamburg than anywhere else, for here the common man gets an easier and more abundant profit from his work than in other large and small towns. The greater number of the lower classes support themselves by peddling, sitting in stalls or cellars, or wandering about in the alleys offering their goods for sale. Because of this, parents often remove their children from the charity schools and send them into the alleys, even if only with tinder sticks or ribbon, twine and all kinds of toys, where they loudly hawk their wares to passers-by all day long, or storm into houses and beg without ceasing until one buys a little something out of pity and often just to get rid of them.

This early mercantile spirit often gives them a tendency to cheat from youth onwards.

They try to take advantage of the buyer and hide from their parents the profit they make over the set price, buying treats for themselves to devour with their comrades. But the impressions made by these early swindles and wanderings about are a permanent harm to this class of people.

Nowhere have I found the children of the lower classes to be raised so idle as in Hamburg. In other places, such as Berlin and Braunschweig, children have to support their parents with handicraft, sewing, knitting, and spinning from an early age, for their parents cannot make such an easy and abundant profit from trade.

Spinning, for example, one of the most useful jobs for the lower classes, is extremely rare in Hamburg, for they do not find this work profitable enough. Regardless of what our insightful heads of the excellent poorhouse have done to motivate them to take it up, they do not want to go on with it, and deign to spin only when they must, for peddling gives them a more abundant and comfortable profit. The parents and children become accustomed to a disorderly way of life with all this peddling and wandering about in alleyways. The food of the poor consists almost always of tea, coffee, and white bread. They seldom cook proper meals. Yet this food is more expensive and does not give them any strength. But now they are used to it, and so they spurn the Rumford's soup that the government charitably provides for them at a small price.

Our better industry schools, still less the imperfect poor schools, will not be able to bring about the moral improvement of the common people if they continue to neglect the difference between education and mere teaching.

And yet the difference between the two is very great. Education is formation for morality, with constant regard for the student's future vocation. The lessons must be completely in keeping with this vocation and only for that purpose. But both can only take place in the parental home or in the institute, where the pupil is constantly observed, and where one can continue to shape his actions and habits outside the lessons. No school can do this, and therefore its sphere of influence remains very limited.

Apart from domestic education conducted under the eyes of wise and moral parents, an institutional education is certainly the next best thing. And yet for some reason Herr Büsch, even though he had himself been the head of an educational institute, rebelled against the institutes shortly before his death.[3] A whole crowd of disciples followed him for various reasons. They wanted to abolish the institutes and promote the schools instead, without considering the permanent damage they would cause the state.

Virtuous and deserving men who devote themselves to this difficult, arduous, and often unrewarded business deserve all kinds of encouragement from their fellow citizens and the government. It would be possible to write a whole book about the reasons why deserving men are sometimes deterred from it, and seldom can hold out for long.

The fact that so many push their way into this business who are not up to the task, who possess little or none of the required knowledge and moral traits, is an occurrence that creeps into all tiers of society and means of subsistence among human beings. The public can prove its power of judgment by selecting better candidates.

Instead of pulling down the institutes, the state should seek to maintain and promote them in every possible way. Indeed, the state should do so while treating this matter as one of great importance to itself, and it should make sure that those who establish such an institute should have first provided evidence of their competence to do so.

The state would do infinitely much for the moral improvement of the lower classes if it were possible to establish institutes for the poor instead of schools, where they receive education, food, and teaching with special regard for their future roles as servants. Of course, it would be difficult to find headmasters for such institutes. For in my view, it is far more difficult to educate children of the lower classes according to their vocation than those of the higher classes.

We have one such institute in our excellent orphanage. Yet it too is subject to the accusation levelled against all orphanages, that the number of students is too large to receive proper supervision and that therefore the purpose of their moral education cannot be fully achieved.

Another cause of the corruption of our servants is the extraordinary expenses that are so numerous in Hamburg's wealthy houses: the calling fee, the so-called cloaking fee, mourning and wedding gifts, and tips.[4]

To the credit of our enlightened citizens, it must be said that some of these expenses are already being abolished. But to satisfy the servants, the lords and masters need to provide them with a substitute out of their own means. But as far as tips and cloaking fees are concerned, they have risen with increasing extravagance.

Nevertheless, it is equally discreditable to both lords and servants if the latter, when it is time for the guests to leave, place themselves in the way of the former to have them pay for their food. Nowhere is this nonsense more common than in Hamburg and in Holland.

These tips are the reason why all the servants flock to the so-called great houses. Those who do not want to make themselves poor by hosting large parties, which bring their servants great wealth, can hardly obtain any. And if the servants are forced to go to less well-off houses, they are completely unsuitable.

Would it not be far more expedient if our enlightened citizens were to go a step further and agree to abolish all these expenses, and in exchange give an equivalent of rewards for their good conduct over the period of a year? The greatest prize would be given to the one among them who had distinguished him- or herself during this period of time through loyalty, moral conduct, and diligence; the next one the second, and so on. These rewards would then be increased with each year that they serve in the same house, and the money securely allocated to them for their future provision or establishment. For it is certainly not good for this class of people, most of whom have not developed their understanding beyond childhood, to receive too much money all at once. Like children they almost always lack a concern for the future, and one does well to act as their guardian.

The labourer is worthy of his wages; a proverb inspired by true humanity.[5] It is certainly one of the most sacred duties of the true master of the house and the loving housemother not only to make their servants happy and joyful but also to take care of their future, to strive for their ongoing provision with true human love. And we will fulfil this duty with a willing heart the more we strive to provide for these our brothers and sisters, in a human sense, and for the advancement of their morality.

I will be forgiven for this small digression because of the importance of the subject. Every housefather and housemother knows how much good and faithful servants contribute to the quiet enjoyment of domestic pleasures, and, by the same token, how much bad and deceitful servants can cloud them. Our good M. Luther knew this well; in the seventh prayer he teaches us to pray for good and faithful servants.[6]

But even in this relationship with the servants, we as women are again in the happy position of being able to do good and charitable work. In this we have far more opportunity than men to have a benevolent effect on the servants. The small matters of the domestic economy bring us more often together with this class of people as we arrange their work, see that it is done, and even work alongside them. If we understand the great art of winning their hearts with love and authority, we find many opportunities in this calling to have a benevolent and charitable effect.

In terms of understanding, we will always treat our servants as children. By giving them our orders, we can incidentally and without any intention on their part scatter certain motives that lie within their grasp, and repeat them so often that they become familiar with them and feel their meaning. In particular, we can show them the great benefit of ever-purposeful activity through our example and through our comprehensible instructions. We will very often have the opportunity, without pedantry, to correct their concepts regarding their relation to God, to their neighbour in general, and to their dominion in particular, and about their hopes and prospects in this life and the next so that false concepts are gradually pushed aside.

And what a joyful, reassuring awareness it is for a good housemother to have won even one of this class for humanity! It will not be so difficult for us to strive for this noble pleasure as one might believe. In small towns, and even more in the country, we will often be able to attain it, and serenity and quiet peace will pour over our domestic affairs.

In large cities, where the striving for abundant and easy gain to fulfil the desires of the lower and rough sensuality has already subdued this class of people and is expressed in the grossest self-interest, we will admittedly almost always have to do without the noble pleasure of having a positive influence. Yet even in this unpleasant situation the wise housemother does not despair. The educated woman will, as everywhere, know how to adapt to the challenging circumstances. She finds the servants more or less corrupt. She cannot escape this discomfort entirely; she cannot immediately change people but must take them as they are for the time being. Frequent reversals have taught her that they sometimes go from bad to worse, so she tries to make this evil as harmless to herself and her household as possible. With a clear outlook she embraces the small and large matters in her relations with them, and nothing escapes her keen eye. Her servants soon realize that she is not easily deceived. The wise woman finds it shameful to be taken advantage of or cheated. She would rather give away a thaler than be cheated a shilling. She knows the price of groceries, she investigates their quality and inquires where the best can be most easily obtained. She supervises their purchase, for nothing that lies within her sphere of influence is too small for her. She knows that what she saves is a gain for her husband, for her children, and for the needy.

If her husband is in a situation where he has only a meagre living, she knows how to handle the circumstances here too. She undertakes the tasks herself and is not afraid of spoiling her beautiful hands when work has hardened them. She knows that the strength of the human being lies in knowing how to adapt to every situation; her honour is the fulfilment of her duties.

She and her husband have entered into a covenant of mutual happiness and common interest. She feels the full weight of this commitment. Through order, thriftiness, and purposeful activity she prepares serene and joyful days for herself, her husband, and her children. She knows that worrying about the food quickly dwindles the peace of the house. It upsets the minds of those who would have remained quiet if they had been able to live at ease. She thus avoids these discomforts by her modest desires and thriftiness, and, with an outlook that is able to keep track of and reckon the whole, she arranges her household in such a way that pressing worries about food do not frighten her or her cheerfulness away.

I once knew a man who was limited to a very small sum of money, and at first did not think that he could support a wife. He entrusted the business of the household to a housekeeper and got into debt. Love finally led him to join with a kind woman whose only dowry was an educated mind and modest desires. Not only did she relieve him of his debts, but afterwards he lived comfortably and without worries, and with a large family that he could not have afforded before. And yet this woman found time to work on her own ever-higher education and to complete the education of her children herself. The rich store of her knowledge meant savings for her husband. If she had not done so, her children would have grown up without any better knowledge, for her husband was not in a position to pay for teachers and had so much arduous business to see to that he could not take over the matter of their education himself. The extensive and varied knowledge she was able to pass on to her children put them in a position to make a decent way in the world. What a gain for this man to have found such a wife, and how lucky these children were to be educated by such a mother!

The educated woman knows in every aspect of life how to take hold of her circumstances and adapt herself to them. Even when the rank or wealth of her husband requires that she increase his influence through gatherings and feasts, she will distinguish herself in a beneficial way.

In the arrangement of her feasts, taste rather than splendour, abundance and yet economy, will reign. She scorns the petty pride of lauding it over her sisters by a display of riches. She knows that, of all the world's merits, wealth is the most fortuitous and insecure. She will always be mindful that the needy are entitled to part of her wealth.

If she hosts banquets, the educated woman will not believe that she has done enough if she has overburdened her guests with a lot of expensive and poorly matched dishes, which are often laid out not so much to please the guests as to display the host's wealth. She will vividly feel the great duty of sociability to care for the entertainment of her guests. This duty does not merely extend to the wealthy and distinguished among them; her care for their entertainment extends to all. She has invited them to enjoy the pleasures of society, so she endeavours to spread cheerfulness everywhere.

She strives to bring together those who have the same degree of culture. But she displays the fulness and diversity of her mind by talking to each one about matters within his grasp, and by leading the conversation in such a way that he can shine in his sphere, or at least believes he can shine.

If, on the other hand, her husband is in a situation where he is of high rank without possessing wealth, as is very often the case, the inexhaustible source of her mind will then come to his aid. She will be able to maintain the splendour of his house with the greatest economy, without anyone noticing it. An ordinary woman would not know how to help in this situation. The highly educated and knowledgeable woman will nowhere be at a loss. Men can only win and never lose through our highest education.

The worn-out claim repeated (almost to the point of disgust) by all writers who have dared to write about the female vocation—that if a woman becomes acquainted with higher sciences, the soup is oversalted, the vegetables are burnt, etc.—does not deserve refutation.[7]

By virtue of the organization of her mind and the important insight that the duty of humanity requires her to develop all her powers harmoniously, the wise, educated woman studies the sciences not to shine but because she feels it as her calling. Guided by this motive, she will seek to acquire vital confidence in her duties as a human being and as a woman so that she becomes just as confident about the most important matters of human knowledge. Consequently, she finds nothing in her sphere of influence too insignificant for her attention.

The genuinely educated woman will therefore be very eager to take care of the details of her economy. She has mastered the art of cooking, for this science lies within her sphere of influence. She cooks herself when circumstances require it. If her position is so high that she does not need to, she still has the knowledge to give decisive advice when mistakes must be fixed. Many clothes horses of my acquaintance are unable to do this. Their torpid lives flow away into nothing but triviality, and the writers remain silent; only higher female education suffers the scourge of their satire.

Since the purposefully educated woman has acquired the rules of the art of cooking, since she combines them with the rules of nutrition, she does not place food together on the table that would hinder digestion through a conflicting mixture. Her dietary care extends to all her household members; even the servants are not excluded. She knows that they complete their tasks with more serenity and strength in the full enjoyment of their health. Knowing their housemother's care for their health, they seek advice from her if even a small ailment strikes them. And after she has investigated the cause of their ailment, she helps them to regain their diminished health with simple household remedies. I know a woman to whose house the doctor rarely comes, for she follows these rules with insight and precision.

The wise and careful housemother is no stranger to the provisions required to see out the winter. She knows what must be set aside for this rough season, when nature seems to slumber in frost and most sedulously prepares its coming beauty, and she is no stranger to the best way to preserve what the household will need. A future perspective is natural to the educated mind.

Everything concerning respectable and appropriate clothing is also familiar to the educated housemother. She knows where it is best and most convenient to purchase, how the linen should be acquired, how to make her and her children's clothing herself if her situation demands it. If this is not the case, if she lives in such a free situation that she can leave it to others, this knowledge protects her from deception. She knows what belongs to each piece of clothing and how they are most appropriately crafted. She watches over everything with careful attention out of a pure sense of duty. She ensures that the air in her house is pure and healthy because she knows its healing influence. In all her rooms there is cleanliness and order, though without exaggeration. She rearranges them according to the climate. If she lives in a humid region, she does not increase the humidity through wet mopping, even if she offends the prevailing custom by this omission and is criticized by her neighbours. She does not depend on the judgment of others in these trifles. She has devised a plan of life that is close to the golden mean allotted to us sublunary people in all affairs.

But if the educated woman is so busily occupied with all the earthly needs of her household, she also feels that she is not called to move solely in the narrow circle of the kitchen, cellar, and pantry to care exclusively for pleasing the palate, satisfying the stomach, and clothing the body. In whatever stage of life it may be found, the small mind may be satisfied with this petty business alone. Its gaze does not reach beyond this span of life. It is not familiar with the purpose of its existence, and does not know how to grasp its relation to the whole. The woman of high spirit knows that she is there for something better. She breathes and works in the consciousness of her high calling. The right and the fine deed and the liveliness of her mind give her independence and character. Everything that she starts and completes happens in a way that is appropriate to the matter at hand. She treats the small things with ease and favour, the large things with seriousness and dignity.

She carries out economic matters easily, quickly, and at the right time. Her outlook, which is accustomed to order and quickly surveys the whole, immediately grasps everything from the right point of view. She has already completed the task when the woman with a limited mind is still talking about it and is still busy with preparations.

To the untrained mind, limited to a small circle, everything becomes difficult. To the trained mind, which surveys the whole, everything becomes easy. Thus, even in the most self-driven, strict fulfilment of her domestic duties, the educated woman will still have enough leisure to continue to work on her own education, to educate her children, to be an uplifting and witty companion for her husband, to be a wise advisor to him in matters of business, and, on occasion, to enjoy with him the pleasures of sociability in an intimate circle of close and dear friends.

Nevertheless, some writers call out to us so loudly that there is simply not enough time to fulfil our duties as housewives and at the same time to complete our higher education with restless zeal. Oh time! I am disgusted to have to repeat this interjection so frequently: time will always be found if we understand the art of using it properly, if we hold the ennoblement of our better selves as a truly important matter, if we duly appreciate all our duties and are deeply imbued with the desire to fulfil them.

Then so many weaknesses, so many trivial things that have often and justly made our sex the subject of satire, will fall away. The woman who so restlessly strives for a purposeful, noble education has so many subjects of interest that occupy her mind and heart in a pleasurable way that boredom, the greatest plague of mortals, is completely unknown to her. Her neighbours and acquaintances are left in peace from the petty criticisms of the most insignificant actions. What does she care for what they do in their houses? She has enough to do with herself and managing her own home. Unless a special interest in common matters brings her close to her neighbours, she does not even know them by name. She is not chased from her pleasant domestic circle to pass time and to run after news of city and fashion by the emptiness of her head or heart.

She indeed plays the liveliest part in the progress of culture, in the moral growth or decline of the whole of humanity. If some people attempt to revive antiquated mysticism as the greatest antipode of true enlightenment, she sees this as an outgrowth of exaggerated fantasy and overdeveloped sensibility. With an anxious heart, she waits to see if these fanatics will prevail over healthy reason, or whether their better genius will bring them back from such aberrations so that these writers will with their great talent have a nobler and more useful effect on humanity, making up for the damage they may already have stirred up in weak minds.

The educated woman takes the warmest part in everything that interests humankind. Evil, immoral, ridiculous, and wrong actions attract her attention. She notes them with feeling and endeavours to suppress them with better concepts and by exposing their harmfulness and ridiculousness, avoiding all inflated personalities. 'Foolishness stings me, and lack of good faith offends me,' says Madame de Sévigné.[8] What creature who truly feels the good of humankind does not feel as she does? This vivid interest in the ennoblement of humanity never degenerates into slander. She feels regret for those who are on the wrong track, pities the fools, does what she can to circulate better concepts, and then lets the world go as it wants to and can, content if she is what she is supposed to be.[9]

It is you, my educated women friends, that I address. In all your actions refute the writers who think that the higher education of our mind cannot exist together with the fulfilment of our individual duties. Be restless in the education of your mind. The more you strive for this great purpose, the more you strive to fulfil all the duties of your threefold calling in the most rigorous way. This is the best way to silence those prejudices.

And you, my women friends who until now have regarded your circumstances from a restricted point of view, look around you in all the field of your duties and strive to fulfil them all! Become human beings in the most fundamental sense of the term. And at the same time become noble, educated women, and thus save the honour of our sex.

5

On the Education of Woman in the Unmarried State

We have so far only spoken about the higher education of women who fulfil the purpose of their existence as wife, mother, and housewife. We have seen that the highest education honours, ennobles, and elevates the threefold calling of woman. Let us now consider those among us who have been prevented by their situation from fulfilling this vocation that nature has given them.

In our luxurious times, when a certain immoral freethinking is in vogue, the sanctity of marriage is ever in decline, and marriage is all too often the product of the basest self-interest.

On the one hand, the cost of maintaining a household is getting higher and higher, and the means of acquisition more and more difficult given the crowd that rushes after it, such that many men dare not follow the sweet drive to tie the bonds of marital fidelity with a loving wife, and are unable to follow their wish for quiet domestic pleasures.

On the other hand, many men are deterred from entering the bond of marital fidelity and love by their prevailing sensuality, which is now so easily satisfied outside of marriage, and by their numbed feeling for the worthy bonds of nature and society.

At the same time, women cannot and may not ask men to marry them and must wait until they are courted. So is the custom, and so is feminine tenderness. Thus, it cannot be avoided that many women will remain unmarried.

According to the prevailing custom, the first motive in choosing a wife is money. It seems that all nations that sank to excessive luxury and then to decadent immorality through the inappropriate refinement of their way of life and the false culture of their minds have been led by the same motives. In Terence, the miserly old man always asks his enamoured son, who speaks with delight of the charms and perfections of his beloved: and what does she bring with her?[1] He does not hear his son's lofty praise for the girl of his dreams, and constantly beats his son's enthusiasm with the cold question, what does she bring with her? But we seem to have come even further in this kind of enlightenment than the Romans in the days of Terence. These days, many of our young men do not need a reminder of the kind that the concerned old man was dishing out back then. For them, the dowry is always the first motivation when choosing a wife.

No matter how deformed a girl or a widow may be in mind and body, if she is the owner of great wealth, the heir to a considerable fortune, she will have the choice of many insistent men. Even if her reputation has many stains, such trivialities will be overlooked. After all, he is only after her money. Since that cannot be obtained without her person, he takes her as his wife, thus deceiving nature, civil society, the woman, and himself out of base self-interest and a lack of self-esteem.

Often a thoughtful person cannot help but smile with pity when he listens to the speculations of men who are eager to marry, how they strive to get hold of the money and the woman by less than delicate means. They do not realize that they are degrading themselves by making wealth their idol and at the same time admitting their ineptitude in acquiring sufficient wealth for themselves to be able to please and feed a lovable wife of their own free choice.

Even men who already possess sufficient wealth strive to accumulate more through an advantageous marriage, for everyone longs for the sensual enjoyment of life without effort.

After wealth follows feminine beauty as the reason for choosing a wife. It is not blameworthy that the beauty of women makes a deep and vivid impression on the hearts of men, for it is entirely in their nature.

Who can resist the charm that nature has poured out on a beautiful woman? If beauty is accompanied by the education of the mind and the gentle human virtues—then we see in a beautiful woman the masterpiece of earthly creation. Happy is the man who enters into the covenant of marital fidelity with her!

But if beauty stands alone, if the one who possesses beauty believes herself by this privilege to be freed from the task of striving for moral and intellectual education, because she knows her omnipotence over the hearts of men; if she becomes proud, vain, and flirtatious due to her beauty, and yet it alone is the motive for the choice of a man deceived by his sensuality; then he cannot complain when he has to atone for his brief sensual indulgence with the long agony of a failed and unhappy marriage. A woman who is nothing but beautiful cannot maintain her influence over a man's heart for long. Habit blunts everything. In contrast, experience tells that if a woman succeeds in capturing a man's heart by the inner charm of a beautiful soul, she would claim it forever and yet gain still more, even if she loses all external charm. The inner beauty of the mind and the heart is an unending source which feeds into every action with new charm and grace. Its diversity always offers the mind new material for contemplation, and its benevolent influence attracts the heart with indissoluble bonds.

Even the woman with few physical charms often succeeds in surprising the sensuality of men and capturing a husband. Men, who are fond of accusing the female sex of vanity, often suffer no less from this infirmity themselves. They are flattered to believe that a woman has fallen in love with them so violently that she forgets her feminine delicacy and makes the first move out of love for them. And the coquette knows how to hide the nets with which she entangles their sensuality and vanity so cleverly that, stormed by these two passions at the same time, they cannot escape her.

Money, beauty, and the arts of seduction are thus the primary means by which women of the ordinary kind generally lay their siege and acquire the possession of a husband. Impoverished virtue trails behind them. A gentle girl in possession of neither striking beauty nor money, and who feels her feminine dignity too vividly to reduce herself to the arts of seduction, can only be prized by the man who is able to value and sense her silent worth. And she does not always meet such a man on her way through life. If she happens to meet him, situation and circumstances all too often make a marital union impossible. Thus, she remains unmarried.

In other cases, the death or unfaithfulness of the first beloved can wound the heart of a noble woman so deeply that she cannot consider a second, similar union.

If there are many causes that deter women from their vocation as wives and mothers, if devastating wars and diseases, which are deadlier to men than to women, leave so many of us as spinsters, what then will be women's defence against the ridicule that is so readily spread against their status? What will make them capable of a benevolent effect on humankind in this situation as well? Nothing but the sciences in the highest perfected education of humankind.

If the woman has attained her education from the only true perspective towards complete, beautiful humanity, then she is not lost to any area of life and adjusts herself to any sphere of influence. If she cannot be useful to the world in one way, she will be useful in another. She is satisfied if, at the close of her life, she can thank the one who assigned her a role to play and exit the stage gracefully, mindful of his and virtuous people's applause, in anticipation of her future reward. She is intimately aware that she paid tribute to humanity by multiplying and expanding that which is morally beautiful and good in the sphere of influence wherein she was placed.

According to the present arrangement of things, in which men have taken all the lucrative offices and trades for themselves, only a few opportunities for income remain for the unmarried woman without a fortune.

These are: the education of young people, the males only to a certain age and the females until its completion, then housekeeping and chaperoning, and finally providing for themselves through handiwork, especially in the field of fashion and luxury.

Each one will choose from these means of provision one to which her education, talents, and inclination dispose her.

Let us consider the most useful and honourable, and especially the most readily available, position: the educator.

It has not yet been sufficiently recognized how greatly women contribute to the world's good or ill through this activity.

Everything I have said in the chapter on the educated mother applies here as well, and to an even greater extent.

If a woman as a mother, as the educator of her children, needs the highest education, it is certain that the teacher, who does not have the motives of maternal affection, must be educated to a yet higher degree, and imbued even more with the intimate and deep feeling of duty than the mother who is inspired by natural feeling.

She must understand with conviction that the position she chooses as educator is the most honourable and important one in the whole of humanity.

All knowledge that is necessary to this end will become important to her, and she will strive unceasingly to acquire it. Her own perpetual moral education will be the most important business of her life. For she is not only a teacher but also a role model to the young people entrusted to her. She knows and feels that teaching without an example has no effect, none at all. And this serious appreciation of her important calling, this perpetual striving for her own perfect education, occupies her with such nobility that she avoids all the ridiculous things of which spinsters are often rightly accused.

If ever a woman requires the highest degree of education, it is in this situation. She, who is not joined with humanity by the beautiful bond of spousal and motherly duty, must be a true citizen of the world. This she can only achieve through knowledge. She considers all of humanity her family. She knows that, as an active member of this great chain, her judgment matters.

Her kind heart and her bright mind tell her that every member must contribute its own share to the great sum, and she restlessly strives to settle this great debt to humankind.

Then an immense feeling of fulfilled duty consoles her for the want of the higher degree of happiness, which she does not have as wife and mother.

The children entrusted to her become her own. They may not owe her their physical existence, but they still owe her their moral one. In her sphere of influence, she has so many opportunities to remove the antiquated prejudices of yore and wealth and to replace them with true concepts, and thus to have an effect even on distant generations. Prejudices and true concepts are like an avalanche: small and imperceptible material is caught up together and rolls an incredible distance, all the while taking up similar bits and pieces until they become a great mass, either terrible or benevolent, such that their influence can no longer be reckoned. Suffused with this great view of her calling, she tries to win the hearts of her pupils and to spread many fertile ideas. And the more she attends to the germination of these ideas, the more these moral children thrive, the more she loves them, and the more zealous she becomes for their education.

These humane feelings remove any hardness towards her pupils, of which spinsters, who have never known the sweetness of the tender motherly feeling, are often accused. The view afforded by the high degree of education that comes with her calling causes her to regard her duty and her relationship to humanity from the most sublime point of view.

Such a woman cannot have too much knowledge. Her knowledge can be regarded as the contact point by which she meets humanity, thus avoiding the pitfalls that are found on her path more frequently than that of a married woman. And when she has gathered treasures at the hand of science and her own contemplation, will it then be considered a crime against the offended majesty of men to leave the fruits of her reflection to the world as a late blessing? If her efforts will still be of use long after she is gone? And is this occupation not far more noble than if, at an age when it no longer befits her to expect the courtship of men, she nevertheless continues to make men the first business of her existence, and thus chooses attire that is supposed to conceal her age but in fact does nothing but ridicule her and attract the contempt that, rightly or wrongly, attaches to her status?

Is it not far more noble than spying on the actions of her younger sisters, eavesdropping on their steps with a hawkish eye, and misleading them with great malice, for she cannot forgive them for enjoying the pleasures that have been denied her? Is it not more noble than putting on a mask of piety to deceive the world all the better, to more cleverly hide the guile and envy that torment her?

The human being, brought up in relations that intersect with the manifold interests of refined humanity, longs for occupation. If it stands on a low level of culture, its occupation will be low and without purpose. If it stands on a high level, its activity will be purposeful and noble.

Whoever is attentive to the aspirations and actions of human beings in the various degrees of their culture will be able, after choosing their pleasures and favourite occupations, to determine the level they occupy in the series of cultured beings.

Only in the lack of education or miseducation of women can we find the unjust source of most of their deficiencies. Insolence, gossip, envy of insignificant trifles, undue concern for one's appearance, coquetry, a penchant for unruly pleasures, quarrelling, and addiction to gambling all flow from an empty and uneducated soul.

I cannot repeat it enough. The study of the sciences must always keep pace with the highest education towards humanity, lest we degrade science, making a parade dress out of it that we put on merely to deceive others; then the poor dress of noble naïvety will certainly look far better.

But even among unmarried women the degree of culture will vary according to their physical and intellectual powers. Nature observes the greatest diversity in all of its forms. The great chain goes from the lowest to the highest. But if the education of women is begun from the right point of view and pursued with a constant tendency towards the morally beautiful and good, then the woman will gladly take a low or high intellectual position, and she will certainly avoid the deficiencies for which our sex is so often reproached, especially those laid against unmarried women.

If the female sex should ever come to the view that the development of its predispositions and powers is a business and a duty, the whole of humanity would receive a great, immeasurable profit. Given the present state of things, women can have no other fruitful purpose for their higher education than the benefit of humanity. This, or the desire to shine, can be the only motives for their education—one right, one wrong. And would I convince my women friends that they humiliate themselves, and the sciences, by using them for this frivolous purpose!

APPENDIX 1
Biographical References

Johann Beckmann, *Vorrath kleiner Anmerkungen über mancherley gelehrte Gegenstände*, vol. 3. (Göttingen: J. H. Röwer, 1806), 549–50

Amalia Holst belongs among our esteemed writers, but her name is still overlooked in learned Germany because, out of modesty, she has not made it known. But now I believe I may reveal that she is the author of *Bemerkungen über die Fehler unserer modernen Erziehung von einer praktischen Erzieherin*, published by the writer Siegfried v. Lindenberg, Leipzig 1791. According to the reliable judgment of the reviewer for the *Götting. gel. Anzeigen* 1791 [sic] p. 545 [p. 117], which did not disclose the name of the author, the work not only displays astute observations but also seems to be written by a male rather than a female scholar, due to the way it is written and the presentation of its ideas.

As a scholar, Amalia von Justi can claim the privilege of being called by her own name. She was kind enough to disclose certain news to me, admittedly not as extensive as my readers would wish, but news whose reliability cannot be doubted, even if one must assume that the daughter has concealed certain things that could be detrimental, if not to the merit then to the honour of the famous father. I would therefore have published an excerpt from the letters I had the pleasure of receiving, according to the permission granted to me, if the author had not given me the hope of describing the life of her father in detail herself from the correspondence that she has in her possession. I tried in vain to execute this intention. The reason why I had to postpone it for another occasion was to honour the consideration she gave to her mother, who was still alive at the time. I do not want, she wrote, to sadden the unhappy woman still more by reminding her of the events she has suffered. I do not know whether the widow is still alive, and whether Amalia will carry out her plans; but I do not think I can wait any longer to faithfully act on the news I have received.

Obituary in *Neuer Nekrolog der Deutschen*, 7(1) (Ilmenau: Voigt, 1829 [1831]), 63–4

Amalie Holst, née von Justi.

Independent Doctor of Philosophy and writer at Greater Timckenberg in Mecklenburg, Schwerin.

Born in February 1758, died 6 January 1829.

She was the daughter of the unfortunate J. Heinr, Gottlob v. Justi, from his second marriage, entered into in 1757, who is known by his fate, last employed as the

Prussian mining officer and chief supervisor of the glass and steel works, and who died on 21 July 1771 as a state prisoner at Cüstrin before the investigation proceedings against him had concluded. For a long time it remained unknown that she was the author of *Bemerkungen über die Fehler unserer modernen Erziehung*; she wished to remain anonymous out of modesty. It only became known when Beckmann, to whom she also communicated the news about her father in his *Anmerkungen über gelehrte Gegenstände*, revealed her name. She also intended to document her father's life in detail, based on the letters she had gathered; but a tender childish feeling not to further sadden her already unhappy mother by recalling the misfortunes she had suffered prevented her from carrying out this plan, however much she was encouraged to do so. She then married Dr Holst, and after his death ran an educational institute in Boizenburg for several years, then in Hamburg and finally in Parchim, where her three married sisters lived. For the last ten years she lived in Groß Timkenberg on Telbau near Boizenburg, a small developed peninsular on the Elbe, with her only son, Eduard H., who has been married to Henriette Conradine née Grelcke, who owns the estate, since 1818. Of her two daughters, Emilie and Mariane, who faithfully assisted her in her educational work, the former has been married to the mayor, lawyer August Ehlers, in Neubukow since 20 September 1822. – The deceased was a woman of equal distinction in mind and heart, and, it is claimed, received a doctorate from Kiel, not through her husband but acquired herself. – She parted silently and gently in her 71st year and rests in the parish churchyard in Blücher on the banks of the Sudenstrom.

Her publications: *Bemerkungen über die Fehler unserer modernen Erziehung von einer praktischen Erzieherin*. Edited by the author of *Siegfried v. Lindenberg*. Leipzig 1791 (anon.). – *Über die Bestimmung des Weibes zur höhern Geistesbildung*, Berlin 1807 [sic]. – Essays in A. Lindemann's *Musarion* (Altona 1799), Parts 4, 5. *Beurtheilung über Elisa, oder das Weib wie es seyn sollte*. – C.f. (Beckmann's) *Vorrath kleiner Anmerkungen über mancherley gelehrte Gegenstände*. 3rd collection. Göttingen 1806. pp. 548 ff., where she shares news about her father. – Schindel's *Schriftstellerinnen*, vol. 1, p. 226, and vol. 3, p. 170.

Schwerin, Dr Brüssow

Obituary in *Freimütiges Abendblatt*, no. 557 (Rostock, 1829), cols 741–2

On 6 January 1829, the writer and former headmistress of a girls' school in Parchim, Amalie Holst, née von Justi, died at Greater Timckenberg, near Boizenburg, in her 71st year. She was the daughter of the unfortunate Johann Heinrich Gottlob von Justi from his second marriage, which took place in October 1757. Known by his fate, von Justi was last employed as a Royal Prussian mining officer and chief supervisor of the glass and steel works, and died on 21 July 1771 as a state prisoner in Cüstrin after the end of the investigation proceedings pending against him. The eulogist is unable to give any details about her upbringing, education, and earlier living conditions, or about her marriage.

Later she ran an educational institute in Boizenburg for several years, followed by Hamburg and then Parchim. For several years she lived in Groß Timkenberg with her only son, Eduard, who has been married to Henriette Konradine Grelcke, owner of that estate, since 11 November 1818. Of her two daughters, Emilie and Mariane, who faithfully assisted her in her educational work, the former has been married to the mayor, lawyer August Ehlers, in Neubukow since 20 September 1822. Amalie Holst held the title of doctor, and it is claimed that it was not acquired through her husband but independently, as was the case with Erxleben, Leporin, von Rodde-Schlözer, von Siebold, etc.

For a long time it remained unknown that the deceased was the author of the work *Bemerkungen über die Fehler unserer modernen Erziehung*; she wished to remain anonymous out of modesty. It was Beckmann, to whom she also communicated the news about her father, who finally revealed her name in his *Anmerkungen über gelehrte Gegenstände*. She also intended to document her father's life in detail, based on the letters she had gathered. However, a tender childish feeling not to further sadden her already unhappy mother by recalling the misfortunes she had suffered prevented her from carrying out this plan, however much she was encouraged to do so. This description of his life would certainly have cleared up several obscurities and contradictory narratives, and would have been an interesting work in general, since in the writings she published she proved herself to be a writer of dynamic expression and astuteness, and was distinguished with equal faithfulness on the part of both mind and heart.

As far as the deceased's work as a teacher is concerned, her school was held in general esteem, for she did not educate her female students merely for domestic service, or for society, or for the so-called refined side of life. Rather, she educated them for life as a whole, opening the wellspring in mind and spirit for a loving and intelligent fulfilment of everything that the female vocation demands of woman in religious and cosmopolitan respects. Household management and maternal care, faithfulness in large and small matters, sensitivity and strength, sense and understanding to delight the circle of society, the propensity to do the right thing, the skill to do it well and without mishap, quiet charity, modest activity with all the knowledge and artistry of female education, and in all this a noble feeling that does not allow the sense of the infinite to be lost in earthly activity, and in which the mind remains free and firm above the colourful essence of all worldly activity: that is what distinguished those who remained in her hands and were left to her guidance until they reached a certain goal. Many parents, young women, husbands, and mothers certainly still thank her for this. Her educational work will remain a blessing for generations to come. As a writer she is known for the following works:

1. *Bemerkungen über die Fehler unserer modernen Erziehung*, edited by the writer Siegfried von Lindenberg (i.e. Dr Phil. Johann Gottwerth Müller, died at Itzehoe on 23 June 1828, aged 86), Leipzig 1791. 8. (anon.)
2. *Über die Bestimmung des Weibes zur höhern Geistesbildung*, Berlin 1807 [sic].
3. *Beurtheilung über Elisa, oder das Weib wie es seyn sollte*, in A. Lindemann's *Musarion, Eine Monatsschrift für Damen*.

C.f. a) (Beckmann's) *Vorrath kleiner Anmerkungen über mancherley gelehrte Gegenstände*. 3rd collection. Göttingen 1806. pp. 548 ff., where she shares news about her father. b) Ersch, *Gelehrtes Teutschland*, p. 346, and d) [sic] C. W. O. A. Schindel's *Schriftstellerinnen des 19ten Jahrhunderts*, vol. 1, p. 226, and vol. 3, p. 170.

Fr. Br.

Bibliographical entry in *Damen Conversations-Lexicon*, vol. 5 (Adorf: Bureau, 1846), 318–19

Holst, Amalie, the author of two excellent works on women's education, was the daughter of the Prussian mining officer von Justi. Born in 1758, her predilection for scientific pursuits pushed back every other activity in her lively mind at an early age. With untiring diligence, she trained the rich faculties of her mind to such a pleasing education that even her first publication, *Bemerkungen über die Fehler unserer modernen Erziehung*, Leipzig, 1791, was received with the greatest approval. Even wider was the recognition received by her second book, *Über die Bestimmung des Weibes zur höhern Geistesbildung*, Berlin, 1807 [sic]. Married to Dr Holst, she lived only to support his children until his death and then took over the management of several educational institutions in Boizenburg, Hamburg, and Parchim. Her outstanding achievements were publicly recognized in her old age when she was awarded a doctorate in philosophy by the University of Kiel. The highly deserving woman met her maker on the small peninsula of Teldau near Boizenburg on 6 January 1829, where she spent her final years with her son at Groß Timkenberg. R.

Bibliographical entry in *Das Lexikon der hamburgischen Schriftsteller*, ed. Dr Phil. Hans Schröder (Hamburg, 1857), 329–31

Holst, née von Justi (Amelie). Born 1758 at..., daughter of the unfortunate J. Heinr. Gottlob v. Justi, from his second marriage, entered into in 1757, who is known by his fate, last employed as the Prussian mining officer and chief supervisor of the glass and steel works, and who died on 21 July 1771 as a state prisoner at Cüstrin before the investigation proceedings against him had concluded. She received thorough schooling and a learned education; however, the claim that she independently earned a Doctorate in Philosophy at Kiel is probably based on an error; her modesty speaks against it, as she was still a completely anonymous writer in 1791. At that time she called herself a practical educator and probably already lived as such in Hamburg. Here she married—it is not known in which year (but it must have been before 1802)—the Doctor of Laws Johann Ludolf Holst, who, like her, dedicated himself to the field of education. She is said to have spent the final ten years of her life at Groß-Timkenberg on the small peninsula formed by the Elbe and Sude rivers near Boitzenburg, with her only son, Eduard Holst, who had been married to

Henriette Konradine Grelcke, owner of that noble estate, since 1818. Her two daughters, Emilie and Mariane Holst, faithfully assisted their mother in her educational work. The eldest was married in 1822 to the mayor and lawyer Aug. Ehlers in Neubukow. Our writer had three married sisters in Parchim. She died quietly and gently at the age of 71 and is buried in the parish churchyard in Blücher on the Elbe. She was distinguished equally by her head and her heart.

APPENDIX 2

Reviews of Holst's work

Review of *Observations on the Errors of Our Modern Education from a Practical Educator*, in *Göttingische Anzeigen von gelehrten Sachen* 55, 7 April 1792, 545–7

Leipzig. By C. Fr. Schneider: *Bemerkungen über die Fehler unserer modernen Erziehung, von einer practischen Erzieherin*. Published by the writer Siegfried von Lindenberg. 1791. 96 pages octavo.

The text displays much insight. Based on the presentation of ideas, the tone, and the language, the reviewer would not conclude that it is written by a woman. Yet, according to the certain assurance of the editor and writer of the foreword, such an author is to be assumed. She does not fail to recognize the strengths and merits of the method of education developed by Locke, Rousseau, Basedow, and their successors. Nor does she directly confront the theory of these men with the errors committed in the application of their prescriptions, which she condemns in the text. Yet some of the most renowned recent theorists and writers in the field of pedagogy seem to her to have had much to do with these errors; for in the various applications they have made of their theory, especially in regard to the means of education (the writings and libraries for children, which they supply in large quantities), they violate the essential foundations of the philosophy of education, or at least gave stimulus and opportunity to those errors. In contrast to the blind faith and obedience formerly demanded of children, the new educators reason with them too extensively; they draw out too much from their pupils too soon, allowing social expectations to squash them into adults; they grant them too much freedom; they prescribe them comprehensive lessons, together with the trifling relief of history and poetry in which their lessons are constantly dressed; these errors, and the immodesty arising from them (the all-too-early awakening of the imagination with all its impulses, hurried volatility and saturation without digestion, stimulation without adequate force and vigour in the pupils brought about by their practice), are all covered in this study. On the whole, the reasons given by the author, which are very well developed from the nature of education and the corroborating experience of others, sufficiently justify her aim and judgments. Yet it seems to the reviewer that in some respects she has gone too far. How, for example, can one accept a sweeping judgment that poems are still incomprehensible for children after several years of schooling (p. 67), given the notion of poetry as it is to be taken here? Moreover, the reviewer would have judged differently, or more definitively, about the rule of telling young children the reasons for the precepts and prohibitions that are given to them. He too knows from much experience that the rule can be practised with good success; children can understand how and why. For a child's understanding depends solely on the reasons one gives and how one gives them. For most of the necessary precepts and prohibitions, a reason can be given that is comprehensible for the child; provided one understands the matter properly oneself. And if this reason is given with such calm resolution and cheerful earnestness that the child notices that the compliance required of him is an endeavour that a reasonable creature is not indifferent to, and can be made even more pleasant when accompanied by other signs of love, then obedience is not made any more difficult than it should be, and love is promoted. There is no harm if the child does not immediately understand this reason completely. Everything, every word and every sentence, must have been said many times before it is understood. It has always seemed to the reviewer an exaggeration on the part of the pedagogical theorists that all teaching, in religion and the like, should be started only when it can be understood all at once. This conflicts with the nature of human knowledge. Nor do they seem to have always distinguished sufficiently between the factors of age and the effects of education. In a time when everything established by convention and the symbolic order of things has lost so much of its prestige, and everything is supposed to be arranged according to nature, it is impossible to produce and maintain such respect for tradition and mystery among the young, given the contrary spirit of the times. Finally, in judging particular methods one must not forget that each one has its inconsistencies, that nothing in the world is perfect, and that human wisdom consists largely in the art of choosing between several evils. In spite of all this, the reviewer does not intend to divert the author away from the literary-pedagogical efforts to which she has declared herself inclined. Rather, he wishes to see them continue.

Review of *On the Vocation of Woman to Higher Intellectual Education*, in *Beilage des Hamburgischen Correspondenten*, February 9, no. 23 (Hamburg, 1802)

Über die Bestimmung des Weibes zur höhern Geistesbildung, by Amalia Holst, née von Justi, Berlin 1802, H. Frölich.

In this work of hers, the highly estimable author has taken it upon herself to defend the noble and often contested rights of the female sex. Her vast and broad knowledge, much revered in her circles, certainly entitled her to do so. She does not merely keep pace with those men—Pockel [*sic*], Meiners, Hippel, Brandes, and Mouvillon—who have examined the present subject, which is of the upmost importance to humanity, but not infrequently she surpasses them in thoroughness, clarity, and persuasive force. But what raises the respect for the author in the eyes of one who knows her more personally is that it is only when she has performed the duties of a loving mother, the duties of a faithful educator of her children, when she has actively attended to her husband's business throughout the day, that she then, in the late evening, gives herself over to the contemplations of such a cultured mind. Blessed is the man to whom such a wife was given; blessed is the female sex for whom such a beautiful model is displayed in her.

K – r.

Review of *On the Vocation of Woman to Higher Intellectual Education*, in *Kaiserlich-Privlegirte hamburgische Neue Zeitung*, 34, Stück 27, February 1802 (Berlin: Heinrich Frölich), 12

Über die Bestimmung des Weibes zur höhern Geistesbildung, by Amalia Holst, née von Justi, 300 p.

Even if one grants the capacity for higher intellectual education to the female sex, as soon as one considers its calling as wife, housewife, and mother it is impossible to concede that it is destined to rise to the scientific culture of men. The woman who wants to fulfil her manifold and, at times, difficult duties in domestic and married life obviously lacks the leisure that is indispensable for the thorough and continued study of the sciences. As much as the author of *Über die Bestimmung des Weibes* wants it to be known that she entrusts herself with that higher intellectual education, and as much as she would like to join the ranks of Meiners, Pockels, Ewald, and others, it is nevertheless obvious that her domestic duties prevented her from obtaining the necessary instruction in the subjects she talks about. For one cannot help but be surprised that truths to which the most learned and virtuous philologists and theologians have dedicated their noblest powers and their entire lives are dismissed by the author with a few scornful remarks. One must be astonished when one hears her claim, 'The story of creation is a childish fable; creation from nothing is an absurdity; according to the Mosaic account, it occurred to the Godhead six thousand years ago to bring the entire universe into being (where did Moses claim this, and how can his writings speak of our time calculation?); the whole Old Testament is a mixture of some great ideas of the ancient philosophers, which contrast strangely with the petty concept of a national god, as he is described everywhere else, who imposes his will regardless of the cost and rules like an oriental despot; Paul's teaching is invalid, because he poisoned the gentle and loving religion of Christ with the spirit of sophistry and intolerance, etc.' If one considers that such principles and assertions, which in fact offer nothing for the improvement of humanity yet which the author would like to supply, easily leave a most corrupting impression on weak minds, one must be filled with regret and lament. For her, as with many other brazen deniers of revelation and Christianity, this freethinking is probably the consequence of a lack of religious knowledge, which is clearly apparent in her claim that 'the good Luther taught us in the seventh petition to pray for good servants'. The reverence that the reviewer believes is due to the female sex cannot extend so far that he should forgo the truth, that he should disrespect the public before whose tribunal she has seen fit to appear, and withhold his judgment. The author, by the way, is to be advised to continue the praiseworthy business of developing her mind in such a way that her actual female vocation does not suffer from it; but also to guard herself, due to her desire to charm gallant men by showing off her immature intellect, from seeking flattery at the expense of pure truth.

Review of *On the Vocation of Woman to Higher Intellectual Education*, in *Hamburg und Altona: eine Zeitschrift zur Geschichte der Zeit, der Sitten und des Geschmacks*, 3 (7–9) (Hamburg: Nestler, 1802), 95–7, 205–12, 356–60

Über die Bestimmung des Weibes zur höhern Geistesbildung, by Amalia Holst, née von Justi. Berlin: Heinrich Frölich, 1802.

Madame Holst, better known by the name of Amalia von Justi, a fellow citizen of our small state, holds no inglorious place among writers. The subject she has chosen for this present work is certainly of the utmost importance. Indeed, the educated woman has the most fundamental right to give her voice freely and unabashedly in a matter so important for humanity. Who would and could deny the author this right? She has expressed her thoughts on this matter in a way that testifies to her wit, her knowledge, and her erudition, but at the same time with a good deal of feminine excitability and a lack of deeply penetrating philosophy. But I will first examine before judging. I will do the author full justice, and try to walk a middle way between the gallant and the overly ungallant reviewer in our patriotic public pages. It seems to me that this important investigation should first be preceded by the preliminary question: what is actually to be understood by higher intellectual education? If this question is answered in a clear and sufficient manner, it will certainly not be difficult to settle the matter. Unfortunately, the author has not seen fit to discuss the question first. Her remarks thereon are found scattered freely here and there in the body of the work itself; it is quite tedious to put them together.

Madame admittedly promises on page 56 [p. 28] to undertake this necessary investigation. Yet she only mentions the sciences that can serve women in their higher intellectual education and leaves the question unexamined. To note a few claims in the work, higher intellectual education is: 'learnedness in harmony with true education for humanity' (p. 15 [p. 14]); 'scientific knowledge and genuine human education' (p. 48 [p. 25]); 'harmonious and purposeful training of all our powers' (p. 17 [14; see p. 67], and several other places). In some passages the author explicitly says that learnedness and humanity are one and the same, and claims for women the right to be allowed to penetrate freely and unhindered into all regions of human knowledge.

It is evident that Madame mixes together the terms learnedness, scientific knowledge, humanistic sciences, humanity, etc., despite feeling and here and there saying that they must be separated. According to the conventional use of language and generally accepted concepts, learnedness consists in knowing, or seeking to know, everything in a science according to a particular order that belongs or has any relation to it....

If we could and may act only according to the principle of perfection, then humanity—or *kalos kagathos*, 'love and striving for all that is beautiful', as the Greeks more aptly call it—would have to be the first and only purpose of all our efforts and actions. But the principle of happiness must be coordinated with humanity, and these two coordinated principles modify our purposes. Humanity, or the highest scientific and moral education of humankind, is therefore the ideal to which we must always grow nearer. Yet in its highest perfection it remains unattainable to us. Which humane and educated man would deny women the right to strive for this ideal as the vocation of humankind? In all likelihood this has not even occurred to Herr Pockels, however immaturely and smugly he often raises the subject of woman and her vocation. Our women should and must become humane. After all, we always represent the beautiful, calm, humane virtues, in their perfection, in feminine form. Yes, we concede even the most beautiful grace—loveliness—to woman alone, and the divinity of wisdom is itself a woman.

But a learned woman, in the proper sense of the word, is in herself neither humane, nor wise, nor amiable, any more than the learned man. All learned women, all heroines, all female generals are and remain anomalies, like all tender and sweet men. Nature herself seems to have drawn a very precise and proper border between feminine and masculine occupations. How many occupations that are now assigned to men—how many scientific occupations—would not offend feminine modesty? It is out of feminine modesty that the author herself rightly withholds from speaking about the shameful and unnatural vice of some men; a male ethicist would have been able to treat this with far more expedience and penetration. No man of moderately vivid imagination will be able to conceive of the woman or girl of his heart, bloody knife in hand, rummaging in the entrails of a cadaver in the anatomical theatre, without the anatomist losing her charm. Just as the woman has a threefold vocation, so too does the man as husband, father, and master of the house. The duties that arise for man and woman from their respective vocations are identical with regard to their purpose and differ only in mode.

The vocation for society and the fatherland is again mutual. The duties that arise from it are yet again identical, different only in practice. The Spartan woman did not herself go to war; but she educated her son in such a way that he had to come back from battle either with or on the shield. The vocation to humanity, or, as the author calls it, to higher education, is common to both sexes, and the duties that flow from it are identical in regard to both purpose and mode. Yet learnedness, in the proper sense, is a trade that nature seems to have ordained for man; woman, with the duties that nature and *femininity* have imposed upon her, is permitted no time for it. If the woman wants to be a scholar by profession, she must renounce the name of wife and mother, and even more of *housewife*. None can do this for her other than... nature.

Some matters, which do not really require learnedness but simply mere humanity, nature seems to have ordained for man rather than for woman. The state needs to choose an envoy, and selects a woman for the post. Yet at the moment the envoy must depart, madame is to deliver a child, and is thus detained for three to six weeks at great embarrassment to the state. Of course, the male envoy may also fall ill at the same moment that the fatherland needs him. Yet this alone is what we call chance; in the case of the woman, it is a *necessary* device of nature. One must say either that higher education is learnedness in harmony with humanity—that we must, for our education, draw from the sciences that which makes us humane—or one must say nothing at all. The harmonious education of all our powers is an ideal, like virtue and humanity, and not at all possible for us finite beings on earth. For many of our powers, their development does nothing to make us more humane. The fact that the girl in Potsdam, according to one of the Wagnerian ghost stories, had so developed the power of her large teeth that she could use them to frighten others, does not in any way make her more humane. Rather, it led her to the great inhumanity of deceiving those she loved in the most horrific way. But perhaps the author here means only the powers of understanding, and then this explanation she has given of higher intellectual education is certainly the most correct. Yet because she confuses the concepts of learnedness and humanity, she spends most of her time throughout the work attacking a straw man.

But I think that I have given enough hints to resolve the primary question. I now turn to the book itself, which is divided into the following chapters: 1. 'Does Higher Education of the Mind Contradict the Proximate Calling of Woman as Wife, Mother, and Housewife?' Here the author gives the impression that she is the first of her sex to discuss the topic, and judges very forcefully and critically. She is absolutely right when she says on p. 2 [p. 9] that 'she is deeply convinced that the fulfilment of these (female) vocational duties to the highest degree is not hindered but indeed only dignified and perfected by higher education'. The author admits on p. 5 [p. 10] that women are surpassed by men in physical strength. But by this she admits to some extent that men are themselves capable of *higher humanity* than women, at least in making greater progress in the sciences. For experience teaches that those who are great in mind and body can develop their powers far more harmoniously than those of great mind and little body.

On p. 8 [p. 11] it reads: 'how often can it be noticed that thinkers are generally weaker in physical strength.... And it is only from the irritability of the learned that we can explain the sensitivity and outrage that arises when their writings are criticized, not to mention the vicious abuse they often hurl at one another.' If the author's observation is correct, then it gives an even stronger reason to zealously oppose the learnedness of women. For then the learned women, with their higher irritability, would give us many a scene in the market square.

P. 9 [p. 12]. The author cannot understand 'how educated men can attach such a high value to physical strength. For as soon as humanity passes from the state of nature to the state of culture, physical strength loses its value and can no longer serve as the basis of any law for cultured peoples.' According to what philosophical system might the author make this claim? Certainly not according to sound reason. The human being is not only mind but also body, and as mixed beings we must act according to the mixed principles of perfection and happiness. The same duties that are incumbent upon us in regard to the education of the mind we also have in regard to the education of the body; and so, does one really want to claim that bodily strength loses its value? How can a perfection at any time cease to be a perfection? How can it cease to be the basis of *any* law?—In a sensual world of the body, should all laws lie in the perfections of the mind?

While many thinkers among men admit that they cannot always follow the course of his ideas, on p. 13 [p. 13] Madame judges J. J. Rousseau in a way that one must at the very least call *bold*. On p. 15 [p. 14] she says of this man: 'Although, as a *fanatic*, he was generally *a favourite among our sex*, he could well have found learned women among them whose learnedness was not always bound to the true education for humanity. Such was the case in France in those times, though it is seldom the case now.' So, fanatics are favourites among the female sex? And the author does not even exclude women philosophers? Then indeed there is not much to hope for, or at least from, the philosophy of women. The author once more jumps to conclusions about the women of a nation, which until now was considered the most humane, with a stroke of the pen, a fact that once more demonstrates her dictatorial tone.

On p. 23 [p. 16] the author lists a long series of heroines and notable women from history who have distinguished themselves for good or evil. Yet she does not prove for a single one that she has fulfilled her threefold calling in a humane way. Besides, with a light brush she destroys many historical facts, which we more ponderous men have contested but not yet disproved. So, you can see how greatly humankind will progress in enlightenment when either the philosophers are women or the women philosophize. Where did Madame H. get the report (p. 32 [pp. 19–20]) that among the Greeks women, the beautiful half of humankind, were so completely neglected? Does she conclude this from the great humility and modesty that prevailed among Greek women? The gynaecea of the Greeks were very different to the harems of the Orientals. The former were temples of domesticity and all feminine virtues, where housewives were priestesses; sanctuaries into which only the tested friend, the educated man, was led. That the Greek men and youths had their hetaerae was not the result of the inferior education of their wives but of the lustful aura that surrounded these idle women, and which every noble woman had to ward off. Greek men and youths wanted to *swim in pleasure*, just as Hamburgers do now. In the sanctum of their wives, however, they knew they ought to and sometimes had to be serious. The unnatural vice, of which the Greeks are justly accused, was also found among the Romans, although Roman women, even according to the author, were held in great esteem and had no mediocre education. It is even found among Englishmen, although English women are considered the most charming, amiable, and humane wives. This disgraceful vice has its ground not in the greater or lesser education of women, but in a strange aberration of men, who very often, like women, perhaps even more, act according to their own whims. Among the Greeks, an excellent custom gave occasion if not for the introduction then for the sanctioning of this vice. What is said later about the prestige and power of the Greek priestesses—that they were not degraded or suppressed—is evidence against the writer herself.

P. 40 [p. 22]. 'Everyone knows the influence of women on the primary virtue of bravery during the time of the knights, which was valued almost to the exclusion of the other virtues. They encouraged men to perform acts of bravery, distributed the prizes, and often gave their hand as a reward for uprightness and valour.' Here, then, the women acted according to their proper high vocation; they did not themselves fight, but they encouraged the fighters and gave the prize to the victors. They did not win a man by courage and bravery, but, as noble and virtuous housewives, to courage and bravery they surrendered themselves as a reward. They did not study philosophy, but encouraged the thinker to courageously tread the boundaries of truth and light. With the sweetest grace, they wiped the sweat from the brow of the fighters of both kinds after the work was done. They were the daemons and guardian angels of their husbands, who, like the daemon of Socrates, revealed hidden things to them and guided them through dangers hidden in future's night. Yet women are no longer satisfied with this high celestial role; they want to break through the perilous barriers of renown and knowledge like a man. For the love of heaven, and you faithful companions of it—your graces—prevent this sad catastrophe!...

On p. 68 [p. 32] the author says, 'It would be just as foolish to demand this higher education for the lower classes, who must satisfy themselves with subordinate purposes. It would be ridiculous to demand this education for the wife of a day labourer or tradesman.' Never has a writer of high nobility been so aristocratic, so dismissive and dictatorial towards the most numerous class of people as the author shows herself to be here. Who but Madame could express this in such a way? Humanity is the highest education, and no human being should be excluded from it; as the vocation of our lives, any human being would take pleasure in it. And she despotically commands at least seven hundred million people not to worry about the purpose of their existence? At least seven hundred million people to remain miserable scavengers of sensuality and vice, so that the rest can indulge sensuously and spiritually? The genuinely humane man, and the genuinely humane woman, wish always that humanity may spread over the whole earth. To promote it everywhere and in all classes is their fairest and most blessed activity. And we—those who would like to consider ourselves educated people—are we not infinitely better off if, instead of remaining ignorant, crude, and immoral, all people with whom we are in some way connected have their share of humanity? The humane cook of the learned Frau Doktor will certainly prepare a far tastier dish than the one who is crude and immoral; at least she will serve it in a far kinder way. Noble von Rochow! You care not only for the understanding and heart of your working men but also for your working women. And yet such folk always only satisfy themselves, according to the author, with *subordinate* purposes. But what does the author mean by subordinate purposes? There is no one on earth who could live only for the higher purpose of humanity; we must also occupy ourselves with sensual, subordinate purposes. Supposing that humanity and learnedness are one and the same, can we exclude at least seven hundred million people from scientific learning? That every human goes as far as they can in the education of their mental and physical powers and as far as their circumstances permit: this is the law of nature and must also be the law of social life. The author is right that it is foolish to demand such education from the so-called lower classes as we are entitled to demand from the higher classes; but education and enlightenment ought to be spread and promoted in all classes. How the author, who lives in a free state, speaks of the *wives* (in this sense, mind you) of day labourers and tradesman is not very humane. We know only female citizens in our state, in which tradesmen constitute a very respectable and honourable class.

2. 'Woman Considered as Wife.' Here, first of all, the creation story of Moses is briefly and well destroyed and declared to be a childish oriental fable. From this source, the opinion that men have superiority over their wives often flows (the author claims on p. 109 [p. 43]). Yet this opinion is certainly much older than the Mosaic creation story, for it is based on a natural law, on the law that the author and others find so terrible: the *right of the stronger*. This right of the stronger is certainly valid in the state of nature; yet it is still valid in every social connection, and will be valid until the real moral law is generally and everywhere recognized and obeyed; as long as we need civil, police, and criminal laws, in short, as long as we are human beings. While this might seem to be an inflated and paradoxical assertion, on closer

examination of the matter it is not so. Just consider that there is not only strength of the body but also strength of the mind. If the law seems to prevail in a civilized state, this is in fact achieved only through power, for the majority of the nation always offers its head and hands to the enforcer of the rule in order to make the rule valid. To take the present case into consideration, in a cultured state it is presently not the man but in fact the woman who more often leads the domestic regime. In such a case the strength of mind comes into play. So, if at the transition from barbarism to the cultured state the physical powers of both sexes were equal, plus the mental powers, the greater strength would consequently lie on the side of women, such that, if not the government in particular, then nevertheless the greatest prestige, would be given to women. The latter assertion is not idle speculation. History confirms it. It tells us that the Ethiopians honoured their sisters above all, and that the kings bequeathed their kingdoms not to their sons but to the sons of their sisters. The Sarmatians obeyed their wives in all things, and the virgin among them did not marry until she had slain a worthy man. The Lydians esteemed their wives more highly than the men, and named themselves after the mother rather than the father. They left their goods to the daughters, not to the sons.

P. 111 [p. 44]. 'Thus woman does not exist for the sake of man, nor man for the sake of woman; they are created one for the sake of the other in completely equal relationship.' If this claim is not sparkling with nonsense, then I understand nothing of the whole matter.

But I have already let myself be carried away too far by the brilliant thoughts of the lively, often elegant, style of the author, and have long since exceeded the limits of my review. I am here in the trap that one constantly enters with a witty woman; one never tires of listening, although what one hears does not always deserve the approval of our reason. I must break off, as much as it frustrates me; only that I must mention that the third chapter is entitled 'The Educated Woman as Mother'.

I have long since conceded to the author that it is only *humanity* that makes woman in all her circumstances uniquely lovely. But the author must concede to me that *true learnedness*, which is often diametrically opposed to charm and grace, cannot be present in *charming women*, if she properly separates both concepts from one another. She could well have added another chapter: *The Educated Woman as Matron*. For it is precisely the matron and the old man who must first show and prove how much they are capable of through humanity.

Some passages in the book, which I can no longer quote, seem to me to prove that the author may have used some English or French work without indicating this to her readers.

Everything I have said so far about the interesting work of Madame Holst seems to be more censure than praise. For this reason, I must honestly and frankly confess that I have found much in it that is thoughtful and instructive. I am glad that one of my fellow citizens had the courage to write such a book, and I hope that in an eventual new edition she may use every rational thought and deliver a completed work.

Notes

Preface

1. *On Improving the Status of Women* (1792) never reached anywhere near the popularity of *On Marriage* (1774), which ran to four separate editions during Hippel's lifetime and seven reprintings by 1841. This imbalance was partly due to the fact that, in the former, Hippel spells out the civic implications of the latter, with results that were too radical for many to accept. Yet is also due to the conservative reaction against the social fragmentation following the French Revolution, such that the moment in which Hippel's *On Improving the Status of Woman*, the second and third editions of *On Marriage*, and the German translation of Wollstonecraft's *Vindication of the Rights of Woman* could be published in the space of one year (1792/3) had decidedly closed by the time Holst published *On the Vocation of Woman* in 1802.

Chapter 1

1. Holst's depiction of herself as a lone advocate of women's education is puzzling, given that she was aware of other women writers who had made similar claims, including Wollstonecraft, Wobeser, Genlis, and Gouges. It suggests that she is primarily concerned with the local debate concerning the 'vocation of woman' in the German pedagogical literature. Considered in this context, Holst was indeed the first woman to criticize the Philanthropinists' gendered reform of the education system.

2. While Holst seldom invokes the idea of women's rights directly, her opening paragraphs resonate with Wollstonecraft's prefatory remarks in *A Vindication of the Rights of Woman*. For example, Wollstonecraft claims that 'the Rights of Woman may be respected, if it be fully proved that reason calls for this respect, and loudly demands JUSTICE for one-half of the human race'; Wollstonecraft, *A Vindication of the Rights of Woman*, 14. We should not, however, rush to the conclusion that Holst is drawing specifically from Wollstonecraft. Holst never cites Wollstonecraft or mentions her name, and similar claims can be found in texts that she does mention. For instance, Gouges opens *Declaration of the Rights of Woman and the Female Citizen* (1791) with a direct challenge to men: 'Man, are you capable of being just? It is a woman who is asking you this question, and you will not take away her right to do so. Who has given you the sovereign right to

oppress my sex?'; Gouges, *Déclaration des droits de la femme et de la citoyenne et autres ecrits*, 5.
3. The male writers Holst criticizes here infer the inferiority of the female intellect from woman's inferior strength and sickly constitution. For instance, see Campe, *Väterlicher Rath für meine Tochter*, 18–19 (cited above on p. xxi), which Holst evidently has in mind in the following paragraphs. See also the second review of *On the Vocation of Woman* in Appendix 2, in which the reviewer rejects Holst's attempt to separate the intellect from physical strength (p. 114). Holst's argument has precursors in the British context. In her third letter on education, for instance, Macaulay attacks the Rousseauian idea that physical strength has a bearing on the intellect. While she accepts that women have inferior strength in comparison to men, Macaulay refuses to concede inferiority on any other grounds. It is for this reason that education, both moral and scientific, cannot be peculiar to either sex. See Macaulay, *Letters on Education*, 15–24.
4. Holst cites Homer in Johann Heinrich Voß's translation. I have used Augustus Taber Murray's. Homer, the *Odyssey*, III 198–9.
5. Holst anticipates Nietzsche's observation in *On the Genealogy of Morality* that, when we look to the gods of antiquity, we discover that when the Greeks reflected on noble and proud men, 'the *animal* in man felt deified, did *not* tear itself apart and did *not* rage against itself!' Yet in contrast to Nietzsche, who praises the natural state in which the brave Greeks '*allowed* themselves as a reason for much of what was bad or calamitous', Holst argues that the state of nature is necessarily superseded by culture. Nietzsche, *On the Genealogy of Morality*, 69–70.
6. Similar arguments are widely found in nineteenth-century feminism. For example, Mill and Taylor argue that while brute strength is the origin of male domination, the state of culture has now advanced beyond that stage. Thus we ought to do so with respect to gender as well. See Mill, *The Subjection of Women*, 127–31.
7. In *Account of the Prussian State under Friedrich II* (*Schilderung des preußischen Staates unter Friedrich II*, 1793–5), Jakob Mouvillon criticizes the poor education of women and blames the ongoing negative treatment of women on works such as Brandes's *On Women*.
8. *Schwärmer*, translated here and elsewhere as 'fanatic', was used by Enlighteners as a pejorative term to differentiate their ideal of a rational, measured subject from the enthusiasm associated with the *Sturm und Drang* movement.
9. Holst's critique of Rousseau reflects the ambivalence found in several feminist writings following Staël's *Letters on the Works and Character of J. J. Rousseau* (*Lettres sur les ouvrages et le caractère de J. J. Rousseau*, 1788). For instance, Macaulay praises Rousseau's emphasis on the early years of moral formation, yet criticizes his claim that virtue is determined by the physiology of one's sex. The contradiction Rousseau introduces between reason and nature, Macaulay declares,

'has lowered the man of genius to the licentious pedant'. Macaulay, *Letters on Education*, 129. Similarly, Wollstonecraft affirmed Rousseau's inquiry into the origins of inequality and yet claimed that 'instead of properly sifting the subject' he 'threw away the wheat with the chaff, without waiting to inquire whether the evils which his ardent soul turned from indignantly, were the consequence of civilisation or the vestiges of barbarism'; Wollstonecraft, *A Vindication of the Rights of Woman*, 22. Hippel asserted that the 'development of human society, which gave the human race as a whole such an astounding impetus, was nevertheless so disadvantageous to one half of this same race'; Hippel, *On Improving the Status of Women*, 86.

10. This reference indicates that Holst was working with the third edition of *On Marriage* published in 1793, in which Hippel develops an egalitarian vision of marriage that is more radical than that found in the first two editions.

11. While other writers in the late eighteenth century offered counter-narratives to Rousseau's account of the social contract, including Hippel and Wollstonecraft, Holst's narrative introduces the anthropological dimension of need, and thus anticipates the materialist conception of history developed by nineteenth-century critics of Enlightenment. In the first chapter of *German Ideology*, for example, Marx argues that spiritual development, at first, follows from the frustration of a natural need. See Marx, *German Ideology*, 48–52.

12. Holst may have such lines from *The Prince* in mind: 'I certainly think that it is better to be impetuous than cautious, because fortune is a woman, and if you want to control her, it is necessary to treat her roughly'. Machiavelli, *The Prince*, 87.

13. Holst is referring to Gouges's *Declaration of the Rights of Woman and the Female Citizen*, which appeared shortly after Louis XVI ratified the French Constitution of 1791. Gouges presents a radical vision of a world in which women enjoy political, legal, educational, and professional equality with men. While she revolts against the Rousseauian ideal of femininity endorsed by the Jacobin government, which denied equal rights to women and suppressed their involvement in political activities, she was nevertheless inspired by the feminist implications of the egalitarian vision set forth in Rousseau's *The Social Contract*.

14. The following section of the chapter extends the eighteenth-century genre of cataloguing learned women. Works such as Peter Paul Finauer's *General Historical Inventory of Learned Women* (*Allgemeines historisches Verzeichnis gelehrter Frauenzimmer*, 1761) and Christian August Wichmann's *History of Famous Women* (*Geschichte berühmter Frauenzimmer*, 1772) document the lives of notable women to show that a woman's dedication to study and other achievements is not inconsistent with fulfilling her particular duties. Yet as Ebbersmeyer notes, this tradition ends with Wichmann's *History of Famous Women*; Holst's catalogue revives a suppressed genre. See Ebbersmeyer, 'From a "memorable place" to "drops in the ocean"', 445–8.

15. Semiramis is the mythological wife of Onnes and Ninus, who succeeded Ninus on the Assyrian throne, as documented in Mosēs Khorenats'i's *History of the Armenians*. The fable refers to the historical figure Shammuramat, who ruled the neo-Assyrian empire for five years following the death of her husband Shamshi-Adad V in 811 BC. See Khorenats'i, *History of the Armenians*, chs 15–19.
16. Dido was the founder and first queen of the Phoenician city state of Carthage. The most extensive documentation of her life is found in Virgil's *The Aeneid*, though the historicity of his account is contested. See Virgil, *The Aeneid*, Book IV.
17. For the English pagination, see Alexander, *The History of Women*, I 129–30.
18. See Alexander, *The History of Women*, I 115–16.
19. Deborah is the only female judge mentioned in the Book of Judges. Her prophesy led Barak into battle at Mount Tabor, where the Canaanites, ruled by Sisera, were completely defeated. See Judges 4:1–5:31.
20. Judith is an apocryphal book found in the Septuagint. It tells the story of Judith, a Jewish widow who uses her beauty to seduce Holofernes, the general of King Nebuchadnezzar's army. As he lay drunk in his bed, she removes Holofernes's head, thereby dismantling the Babylonian army and saving Israel from invasion. The Book of Esther, found in the Hebrew Bible, tells the story of a young woman chosen for her beauty to become the queen of the Persian king Ahasuerus. Esther used her influence as queen to save the Jewish people from genocide.
21. Holst's argument here resonates with her father's case for the establishment of academies for women. In 1747, Justi noted, 'I confess that, in the case of women's education, I have found the Republic's provision for common people to be more careless and deficient than anywhere else, as if the Republic had no concern for something that makes half of its population more rational, and has so great an influence on the other half of the population and on the Republic itself.' Justi, 'Vorschlag von Errichtung einer Akademie vor das Frauenzimmer', 315.
22. Artemis (and Diana, her Roman equivalent) is a Greek goddess whose temple stood in Ephesus. Zenobia (*c.* AD 240–74) was queen of the Palmyrene Empire in Syria. Cleopatra (69–30 BC) was ruler of the Ptolemaic Kingdom of Egypt.
23. On the women of Sabine, see Alexander, *The History of Women*, I 146–8.
24. Lucretia (died 510 BC) was a noblewoman in ancient Rome. Her rape by Tarquinius Superbus, and her subsequent suicide, sparked a rebellion that overthrew the Roman monarchy and the formation of a republican government.
25. When Coriolanus stood with the Volscian army before the walls of Rome, the senate set out several waves of supplicants. After the ambassadors and priests had failed, Coriolanus's mother, Veturia, and wife, Volumnia, implored him to desist with the attack. Coriolanus was overcome by their pleas and ended the siege on the city.
26. Cornelia (190s–115 BC) was unique among the virtuous Roman women due to her interest in literature and her dedication to the political careers of her sons.

27. Livia was Empress of Rome from 27 BC to AD 14 as the wife of Emperor Augustus. She had a significant influence over her husband and was rumoured to have been responsible for the assassination of several of his notable relatives.
28. Elagabalus was Emperor of Rome from AD 218 to 222. His mother, Julia Soaemias, and grandmother, Julia Maesa, were the first women allowed into the senate, and both received senatorial titles.
29. In *History of the Female Sex*, Meiners presents an anthropological survey of the female sex through an examination of historical literature, modern travelogues, and missionary diaries. He includes a chapter on the 'State of the Female Sex Among the Greeks', in which he speculates that the poor treatment of women among the ancient Greeks suggests a greater oriental influence than is often recognized. Meiners, *Geschichte des weiblichen Geschlechts*, I 313–17.
30. Herodotus records that Leaena was the mistress of Harmodius, and was tortured by Hippias to compel her to reveal the accomplices in the assassination of Hipparchus. Distrusting her fortitude, she bit off her tongue in an act that was later honoured by the Athenians with a statue. Herodotus, *Terpsichore*, LVI.
31. Phryne (c.371 BC–after 316 BC) and Lais of Hyccara (died 340 BC) were hetaerae in the fourth century, and reportedly were rivals. While the hetaerae were overlooked during the Renaissance, interest in their extensive learning and influential role in political life rose during the late eighteenth century. Angelica Kauffmann's *Praxiteles Giving Phryne his Statue of Cupid* (1794), for instance, depicts Phryne as a tender and inspirational companion rather than an object of desire.
32. Aspasia (470–400 BC) was the partner of the Athenian statesman Pericles, and reportedly attracted the greatest thinkers of her time, including Socrates, to her salon.
33. Holst's claim is inaccurate, as Galli were eunuchs. There is a funerary relief of a high priestess of the Cybele named Laberia Felicia in the Musei Vaticani in Rome, which is the source of scholarly debate regarding the practice of Cybele's cults. See Latham, 'Roman Rhetoric, Metroac Representation', 67–72.
34. Again Holst's claim is dubious. The only ancient source that mentions a priestess called Pelias is Maurus Servius Honoratus. Her claim might be a faulty generalization of a fragment from Strabo's *Geography*, which states that 'among the Thesprotians and the Molossians old women are called "peliai"', which means 'doves'. Strabo, *Geography*, VII Fr. 1a.
35. Plutarch records that when Alexander the Great consulted the Delphic oracle in 336 BC, Pythia refused to comment and asked him to return later. When Alexander furiously dragged her out by the hair, she cried, 'my son, who can resist you?' He responded, 'Now I have my answer'. Plutarch, 'Alexander', in *Plutarch's Lives*, 14.6–7.
36. Holst is referring to Meiners, *Geschichte des weiblichen Geschlechts*, I 213.
37. The 'courts of love [*Gerichtshöfe der Liebe*]' were women-led tribunals established in southern France during the twelfth century to resolve the amorous

quarrels that frequently broke out between knights and ladies, such that decisions in matters of love should have full legal force. Isabelle of Bavaria, the wife of King Charles VI, established the *Cour d'Amour* in 1380, which was administered by members of court from all ranks. See Meiners, *Geschichte des weiblichen Geschlechts*, I 298–300.

38. Brunhilda (*c*.543–613) ruled the eastern Frankish kingdoms of Austrasia and Burgundy from 575 to 583. Her forceful personality brought her into conflict with the nobles and the Church. Her bitter feud with Fredegund, mistress of Chilperic I of Neustria (who murdered Brunhilda's sister), ended with Fredegund's death in 597. Fredegund's son, Chlothar II, defeated Brunhilda in 613, and had her executed.
39. Either Holst or her source is confused here. Flavia Julia Constantia (*c*.293–330), who was the half-sister of Constantine, converted to Christianity and played a key role in Constantine's agreement to the Edict of Milan, granting full tolerance of Christianity in all regions of the Empire. She married the co-emperor, Licinius, who was a close friend of the future emperor Galerius.
40. Dobrawa of Bohemia (*c*.940–77) played a key role in the Baptism of Poland, which occurred when her husband, Mieszko I, was baptised in 966.
41. Bertha (*c*.565–601), the Christian daughter of Charibert I, was the wife of Ethelbert, King of Kent, the first English king to convert to Christianity.
42. These claims stretch the truth somewhat. Mary is venerated in the Catholic Church but is certainly not deified. Hannah was one of Elkanah's two wives, and the mother of Samuel. After having been barren for many years, Hannah went up to the tabernacle and prayed with great weeping, asking for a son and, in exchange, vowing to give the son to the service of God. She was blessed by Eli and soon conceived, bearing a child she named Samuel, which means 'heard by God'. See 1 Samuel 1:2–2:21.
43. Marie de' Medici (1575–1642) was Queen of France as the second wife of Henry IV. Anne of Austria (1601–66), a Spanish princess and Austrian archduchess, was Queen of France as the wife of Louis XIII.
44. Through her marriage to King Henry II, Catherine de' Medici (1519–89) was Queen Consort of France from 1547 until 1559 and mother of Kings Francis II, Charles IX, and Henry III. She was renowned for having an extensive influence on the political life of France through her sons.
45. Holst seems to be referring to Charles VII, who was married to Marie d'Anjou and yet remained in love with his mistress, Agnès Sorel.
46. Joan of Arc (1412–31) received visions instructing her to support Charles VII to recover France from English domination, and played a decisive role in several key victories that led to Charles's coronation in Reims.
47. Henry's womanizing was legendary, earning him the title of *Le Vert Galant* (the verdant gallant). He kept several mistresses and often required the assistance of his favoured counsellor, the Duke of Sully, to settle arising complications. Sully played a key role in securing Henry's second marriage to Marie de' Medici.

48. Françoise d'Aubigné, Madame de Maintenon (1635–1719) was secretly married to Louis XIV in 1683. Her strong religious convictions had a marked effect on her husband, who no longer held open mistresses and banned operas during Lent. She also secured the children of the king's first marriage to high positions at court.
49. Jeanne Antoinette Poisson, Marquise de Pompadour (1721–64), and Jeanne Bécu, Comtesse du Barry (1743–93) were royal mistresses to Louis XV, making political enemies for Louis and securing royal titles for their family members and friends.
50. Charlotte Corday (1768–93) was executed by guillotine in 1793 for assassinating the Jacobin leader Jean Paul Marat, who was partly responsible for the radical course taken by the Revolution. Her act sparked extensive debate regarding the role of women in political history.
51. Joan of Penthièvre (1319–84) fought alongside her husband, Charles de Blois-Châtillon, against the House of Montfort in the Breton War of Succession. Charles was imprisoned by the Kingdom of England for nine years, during which time Joan continued the campaign. Joanna of Flanders (1295–1374) led the Montfortist cause after her husband, John of Montfort, was captured in 1341 and imprisoned in Paris.
52. Philippa of Hainault (1310–69) was Queen of England as the wife of Edward III.
53. Margaret of Anjou (1430–82) was Queen of England and nominally Queen of France through her marriage to Henry VI. Her husband's frequent bouts of insanity meant that she ruled the kingdom in his place.
54. Elizabeth I (1533–1603) was Queen of England and Ireland for forty-four years. The Elizabethan era is remembered as a time of cultural and economic prosperity.
55. Anna and Elizabeth Petrovna were the daughters of Catherine I, Empress of Russia, from 1725 until her death in 1727. Anna was Grand Duchess of Hollstein-Gottorp from 1725 to 1728. Elizabeth reigned as Empress of Russia from 1741 until her death in 1762.
56. Holst's argument is similar to Hippel's critique of gendered conceptions of virtue. Paraphrasing Augustine's *City of God*, Hippel claims that 'our vices are nothing more than ill-bred virtues'. Hippel, *On Improving the Status of Women*, 149.
57. Holst is attuned to the fact that the status of women will only change for the good with the cooperation of both men and women. Like Hippel, she emphasizes the gain that men can expect from women's higher education. What sets her apart from Hippel is that she also appeals to her women readers to shatter male prejudice by pursuing their own higher education and thereby extending their sphere of influence within oppressive social norms.
58. Holst cites two verses from *Nachten Göckingk* (1777), which became a symbol for progressive women in the 1780s and 1790s and was fiercely debated in

popular periodicals. It was still so well known in 1802 that Holst felt no need to introduce the text or cite it in full. The poem was originally composed by the renowned lyric poet Leopold Friedrich Günther von Göckingk by collating lines from letters he had received from his fiancée, Sophie Ferdinande Maria Philippine Vopel. For the full text see Herminghouse and Mueller, *German Feminist Writings*, 2–5.

59. 'An immeasurable pity for woman! Her purity must not become virtue but remain nature, for her sex is not made for virtue but for innocence. She must use her fine power to refrain from certain immoralities; she does not have to depart from what is naturally her own. Her innocence is already half-defeated when it has to fight against a certain sensuality.' Ewald, *Die Kunst, ein gutes Mädchen, eine gute Gattin, Mutter und Hausfrau zu werden*, I 48–9.

60. Holst's attack on Basedow and Campe's elementary books echoes Wobeser's lament in the Preface to *Elisa*: 'Half-enlightenment is always harmful, but why should women always be half-enlightened?' [Wobeser,] *Elisa, oder das Weib, wie es seyn sollte*, xi.

61. Holst's diagnosis of the possible motivations for women to study resonates with Staël's analysis of the possible motivations for women to write in *The Influence of Literature on Society*: 'Men can always hide their self-esteem and their desire to be applauded under the appearance or reality of stronger and nobler passions. But when women write, one always assumes that it is in order to display their abilities.' Staël, *De la littérature considérée dans ses rapports avec les institutions sociales*, 296.

62. Holst appears to view social inequality as a necessity determined by nature, a view that attracts the scorn of one of her reviewers (see p. 116). While she criticizes Campe's claim that women must fulfil their vocation as human beings 'with constant respect to the sphere of influence assigned to them by foresight and human society', she seems to repeat the same idea with respect to class. See Campe, *Väterlicher Rath für meine Tochter*, 8–9.

63. Anne Dacier (1654–1720) was a commentator, translator, and editor of classical texts, famous for her French translations of the *Iliad* and *Odyssey*.

64. Ernestine Müller, wife of philologist Johann Jakob Reiske (1716–74), was a scholar of Greek and assisted in her husband's collations.

65. Anna Maria van Schurman (1607–78) was a Dutch scholar known for her exceptional learning and her defence of female education. Louisa Maria von Stolberg was the wife of Charles Edward Stuart, the Jacobite claimant to the English and Scottish thrones. Lady Jane Grey (c.1536–54), the subject of Christoph Wieland's tragedy *Lady Johanna Gray* (1758), was an English noblewoman and de facto Queen of England for nine days in 1553, noted for her humanist education and proficiency in ancient languages.

66. Sappho, one of the great lyric poets of antiquity, shaped the study and composition of lyricism throughout history. Korinna is the most famous Greek female poet after Sappho, whose works document local Boeotian legends.

67. The author of *Schwestern von Lesbos* (1801) is the German and Swedish writer and translator Amalia von Helvig (1776–1831). Caroline Rudolphi (1753–1811) was a German pedagogue and poet, whose poems were set to music by Johann Friedrich Reichardt. Emilie von Berlepsch (1755–1830) was a German travel writer, essayist, and poet, and one of the earliest to write about women's rights in Germany (see pp. xxxii–xxxiii). Friederike Brun (1765–1835) was a Dutch poet and salonist. The first wife of Leopold Friedrich Günther von Göckingk was Sophie Marie Filippine Vogel, the inspiration for *Nantchen Göckingk* (1777). The Young Lady of A presumably refers to the English poet and painter Anne Killigrew (1660–85), who was eulogized by John Dryden in his poem *To the Pious Memory of the Accomplish'd Young Lady Mrs Anne Killigrew* (1686), in which he compares her poetic abilities to Sappho's.
68. Antoinette Deshoulières (1638–94) was a seventeenth-century French poet, most famous for her idylls.
69. Voltaire, *Siècle de Louis XIV*, 64.
70. Madeleine de Scudéry (1607–1701) wrote some of the longest novels ever published, several of which are addressed to women and defend women's education. In *Les femmes illustres* (1642), she advocates education over beauty and cosmetics as a means to social mobility.
71. Pockels, *Versuch einer Charakteristik des weiblichen Geschlechts*, III 83–4 n.
72. I can find no record of a French artist from this period named Chenon. It may be the misspelling of a name that Holst had not seen written down.
73. Henriette de Coligny de La Suze (1618–73) was a French poet who, with Paul Pellisson and others, edited a collection of poems entitled *Recueil de pièces galantes*, which became one of the most popular collections of seventeenth-century verse and prose.
74. Pockels, *Versuch einer Charakteristik des weiblichen Geschlechts*, I 383.
75. Émilie de Sainte-Amaranthe (1773–94) organized an influential salon in Paris, frequented by the leading artists of her day. Nantchen Göckingk (1743–81), the first wife of Leopold von Göckingk, published numerous poems in women's periodicals. *Nantchen Göckingk* (cited by Holst on p. 29) was composed by Leopold using lines taken from his fiancée's letters, and captures the tension between a woman's particular duties and her vocation to freedom: 'To cook and spin for a man – / An unworthy profession! / Be it the one for which nature made me / With these senses and with this spirit!'
76. Marie-Madeleine Pioche de La Vergne, Comtesse de La Fayette (1634–93), was a seventeenth-century French writer. Her *La Princesse de Clèves* (1678) was the first historical novel and one of the earliest novels in literature.
77. *Agnes von Lilien* (1793) was the first novel of German writer Caroline von Wolzogen (1763–1847), and tells the story of a young woman, poor but well educated in the classics and modern literature, who discovers and embraces the wider world after meeting an older and wealthier man.
78. Sophie von La Roche (1730–1807) was a German novelist whose books were intended to be morally instructive to young women. Holst presumably has

The History of Lady Sophie Sternheim (*Geschichte des Fräuleins von Sternheim*, 1771) in mind, in which La Roche explores how a woman's education can form the basis for an impermeable happiness that is not subject to external circumstances.

79. *Julchen Grünthal* (1784) was written by the German author Friederike Helene Unger (1741–1813), who also translated Rousseau and published an almanac.
80. Caroline-Stéphanie-Félicité, Madame de Genlis (1746–1830), was a French writer known for her novels and her theory of children's education. Holst refers to Genlis again on p. 41 and p. 91.
81. Unfortunately Holst does not mention the women writers she has in mind. Possibilities include Anna Barbauld and Hannah More, who wrote instructive plays and stories for children.
82. Dorothea Christiane Erxleben (née Leporin) (1715–62) was the first woman to become a medical doctor in Germany, and the first woman licensed to practise medicine in the world.
83. Friedrich Georg Christian Erxleben, 'Nachricht von einigen Lebensumständen der Fr. Dorothee Christiane Erxleben', 350–8.
84. Holst seems to be referring to a book by Erxleben that was in fact published in German under her maiden name in 1742, *Rigorous Investigation of the Causes that Obstruct the Female Sex from Study* (*Gründliche Untersuchung der Ursachen, die das weibliche Geschlecht vom Studieren abhalten*), in which she argues that women should receive the same education as men, including admission to universities. See Section 1.2.3 in the Introduction.
85. Chevalier d'Éon (1728–1810) was a French diplomat, spy, and soldier. Her androgynous physical characteristics enabled her to successfully undertake both male and female roles in her diplomatic activities.
86. Marie de Rabutin-Chantal, Marquise de Sévigné (1626–96), was a French aristocrat noted for the wit and vividness of her letters, most of which were written to her daughter, Françoise-Marguerite de Sévigné.
87. Françoise d'Aubigné, Marquise de Maintenon (1635–1719), was a French aristocrat who secretly married King Louis XIV, founded a school for girls, and was renowned for the taste, tone, and expression of her letters.
88. Anne de l'Enclos (1620–1705) was a French author and courtesan who ran an influential salon and was known for her witty and controversial writings on beauty, love, and religion.
89. *Lettres à Babet* (1683) is an epistolary novel written by the French dramatist and writer Edmé Boursault. Babet became a symbol of female independence; in *Nantchen Göckingk*, for instance, Göckingk cries, 'O, if only I had a Babet! / What I would do with her! / Intensely would we love each other / And each night on one pillow rest'.
90. Anne Louise Germaine de Staël-Holstein (1766–1817) was a French political theorist, novelist, and philosopher. In *Letters on the Works and Character of J. J. Rousseau*, she criticizes Rousseau's conservative take on women readers and writers and calls on women to cultivate their minds. In the fourth chapter of

The Influence of Literature on Society, entitled 'On Women Writers', Staël addresses the general situation of women through the lens of women writers. This text may have been a key resource for Holst's account of the state of women's education in the Enlightened circles in France. In words echoed by Holst, Staël attacks the double standards placed on women: 'Women are permitted to sacrifice their domestic occupations for the sake of worldly amusements, but any serious study is accused of pedantry.' Staël, *De la littérature considérée dans ses rapports avec les institutions sociales*, I 297.

91. *Des Abts Millot Universalhistorie* (1777–94) is a German translation of Claude-François-Xavier Millot's *Élémens de l'histoire général ancienne et moderne* (1772–83) by Wilhelm Ernst Christiani.
92. Angelika Kauffmann (1741–1807) was a Swiss neoclassical painter, and one of two women painters among the founding members of the Royal Academy in London.
93. Herder, *Sämmtliche Werke*, VII 209.
94. Maria Theresia von Paradis (1759–1824) was an Austrian musician and composer, who gradually lost her sight between the ages of 2 and 5.
95. Holst is referring to Regina Strinasacchi (1761–1839); her misspelling may be a result of having never seen Strinasacchi's name in writing. The name is also misspelled in the list of printing errors appended to the book (the original text is 'Steinasaccy', and the correction states that 'Strinosaccy' should be changed to 'Strinasaccy'). Women rarely played the violin in public, yet Strinasacchi toured Italy, France, and Germany as a soloist. She was sufficiently familiar with Mozart that he composed the Sonata in B-flat major for Violin and Keyboard ('Strinasacchi') at her request.
96. Sophia Maria Westenholz (1759–1838) was a German composer, singer, and music educator. She performed mostly in the courts of Schwerin and Ludwigslust, capitals of the Duchy of Mecklenburg-Schwerin.
97. Charlotte Wilhelmina Franziska Brandes (1765–88) was a German singer, pianist, actress, and composer. Friederike Charlotte Bause, daughter of the famous portrait engraver Johann Friedrich Bause (1738–1814), was a talented musician but died when she was only 19.
98. See Euler, *Letters of Euler on Different Subjects in Physics and Philosophy Addressed to a German Princess*.
99. Christina (1626–89) was Queen of Sweden from 1632 until her abdication in 1654. She began a correspondence with Descartes in 1646 through an introduction from the French ambassador Pierre Chanut, and invited Descartes to Sweden. He arrived in 1649, and held daily lessons with Christina on philosophy and religion.
100. Caroline Lucretia Herschel (1750–1848), the younger sister of William Herschel, was an astronomer who discovered several comets. She is said to have been the first woman to receive a salary as a scientist, and in 1828 she became the first woman to receive a Gold Medal from the Royal Astronomical Society.

138   NOTES

101. Baroness Philippine von Knigge (1775–1841), daughter of the satirical author Adolf von Knigge, wrote a philosophical manual for women when she was only 14 years old. See Knigge, *Versuch einer Logik für Frauenzimmer*.
102. Émilie du Châtelet (1706–49) was a French natural philosopher and mathematician, known for her book *Institutions de Physique* (1740), in which she develops a Leibnizian foundation for Newtonian mechanics, and for her translation and commentary of Isaac Newton's *Principia*, published posthumously in 1756.
103. Voltaire, *Le Siècle de Louis XIV*, 46.
104. Holst echoes the experiment proposed by Du Châtelet in the preface to *The Fable of the Bees* (see p. 1). Yet, in contrast to Du Châtelet, whose financial independence and estranged marriage meant that she could move outside the conventional constrains on women, Holst dedicated her life to making this experiment a reality.
105. Hippel similarly points to Kant's celibacy in *On Marriage* to argue that some callings are undeniably good for society despite their incompatibility with biologically determined ends. [Hippel,] *Über die Ehe*, 78–9.

Chapter 2

1. Claims to this end can be found throughout the 'writings by men' that initially prompted Holst to put pen to paper. For instance, in *Emile* Rousseau states that 'Once this principle [of complementarity between the sexes] has been established, it follows that woman is made specially to please man.' Rousseau, *Emile, Or on Education*, 358. In *On Women*, Brandes concludes his critique of the false culture prevailing across Europe by asserting that 'it is in vain one resists recognizing the truth that woman exists for the sake of man'. Brandes, *Ueber die Weiber*, 83.
2. Holst's definition of marriage in this chapter bears close parallels with Hippel's definition in *On Marriage*. In the third edition (which Holst appears to be using), Hippel defines 'the ultimate purpose of marriage [*der Endzweck der Ehe*]' according to the Roman formulation 'arctissimum vitae commercium', that is, 'the closest possible unification of life [*die genaueste Lebensvereinigung*].' [Hippel,] *Über die Ehe*, 93. Similar ideas were developed by other women writers in the late eighteenth century, who argued that the end of marriage consists of the happiness of both parties. In *Letters on Education*, for instance, Macaulay contends that 'the happiness and perfection of the two sexes are so reciprocally dependent on one another that, till both are reformed, there is no expecting excellence in either.' Macaulay, *Letters on Education*, 135.
3. In *The History of Women*, Alexander notes that there is no record of marriage as an institution in Genesis. He argues that it was the rabbis who introduced a ceremonial dimension to marriage, whereby matrimonial engagements were consummated by sexual union. Alexander, *The History of Women*, II 209.

4. It is interesting to note that Holst takes such a disparaging view of biblical sources, which was sure to provoke many of her readers, when Hippel defends the equality of the sexes from the very texts she rejects. For instance, in contrast to the Philanthropinists, who interpreted the Fall as the consequence of unchecked female desire, Hippel located the origins of Enlightenment in Eve's so-called sin. For Hippel, it was Eve who 'shattered the bonds of instinct which had prevented human reason from rising up.... In memory of her words Eve and Reason should be regarded as synonymous.' Hippel, *On Improving the Status of Women*, 65.
5. *Letters on the Most Important Matters of Humanity* (1794–8) is a collection of witty epistles by Christian Friedrich Sintenis, a theologian and popular writer from Zerbst. Pockels cites from a letter entitled 'On Learned Women', in which Sintenis ridicules the notion of a *gelehrte Frau* and argues that women should be educated only to the extent that it aids them to fulfil their threefold vocation as wives, mothers, and housewives. Sintenis, *Briefe über die wichtigsten Gegenstände der Menschheit*, III 261–81.
6. In the first chapter of Genesis, God creates man in God's image; yet here 'man' is plural: 'So God created man in His own image; in the image of God He created him; male and female He created them' (Genesis 1:27). In the second chapter, man is singular: 'the LORD God formed man of the dust of the ground, and breathed into his nostrils the breath of life; and man became a living being' (Genesis 2:7). It is not until Adam has named the animals that it becomes apparent that 'there was not found a helper comparable to him'. God then takes a rib from Adam, which he 'made into a woman, and He brought her to the man' (Genesis 2:20–2).
7. Pockels, *Versuch einer Charakteristik des weiblichen Geschlechts*, II 319–21.
8. The same point drives Hippel's rereading of the Creation and Fall narratives. Yet in contrast to Holst, his interpretation assumes that the Creator cannot act contrary to reason. See Hippel, *On Improving the Status of Women*, 64 ff.
9. While Holst remains silent on the political status of the Jewish community in the German nation, she connects her historical portrait of the uncivilized Jewish nation with her broader claim that the civilizing process, properly understood, irresistibly leads to the progress of women's rights. It is only a short step to Fichte's claim in *Contribution to the Rectification of Public Opinion Concerning the French Revolution* (*Beiträge zur Berichtigung der Urtheile des Publicums über die französische Revolution*, 1793) that Jewish people should be denied civic rights on the basis that they form a 'state within the state' that undermines the civility of the German nation. Fichte, *Sämmtliche Werke*, VI 150.
10. Holst is referring to Jean-Baptiste-Claude Delisle de Sales's multivolume *Philosophy of Nature: Treatise on Human Moral Nature* (*De la philosophie de la nature ou traité de morale pour le genre humain tiré de la philosophie et fondé sur*

140   NOTES

la nature, 1770 ff.), in which he ridicules the 6,000-year creation account presented in the Mosaic texts and argues from astronomical evidence for a 140,000-year-old earth.

11. One challenge of reading Holst's argument as a whole is not to downplay her attempt to blame misogyny on the Jewish origins of Christianity and to reclaim an Arian Christ as the model of true humanity. See Section 2.2.5 of the Introduction.

12. Holst is referring to Sintenis, who was cited by Pockels. In his letter 'On Learned Women', Sintenis cites 1 Corinthians 14:34 to argue that if there is no proper place for women to speak in the state or church, then there is no end for which they should become learned: 'Let your women, says Paul, keep silent in the churches, they belong in the house.' Sintenis, *Briefe über die wichtigsten Gegenstände der Menschheit*, III 274.

13. Holst paraphrases Luke 10:41–2. She writes: 'Martha, du machst dir zu viel zu schaffen; Maria aber had das beste Theil erwält.' In the Luther Bible, the verses read: 'Martha, Martha, du hast viel Sorge und Mühe; eins aber ist not. Maria hat das gute Teil erwählt.' In the New King James Version: 'Martha, Martha, you are worried and troubled about many things. But one thing is needed, and Mary has chosen that good part.' While several new translations of the New Testament were published in the late eighteenth century, the Luther Bible was still used in most ecclesial settings. This is probably one of the reasons that Holst criticizes the recitation of scripture in industrial schools for being 'not at all appropriate for the needs of our times' (p. 95).

14. Holst evokes the lines of Nantchen Göckingk she cited earlier ('If here by pot and spindle I let it [my mind] idly rest'), which continue, 'Is it not enough to spend half my life / As the dutiful Martha? / Is it treason, is it folly, is it all in vain / To pledge the second half to Wisdom?'

15. Here Holst follows up on an argument she began in her letters on *Elisa*. Wobeser's aim was to portray Elisa as a woman who acted in an unjust world from 'pure morality' alone. Holst argues that Elisa becomes an angel-like creature for whom happiness, as an immanent human good, is impossible. The middle path between subordination and transcendence, for Holst, is to critique and ultimately transform the institutions in which human happiness can be realized. See Section 1.2.2 of the Introduction.

16. Several of Holst's contemporaries attacked gendered conceptions of virtue and stressed the unity of morality and reason. In *Letters on Education*, for instance, Macaulay argues that 'there is but one rule of right for the conduct of all rational beings; consequently that true virtue in one sex must be equally so in the other, whenever a proper opportunity calls for its exertion; and, vice versa, what is vice in one sex, cannot have a different property when found in the other.' Macaulay, *Letters on Education*, 125–6.

17. One of Holst's reviewers responds directly to her question. Learnedness, the reviewer claims, 'is a trade [*Gewerbe*] that nature seems to have ordained for man; woman, with the duties that nature and *femininity* have imposed upon her, is permitted no time for it' (p. 121).

18. Holst draws the following extended quotation from Pockels, *Versuch einer Charakteristik des weiblichen Geschlechts*, II 331–44. Here Pockels is still quoting from Sintenis's letter 'On Learned Women'. Pockels's lengthy quotation is clearly an endorsement. He describes Sintenis as 'the honest author of the letters on the important matters of humanity' (319), and, at the close of the citation, praises him alongside the French poet and critic Nicolas Boileau-Despréaux, who composed a satirical poem on 'the learned female fool' (344).
19. The 'following note' Holst mentions is a footnote that Pockels appended to the preceding paragraph.
20. Holst's critique of Rousseau anticipates Marx's attack on the German Romantics: 'good-natured enthusiasts, German nationalists by sentiment and enlightened radicals by reflection, seek our history of freedom beyond our history in the primeval Teutonic forests. But then how does our history of freedom differ from that of the wild boar, if it is only to be found in the forests? Besides, as the saying goes: What is shouted in the forest echoes back from the forest. So peace to the primeval Teutonic forests!' Marx, 'A Contribution to the Critique of Hegel's Philosophy of Right', 59.
21. This passage is typical of an ambiguity that persists throughout the text. Holst seems to be saying that, as members of humanity, men and women have the same status. Yet as members of the state, they are unequal. Against the background of natural equality, however, the normative foundation of this civil inequality becomes questionable.
22. Joachim Christian Friedrich Schulz (1762–98) was a German novelist and writer from Magdeburg, most noted for his novel *Moritz* (1785) and for his eyewitness accounts of political events in France and Poland.
23. Ewald recommends that a girl should not undergo extensive moral training, for the 'innocence of woman is already there at this point, where all morality and virtue should lead: to want and to love purity. Disgust with impurity is her virtue, it replaces all virtues.' Ewald, *Die Kunst, ein gutes Mädchen, eine gute Gattin, Mutter und Hausfrau zu werden*, 49–50.
24. Holst quotes Mozart's *The Magic Flute* here. In Act I, Papageno and Pamina sing the quoted lines in a duet.
25. The late eighteenth century saw an increase in journals intended for affluent segments of German society with sufficient leisure and wealth to pursue fashion and luxury. For instance, the *Journal of Luxury and Fashion* (*Journal des Luxus und der Moden*), founded in 1786 by F. J. Bertuch and G. M. Kraus, promoted luxurious living as a fundamental part of the economic and moral life of the German nation. These journals served as an educational medium, filling in the space left by a woman's discontinued education.
26. Jewell translates the proverb as follows: 'The maid which takes, sells her self.' Jewell, *The Golden Cabinet of True Treasure*, 6.
27. Holst uses the term *Zweieinigkeit* (duel unity) as a play on *Dreieinigkeit* (trinity) to form her own version of Hippel's rendition of the Roman *arctissimum vitae commercium* (see p. liv). The term began to circulate in the 1790s, so it was

142   NOTES

probably not her own invention. Curiously, it was later popularized by the Catholic theologian Herbert Doms, who characterized marriage as *Zweieinigkeit* in *Vom Sinn und Zweck der Ehe* (1935).

Chapter 3

1. Holst's argument resonates with several other women writers in the late eighteenth century who called for 'educator mothers'; mothers that do not simply embody natural goodness but grasp and disseminate the principles of knowledge. Genlis's treatise on education is just one example: 'Destined to run a household, to raise children, and to depend on a master who will expect both advice and obedience, women should be patient, prudent, and orderly, with a healthy and fair mind; it is necessary that they are familiar with a wide range of fields so that they can join in any conversation with ease and grace, that they possess all the traditional feminine accomplishments, as well as a taste for reading.' Genlis, *Adèle et Théodore ou Lettres sur L'éducation*, I 45–6.
2. See [Holst,] *Bemerkungen über die Fehler unserer modernen Erziehung*, 45–6.
3. Holst's radical conception of a child's malleability was shared by other writers who stressed the significance of early education in realizing the project of Enlightenment. Locke opens his treatise on education by stating that 'of all Men we meet with, Nine parts of Ten are what they are, Good or Evil, useful or not, by their Education'; Locke, *Some Thoughts Concerning Education*, 2. In *Letters on Education*, Macaulay declared that 'there is not a virtue or a vice that belongs to humanity, which we do not make ourselves... There is not a wretch who ends his miserable being on a wheel, as the forfeit of his offenses against society, who may not throw the whole blame of his misdemeanours on his education; who may not look up to the very government, by whose severe laws he is made to suffer, as the author of his misfortunes; and who may not with justice utter the hardest imprecations on those to whom the charge of his youth was entrusted, and to those with whom he associated in the early periods of his life.' Macaulay, *Letters on Education*, 7–8.
4. Here Holst returns to the terrain she originally covered in *Observations on the Errors of Our Modern Education from a Practical Educator*. While she affirmed the general sentiment among modern pedagogues that the Latin schools should be replaced with a new curriculum in keeping with bourgeois life, Holst argued that the first wave of reformers (including Gottsched) threw out disciplined memorization and rule-following and replaced it with a verbal approach to learning. The second wave of reformers (including Basedow and Campe) made progress by realigning the curriculum to the natural ordering of cognition. Yet Holst contends that they still relied too heavily on sensory input and elementary books. See Introduction, Section 1.2.1.

NOTES   143

5. Holst plays with the term *Menschenfreund*, translated here as 'philanthropist', which was used by the pedagogues associated with Basedow's Philanthropin to describe their movement. She contends that a true philanthropist should be alarmed by the products of modern education and thus wary of overemphasizing sensory stimulation as the foundation of learning—a problem she identified in Basedow's *Methodenbuch*.
6. '[F]or a young woman of your station and your calling—the calling not to be a Frenchwoman or a lady at court but rather a bourgeois housewife—learning foreign languages is not only useless but also harmful.' Campe, *Väterlicher Rath für meine Tochter*, 120–1.
7. Campe, *Väterlicher Rath für meine Tochter*, 122.
8. Holst is criticizing Basedow's method of language learning, which rejects extensive training in grammar and vocabulary and insists instead that 'the teacher must for the most part teach students by means of conversation'. Basedow, *Ausgewählte Schriften*, 121.
9. In the final chapter of the *Methodenbuch*, 'Of the Encyclopaedia for Instruction and for Readers', Basedow lays down a two-part solution to the errors of modern education. The first part is to produce an *Elementarwerk* that will instruct teachers and provide a basic plan for schools. The second is to create an 'elementary library': 'This small library, which I wish for schools and gymnasia, can and must be so constituted that even beyond the places of instruction the needs of every reader would be remedied though its proper use...by filling the gaps, by instructing themselves in their own necessary areas of knowledge, and to this end helping themselves by reading an elementary, well-ordered, and complete *encyclopaedia*.' Basedow, *Ausgewählte Schriften*, 211.
10. Holst's critique of miseducation shares a concern with several women writers who criticize the tendency of men to generalize from just a few examples of poorly educated women to women as such. In her essay on happiness in marriage in the *Teutscher Merkur*, for instance, Emilie von Berlepsch poses a exasperated question: 'If an error-ridden education... mislead[s] some women into dissolution and foolishness, should the larger number of those who lead a useful, innocent life therefore also be condemned and robbed of their well-earned claims to public respect and domestic trust?' [Berlepsch], 'Ueber einige zum Glück der Ehe nothwendige Eigenschaften und Grundsätze', 83.
11. Holst's stipulation of the essential goodness of nature's laws shares more with the view she criticizes than she admits. The difference is that hers is a distinctly Protestant conception of ends that supersedes the pre-Enlightenment conception of means.
12. The holistic pedagogical vision Holst expresses in this section, which engages the senses and ignites the child's curiosity, has several parallels with Anna Barbauld's educational books, especially her stories and lessons addressed to children. These resources were published in German as a multivolume series,

144 NOTES

The Opened Writing Desk for the Instruction and Entertainment of Young Persons (*Das geöffnete Schreibepult, zum Unterricht und Vergnügen junger Personen*, 1794–5); Holst may have consulted them when preparing her lessons.

13. In contrast to Basedow, who argued in his *Elementarwerk* that a child's understanding of nature should begin with the natural history cabinet (*Naturalienkabinett*), Holst emphasizes the child's independent activity. An educated woman does not direct her students to a preassembled cabinet but invites them to join her in the independent role of collector, organizer, and friend of nature. Similar criticisms of Basedow were made by other pedagogues, including Christian Gotthilf Salzmann and Johann Stuve. Stuve, for instance, argued that the function of the natural history cabinet is not to present the student with 'An Ordered Storehouse of All Necessary Knowledge', to use the subtitle of Basedow's *Elementarwerk*, but rather 'to exercise the children's attentiveness, their ability to differentiate and to compare, their powers of reflection and thought, and their ability to present their ideas correctly and clearly'. Stuve, 'Über die Notwendigkeit', 234.
14. Holst makes two mistakes here. First, the epitaph was written by Alexander Pope, but never made it onto Newton's tombstone. Second, she misquotes the original: 'Nature, and Nature's laws lay hid in night. / God said, Let Newton be! and all was light.'
15. Friedrich Gottlieb Klopstock, *Die Frühlingsfeier* (1783).
16. See the debate between the theist and the atheist in the first volume of Sales, *De la philosophie de la nature*, I 274–83.
17. Holst cites from Ludwig Heinrich Christoph Hölty's *Das Landleben* (1777). I follow Warner's translation in *The Library of the World's Best Literature*. Interestingly, Holst misquotes the first line. Hölty writes, 'Wunderseliger Mann, welcher der Stadt entfloh!' Holst replaces 'Mann' with 'Mensch'. I have altered Warner's translation accordingly.
18. Once again, Holst insists that the means of social reform is not, as the Philanthropinists would have it, the formation of new pedagogical institutes, but the higher education of women.
19. Genesis 3:19.
20. Holst is referring to the Italian dancer and poet Teresa Landucci Bandettini (1763–1837), whose portrait was famously painted by Kauffmann in 1794.
21. Campe recommends that young women should be allowed to develop a useful capacity for the fine arts, especially singing and dancing. Yet he warns that here the hearts of young women are in danger of losing their innocence, and thus advises that they do not pursue the arts extensively. Campe, *Väterlicher Rath für meine Tochter*, 127–8.
22. The use of anecdotal evidence is a basic strategy in the writings of men on the vocation of woman. Here and elsewhere Holst turns the strategy against her male interlocutors, demonstrating that the vices they condemn are more often caused by a lack of education rather than an overindulgence.

23. Breastfeeding was widely discussed in women's writing on education following Rousseau's exhortation that, to strengthen the natural attachment between mother and child, mothers should breastfeed their children rather than hiring a wet nurse. See Rousseau, *Emile, Or on Education*, 44–7. Holst's opinion reflects several women writers of her time, including Genlis and Macaulay: 'Rousseau's address to mothers, so well calculated to inspire sentiments of duty, and to call forth the latent affections of the maternal breast, has introduced a kind of fashion among the great for taking upon themselves the task of suckling their infants; but on this subject, I am entirely of Genlis's opinion, and think that the custom is almost always of more prejudice than good to infants.' Macaulay, *Letters on Education*, 21.
24. In her play *La Bonne Mère*, Genlis contrasts the good mother's selfless regard for her daughters with the *mauvaise mère*, who neglects her motherly duties for social vanities. Genlis, *Théâtre d'éducation à l'usage de la jeunesse*, II 177–242.

Chapter 4

1. In this section we see that Holst's defence of women's rights is closely tied to her Protestant morals. C.f. Max Weber: 'The type of backward traditional form of labor is today very often exemplified by women workers, especially unmarried ones. An almost universal complaint of employers of girls, for instance German girls, is that they are almost entirely unable and unwilling to give up methods of work inherited or once learned in favor of more efficient ones, to adapt themselves to new methods, to learn and to concentrate their intelligence, or even to use it at all.' Weber, *The Protestant Ethic and the Spirit of Capitalism*, 26.
2. Friedrich Eberhard von Rochow (1734–1805) founded an industrial school on his estate in Reckahn following Philanthropinist principles, providing a model for how a school could improve the social and economic situation of the rural population. His book *Der Kinderfreund* (1776–9) sold over two million copies, and became a foundational text in Prussian pedagogy.
3. Johann Georg Büsch (1728–1800) was professor of mathematics at the Hamburg gymnasium. Büsch used his expertise to make theoretical improvements to the conduct of trade in Hamburg, and founded a school of trade in 1767 that became a flagship of its kind across Europe.
4. The calling fee was for announcing the birth of a child. The cloaking fee was for leading the men to the confinement chamber.
5. The proverb is drawn from Luke 10:7, when Jesus sends out the seventy to announce the coming of God's kingdom: 'And remain in the same house, eating and drinking such things as they give, for the laborer is worthy of his wages.'
6. Holst seems to be referring to Luther's interpretation of the Fifth Petition, 'forgive us our debts as we forgive our debtors', in which he expounds the parable of the unmerciful servant in Matthew 18 to illustrate the significance of the

conditional clause (as *we* forgive). One of Holst's reviewers takes her mistake here as a sign of her theological ignorance (see p. 119).

7. For an example of this worn-out claim, see Campe, *Väterlicher Rath für meine Tochter*, 69. Campe argues that a woman with intellectual aspirations will destroy all hope for domestic happiness: 'Do you think that her husband will feel compensated for the salty, burnt, or tasteless dishes she serves him, for the disorder in his household, for the squandering of his finances, for the chaotic management of household matters, for the neglect of his laundry, for the spoiling of his children by leaving them to the servants, etc., by erudite talk at the table, by a poem, a novel or the like, penned by his witty wife?'

8. '[L]a dèraison me pique, et le manque de bonne foi m'offense.' Lettre XLI, 8 Avril 1671. Sévigné, *Lettres de madame de Sévigné*, I 129.

9. This is Holst's ultimate response to Wobeser's *Elisa, or Woman as She Ought to Be*, which she began in her letters in *Lindemann's Musarion*. The housewife extends her sphere of influence through the fulfilment of her duty, changing the normative definition of woman though her higher education. Accepting that her calling is not to redirect the course of the crooked world, she rests content that she has played her part.

Chapter 5

1. Publius Terentius Afer (195–159? BC) was a Roman African playwright of the Roman Republic. Holst is referring to Terence's comedy *The Girl From Andros*, in which Simo attempts to prevent his son, Pamphilus, from marrying the woman he loves.

Bibliography

Primary Sources: the Works of Amalia Holst

[Holst, Amalia.] *Bemerkungen über die Fehler unserer modernen Erziehung von einer praktischen Erzieherin. Herausgegeben vom Verfasser des Siegfried von Lindenberg [Johann Gottwerth Müller]* (Leipzig: Carl Friedrich Schneider, 1791).

Holst, Amalia. 'Erster Brief über *Elisa, oder das Weib wie es seyn sollte*'. In *Musarion: eine Monatsschrift für Damen*, ed. August Lindemann (Altona: Hammerich, 1799), Bd. 1, H. 4, 345–61.

Holst, Amalia. 'Zweiter Brief über *Elisa, oder das Weib wie es seyn sollte*'. In *Musarion: eine Monatsschrift für Damen*, ed. August Lindemann (Altona: Hammerich, 1799), Bd. 1, H. 5, 30–52.

Holst, Amalia. 'Dritter Brief über *Elisa, oder das Weib wie es seyn sollte*'. In *Musarion: eine Monatsschrift für Damen*, ed. August Lindemann (Altona: Hammerich, 1800). Bd. 2, H. 7, 213–27.

Holst, Amalia. 'Vierter Brief über *Elisa, oder das Weib wie es seyn sollte*'. In *Musarion: eine Monatsschrift für Damen*, ed. August Lindemann (Altona: Hammerich, 1800), Bd. 2, H. 8, 326–34.

Holst, Amalia. 'Brief an August Hennings (Hamburg, 29 May 1802)'. Staats- und Universitätsbibliothek Hamburg. Manuscript call number: NHA: 11: 278–88.

Holst, Amalia. *Über die Bestimmung des Weibes zur höhern Geistesbildung* (Berlin: Heinrich Frölich, 1802).

Holst, Amalia. 'Brief an Franz August Gottlieb Campe (Timckenberg, 31 October 1824)'. Staats- und Universitätsbibliothek Hamburg. Manuscript call number: CS 2: Holst: 1–2.

Holst, Amalia. *Über die Bestimmung des Weibes zur höhern Geistesbildung*, ed. Berta Rahm (Zurich: ALA Verlag, 1983).

Other Primary Sources

Alexander, William. *The History of Women, from the Earliest Antiquity, to the Present Time; Giving an Account of Almost Every Interesting Particular Concerning That Sex, among All Nations, Ancient and Modern* (Philadelphia: J. H. Dobelbower, 1796).

Astell, Mary. *A Serious Proposal to the Ladies, for the Advancement of their True and Greatest Interest* (London: Wilkin, 1695).

Barbauld, Anna Laetitia. *Das geöffnete Schreibepult, zum Unterricht und Vergnügen junger Personen*, trans. Christian Felix Weisse (Leipzig, 1794–5).

148 BIBLIOGRAPHY

[Barbauld, Anna Laetitia.] 'What is Education?' *The Monthly* 5 (1798): 167–71.

Basedow, Johann Bernhard. *Basedow's ausgewählte Schriften. Mit Basedow's Biographie, Einleitungun und Anmerkungen*, ed. Hugo Göring (Langensalza: Hermann Beyer & Söhne, 1880).

Beilage des Hamburgischen Correspondenten, Februar 9, no. 23 (Hamburg, 1802).

[Berlepsch, Emilie von.] 'Ueber einige zum Glück der Ehe nothwendige Eigenschaften und Grundsätze'. *Neuer Teutscher Merkur*, Teil 1: April, 63–102, Teil 2: Juni 113–134 (1791).

Brandes, Ernst. *Ueber die Weiber* (Leipzig: Weidmanns Erben und Reich, 1787).

Campe, Johann Heinrich. *Väterlicher Rath für meine Tochter*, 5th ed. (Braunschweig: Schulbuchhandlung, 1796).

Du Châtelet, Émilie. 'Examination of Exodus'. In *Selected Philosophical and Scientific Writings*, ed. Judith P. Zinsser, trans. Isabelle Bour and Judith P. Zinsser (Chicago: University of Chicago Press, 2009), 207–13.

Du Châtelet, Émilie. 'Translator's Preface for *The Fable of the Bees*'. In *Selected Philosophical and Scientific Writings*, ed. Judith P. Zinsser, trans. Isabelle Bour and Judith P. Zinsser (Chicago: University of Chicago Press, 2009), 44–50.

Dohm, Hedwig. 'Nietzsche on Women'. In *Women Philosophers in the Long Nineteenth Century: The German Tradition*, ed. Dalia Nassar and Kristin Gjesdal, trans. Anna C. Ezekiel (Oxford: Oxford University Press, 2021), 128–38.

Erxleben, Dorothea Chrisiane, 'Rigorous Investigation of the Causes that Obstruct the Female Sex from Study'. In *Early Modern German Philosophy, 1690–1750*, ed. Corey W. Dyck (Oxford: Oxford University Press, 2019), 41–53.

Erxleben, Friedrich Georg Christian. 'Nachricht von einigen Lebensumständen der Fr. Dorothee Christiane Erxleben'. *Journal von und für Deutschland* 6 (1789): 350–8.

Euler, Leonhard. *Letters of Euler on Different Subjects in Physics and Philosophy Addressed to a German Princess*, 2 vols., trans. Henry Hunter (London: Murray & Highley, 1795).

Ewald, Johann Ludwig. *Die Kunst, ein gutes Mädchen, eine gute Gattin, Mutter und Hausfrau zu werden* (Frankfurt am Main: Friedrich Wilmans, 1802).

[Feurer, Angelika.] *Die Bestimmung des Weibes zur Hausfrau, Mutter und Gattin* (Campe, 1789).

Fichte, Johann Gottlieb. *Grundlage des Naturrechts nach Prinzipien der Wissenschaftslehre* (1796) (Hamburg: Meiner, 1979).

Fichte, Johann Gottlieb. *Foundations of Natural Right*, ed. Frederick Neuhouser, trans. Michael Baur (Cambridge: Cambridge University Press, 2000).

Fichte, Johann Gottlieb. *Johann Gottlieb Fichte's sämmtliche Werke*, ed. I. H. Fichte (Berlin: De Gruyter, 2018–).

Genlis, Stéphanie de. *Adèle et Théodore ou Lettres sur l'éducation*, 4 vols. (Paris: Maradan, 1801).

Genlis, Stéphanie de. *Théâtre d'éducation à l'usage de la jeunesse*, 2 vols. (Paris, 1847).

Gleim, Betty. *Erziehung und Unterricht des weiblichen Geschlechts* (Leipzig: Göschen, 1810).

Gottsched, Johann Christoph. *Akademische Redekunst, zum Gebrauche der Vorlesungen auf hohen Schulen als ein bequemes Handbuch eingerichtet und mit den schönsten Zeugnissen der Alten erläutert* (Leipzig: Breitkopf, 1759).

Gouges, Olympe de. *Femme réveille-toi! Déclaration des droits de la femme et de la citoyenne et autres ecrits*, ed. Martine Reid (Paris: Gallimard, 2014).

Halberstadt, Wilhelmine. *Über Würde und Bestimmung der Frauen* (A. F. Grossmann, 1808).

Hamburg und Altona: eine Zeitschrift zur Geschichte der Zeit, der Sitten und des Geschmacks 3 (7–9) (Hamburg: Nestler, 1802).

Hamilton, Elizabeth. *Letters on Education* (Dublin: Colbert, 1801).

Herder, Johann Gottfried von. *Sämmtliche Werke* (Vienna: Geistinger, 1813–21).

Herodotus. *Herodotus*, trans. William Beloe (London: Jones & Co., 1830).

[Hippel, Theodor Gottlieb von.] *Über die Ehe*, 1st ed. (Berlin: Christian Friedrich Voß, 1774).

[Hippel, Theodor Gottlieb von.] *Über die bürgerliche Verbesserung der Weiber* (Berlin: Voßischen Buchhandlung, 1792).

[Hippel, Theodor Gottlieb von.] *Über die Ehe*, 2nd ed. (Berlin: Voß, 1792).

[Hippel, Theodor Gottlieb von.] *Über die Ehe*, 3rd ed. (Berlin: Voß, 1793).

Hippel, Theodor Gottlieb von. *On Improving the Status of Women*, ed. and trans. Timothy F. Sellner (Detroit: Wayne State University Press, 1979).

Hippel, Theodor Gottlieb von. *On Marriage*, ed. and trans. Timothy F. Sellner (Detroit: Wayne State University Press, 1994).

Homer. *Odyssey*, trans. A. T. Murray (Cambridge, MA: Harvard University Press, 1919).

Jewell, William. *The Golden Cabinet of True Treasure* (London: John Crosley, 1612).

Justi, Heinrich Gottlob von. 'Vorschlag von Errichtung eines weiblichen Schöffenstuhls'. In *Ergetzungen der vernünftigen Seele aus der Sittenlehre und der Gelehrsamkeit überhaupt* (Leipzig: Breitkopf, 1745), vol. 1, 131–52.

Justi, Heinrich Gottlob von. 'Vorschlag von Errichtung einer Akademie vor das Frauenzimmer'. In *Ergetzungen der vernünftigen Seele aus der Sittenlehre und der Gelehrsamkeit überhaupt* (Leipzig: Breitkopf, 1747), vol. 5, 312–31.

Kaiserlich-Privilegierte hamburgische neue Zeitung 34 Stück, 27, Februar (Berlin: Heinrich Frölich, 1802).

Kant, Immanuel. *Gesammelte Schriften*, ed. Königlich Preußischen Akademie der Wissenschaften (Berlin: Walter de Gruyter, 1902–).

Kant, Immanuel. *Anthropology from a Pragmatic Point of View*. In *Anthropology, History, and Education*, ed. Gunter Zöller and Robert Louden, trans. Robert Louden (Cambridge: Cambridge University Press, 2007), 227–429.

Kant, Immanuel. *Idea for a Universal History with a Cosmopolitan Aim*. In *Anthropology, History, and Education*, ed. Günter Zöller and Robert B. Louden, trans. Allan W. Wood (Cambridge: Cambridge University Press, 2007), 107–20.

Kant, Immanuel. *Observations on the Feeling of the Beautiful and the Sublime*. In *Anthropology, History, and Education*, ed. Günter Zöller and Robert Louden, trans. Paul Guyer (Cambridge: Cambridge University Press, 2007), 18–62.

Khorenats'i, Movsēs. *History of the Armenians*, trans. R. W. Thomson (Cambridge, MA: Harvard University Press, 1978).

Klopstock, Friedrich Gottlieb. *Die Frühlingsfeier* (Cassel: Waisenhaus-Buchdruckerei, 1783).
Knigge, Philippine von. *Versuch einer Logik für Frauenzimmer* (Hanover: Christian Ritscher, 1789).
Leporin, Dorothea Christiane. *Gründliche Untersuchung der Ursachen, die das weibliche Geschlecht vom Studieren abhalten* (Berlin: Küdiger, 1742).
Locke, John. *Some Thoughts Concerning Education* (London: A. & J. Churchill, 1693).
Macaulay, Catherine. *Letters on Education. With observations on religious and metaphysical subjects* (London: C. Dilly, 1790).
Machiavelli, Niccolò. *The Prince*, ed. Quentin Skinner and Russell Price (Cambridge: Cambridge University Press, 1988).
Marx, Karl. 'A Contribution to the Critique of Hegel's Philosophy of Right'. In *Marx: Early Political Writings*, ed. Joseph J. O'Malley (Cambridge: Cambridge University Press, 2012).
Marx, Karl, and Engels, Frederick. *The German Ideology*, ed. C. J. Arthur (New York: International Publishers, 1970).
Meiners, Christoph. *Geschichte des weiblichen Geschlechts*, 4 vols. (Hanover: Helwingsche Hofbuchhandlung, 1788–1800).
Mill, John Stuart. *On Liberty with The Subjection of Women and Chapters on Socialism*, ed. Stefan Collini (Cambridge: Cambridge University Press, 1989).
More, Hannah. *Considerations on Religion and Public Education* (Boston: Weld & Greenough, 1794).
Mouvillon, Jakob. *Schilderung des preußischen Staates unter Friedrich II*, 4 vols (Leipzig, 1793–5).
Müller, Johann Gottwerth. 'Vorrede des Herausgebers'. In [Amalia Holst,] *Bemerkungen über die Fehler unserer modernen Erziehung von einer praktischen Erzieherin* (Leipzig: Carl Friedrich Schneider, 1791), 3–8.
Nietzsche, Friedrich. *On the Genealogy of Morality*, ed. Keith Ansell-Pearson, trans. Carol Diethe (Cambridge: Cambridge University Press, 1994), 57–70.
Plato. *Complete Works*, ed. John M. Cooper (Indianapolis: Hackett, 1997).
Plutarch. *Plutarch's Lives*, trans. Bernadotte Perrin (Cambridge, MA: Harvard University Press, 1919).
Pockels, Karl Friedrich. *Versuch einer Charakteristik des weiblichen Geschlechts. Ein Sittengemählde des Menschen, des Zeitalters und des geselligen Lebens*, 5 vols. (Hanover: Christian Ritscher, 1797–1802).
Rochow, Friedrich Eberhard von. *Der Kinderfreund: Ein Lehrbuch zum Gebrauch in Landschulen*, 2 vols. (Frankfurt: Eichenbergische Erben, 1776–9).
Rousseau, Jean-Jacques. *Émile, ou De l'éducation*, 4 vols. (Paris: Jean Néaulme, 1762).
Rousseau, Jean-Jacques. *Émile oder über die Erziehung* (Berlin, 1762).
Rousseau, Jean-Jacques. *Emile, or On Education*, trans. Allan Bloom (New York: Basic Books, 1979).
Sales, Jean-Baptiste-Claude Delisle de. *De la philosophie de la nature ou traité de morale pour le genre humain tiré de la philosophie et fondé sur la nature* (Amsterdam: Arkstée & Merkus, 1770).
Salzmann, Christian Gotthilf. *Reisen der Salzmannischen Zöglinge*, 6 vols. (Leipzig: S. L. Crusius, 1786–93).

[Schwarz, Sophie.] *Briefe einer Curländerinn. Auf einer Reise durch Deutschland. Zwei Theile* (Berlin: Friedrich Vieweg, 1791).

Sévigné, Marie de Rabutin-Chantal, marquise de. *Lettres de Madame de Sevigné* (Avignon: Chambeau, 1804).

Sintenis, Christian Friedrich. *Briefe über die wichtigsten Gegenstände der Menschheit*, 4 vols. (Leipzig: Bahrdt, 1794–8).

Spalding, Johann Joachim. *Die Bestimmung des Menschen, die Erstausgabe von 1748 und die letzte Auflage von 1794* (Waltrop: Hartmut Spenner, 1997).

[Staël, Germaine de.] *Lettres sur les ouvrages et le caractère de J. J. Rousseau* (Paris, 1788).

Staël, Germaine de. *De la literature consideree dans ses rapports avec les institutions sociales*, 2nd ed, 2 vols. (Paris: Maradan, 1800).

Strabo. *Geography, Volume III: Books 6–7*, trans. Horace Leonard Jones (Cambridge, MA: Harvard University Press, 1924).

Stuve, Johann. 'Über die Notwendigkeit, Kindern frühzeitig zu anschauender und lebendiger Erkenntnis zu verhelfen, und über die Art, wie man das anzufangen habe'. In *Allgemeine Revision des gesamten Schul- und Erziehungswesens: von einer Gesellschaft praktischer Erzieher* [1788], ed. Günter Ulbricht (Berlin: Volk und Wissen Verlag, 1957), 205–45.

Thomasius, Christian. 'Introduction to the Doctrine of Reason'. In *Early Modern German Philosophy, 1690–1750*, ed. Corey W. Dyck (Oxford: Oxford University Press, 2019), 15–40.

Trapp, Ernst Christian. *Theologischer Beweis, daß der Doktor Bahrdt schuld an dem Erdbeben in Kalabrien sei* (Quedlinburg, 1785).

Virgil. *The Aeneid*, trans. D. West (London: Penguin Classics, 2003).

Voltaire. *Le Siècle de Louis XIV*. In *Œuvres complètes de Voltaire* (Paris: Garnier, 1878), vol. 14, 32–144.

[Wobeser, Wilhelmine Caroline von.] *Elisa, oder das Weib, wie es seyn sollte* (Leipzig: Heinrich Graff, 1795).

[Wobeser, Wilhelmine Caroline von.] *Elisa, oder das Weib, wie es seyn sollte*, 3rd ed. (Leipzig: Heinrich Graff, 1798).

[Wollstonecraft, Mary.] 'Review of Translation of *Letters on the Works and Character of J. J. Rousseau*'. *Analytical Review* IV (1789): 360–2.

Wollstonecraft, Mary. *A Vindication of the Rights of Woman* (London: Vintage, 2014).

Zedler, Johann Heinrich. *Grosses vollständiges Universal-Lexicon aller Wissenschafften und Künste*, 68 vols. (Halle and Leipzig: Zedler, 1731–54).

Secondary Sources

Backhaus, Jügern G. 'From Wolff to Justi'. In *The Beginnings of Political Economy. The European Heritage in Economics and the Social Sciences*, vol. 7, ed. Jürgen G. Backhaus (Boston: Springer, 2009), 1–18.

Backhaus, Jügern G. 'Introduction'. In *The Beginnings of Political Economy. The European Heritage in Economics and the Social Sciences*, vol. 7, ed. Jürgen G. Backhaus (Boston: Springer, 2009), xi–xii.

Bäumer, Gertrud. *Handbuch der Frauenbewegung*, Bd. 1 (Berlin: Moeser, 1901).
Beauvoir, Simone de. *The Second Sex*, trans. and ed. H. M. Parshley (London: Vintage, 1997).
Botting, Eileen Hunt. 'Wollstonecraft in Europe, 1792–1904: A Revisionist Reception History'. *History of European Ideas* 39(4) (2013): 503–27.
Botting, Eileen Hunt. 'Nineteenth-Century Critical Reception'. In *Mary Wollstonecraft in Context*, ed. Nancy E. Johnson and Paul Keen (Cambridge: Cambridge University Press, 2020), 50–6.
Cooper, Andrew. 'Amalia Holst'. In *The Oxford Handbook for Nineteenth-Century Women Philosophers in the German Tradition*, ed. Kristin Gjesdal and Dalia Nassar (Oxford: Oxford University Press, 2023).
Dawson, Ruth P. *The Contested Quill: Literature by Women in Germany, 1770–1800* (Newark: University of Delaware Press, 2002).
Desan, Susan. 'Reconstituting the Social after the Terror: Family, Property and the Law in Popular Politics'. *Past & Present* 164 (1999): 81–121.
Dyck, Corey W. 'On Prejudice and the Limits to Learnedness: Dorothea Christiane Erxleben and the Querelle des Femmes'. In *Women and Philosophy in Eighteenth-Century Germany*, ed. Corey W. Dyck (Oxford: Oxford University Press, 2001), 51–71.
Dyck, Corey W. 'Amalia Holst on the Education of the Human Race'. In *Women and the Law in the Eighteenth-Century*, ed. Isabel Karremann, Anne-Claire Michoux, and Gideon Stiening (Stuttgart: J. B. Metzler, forthcoming).
Easley, Alexis. *First Person Anonymous: Women Writers and Victorian Print Media, 1830–70* (London: Routledge, 2017).
Ebbersmeyer, Sabrina. 'From a "memorable place" to "drops in the ocean": On the Marginalization of Women Philosophers in German Historiography of Philosophy'. *British Journal for the History of Philosophy* 28(3) (2020): 442–62.
Felden, Heide von. 'Geschlechterkonstruktion und Frauenbildung im 18. Jahrhundert: Jean Jacques Rousseau und die zeitgenössische Rezeption in Deutschland'. In *Handbuch zur Frauenbildung*, ed. Wiltrud Geiseke (Wiesbaden: Springer, 2001), 25–34.
Foucault, Michel. *The Order of Things* (London: Routledge, 2002).
Fraisse, Geneviève. *Muse de la Raison: Démocratie et exclusion des femmes en France* (Paris: Éditions Gallimard, 1995).
Fronius, Helen. *Women and Literature in the Goethe Era, 1770–1820* (Oxford: Oxford University Press, 2007).
Gardner, Catherine. 'Catharine Macaulay's "Letters on Education": Odd but Equal'. *Hypatia* 13(1) (1998): 118–37.
Gerhardt, Andrea. *Wenn die Frau Mensch wird. Campe, Holst und Hippel im Vergleich* (Norderstedt: Books on Demand, 2017).
Greif, Stefan. 'Theodor Gottlieb von Hippel und Amalia Holst: Kritisch-emanzipative Gegenentwürfe zur bürgerlichen Geschlechterordnung'. In *Geschlechterordnung und Staat*, ed. Marion Heinz and Sabine Doyé (Berlin: Akademie Verlag, 2012), 199–217.
Guest, Harriet. 'Hannah More and Conservative Feminism'. In *British Women's Writing in the Long Eighteenth Century: Authorship, Politics and History*, ed. Jennie Batchelor and Cora Kaplan (Basingstoke: Palgrave Macmillan, 2005), 158–70.

Herminghouse, Patricia A., and Mueller, Magda (eds.). *German Feminist Writings* (New York: Continuum, 2001).

Hull, Isabel. *Sexuality, State, and Civil Society in Germany, 1700–1815* (Ithaca, NY: Cornell University Press, 1996).

Jacoby, Karl. S. *Beiträge zur deutschen Literaturgeschichte des achtzehnten Jahrhunderts* (Hamburg: Lütcke & Wulff, 1911).

James, David. 'Fichte on the Vocation of the Scholar and the (Mis)Use of History'. *Review of Metaphysics* 63(3) (2010): 539–66.

Johns, Alessa. *Bluestocking Feminism and British-German Cultural Transfer, 1750–1837* (Ann Arbor: University of Michigan Press, 2014).

Johns, Alessa. 'Translations'. In *Mary Wollstonecraft in Context*, ed. Nancy E. Johnson and Paul Keen (Cambridge: Cambridge University Press, 2020), 323–31.

Latham, Jacob Abraham. 'Roman Rhetoric, Metroac Representation: Texts, Artifacts, and the Cult of Magna Mater in Rome and Ostia'. *Memoirs of the American Academy in Rome* 59/60 (2014/2015): 51–80.

Lohmann, Ingrid, and Mayer, Christine. 'Dimensions of Eighteenth-century Educational Thinking in Germany: Rhetoric and Gender Anthropology'. *History of Education* 37(1) (2007): 113–39.

Louden, Robert. B. '"Not a Slow *Reform*, But a Swift *Revolution*": Kant and Basedow on the Need to Transform Education'. In *Kant and Education*, ed. Klas Roth and Chris Surprenant (New York: Routledge, 2001), 39–54.

Louden, Robert. B. *Johann Bernhard Basedow and the Transformation of Modern Education: Educational Reform in the German Enlightenment* (London: Bloomsbury, 2020).

Louden, Robert. B. 'A Mere Skeleton of the Sciences? Amalia Holst's Critique of Basedow and Campe'. In *Women and Philosophy in Eighteenth-Century Germany*, ed. Corey W. Dyck (Oxford: Oxford University Press, 2021), 72–91.

Madland, Helga. 'Three Late-Eighteenth Century Women's Journals: Their Role in Shaping Women's Lives'. *Women in German Yearbook* 4 (1988): 167–86.

Mayer, Christine. 'Bildungsentwürfe und die Konstruktion der Geschlechterverhältnisse zu Beginn der Moderne'. In *Das Geschlecht der Bildung—Die Bildung der Geschlechter*, ed. Britta L. Behm, Gesa Heinrichs, and Holger Tiedemann (Opladen: Leske & Budrich, 1999), 13–29.

Mayer, Christine. 'The Struggle for Vocational Education and Employment Possibilities for Women in the Second Half of the Nineteenth Century in Germany'. *History of Education Researcher* 80 (2007): 85–99.

Mayer, Christine. 'Female Education and the Cultural Transfer of Pedagogical Knowledge in the Eighteenth Century'. *Paedagogica Historica* 48(4) (2012): 511–26.

Menhennet, Alan. '"Elisa steht wie eine Gottheit da": Heroic Femininity in the Popular Novel of the "Goethezeit"'. *German Life and Letters* 39(4) (1986): 253–267.

Nassar, Dalia, and Gjesdal, Kristin (eds.). *Women Philosophers in the Long Nineteenth Century: The German Tradition* (Oxford: Oxford University Press, 2021).

Nassar, Dalia, and Gjesdal, Kristin. 'Editors' Introduction'. In *Women Philosophers in the Long Nineteenth Century: The German Tradition*, ed. Dalia Nassar and Kristin Gjesdal (Oxford: Oxford University Press, 2021), 1–20.

O'Neill, Eileen. 'Disappearing Ink: Early Modern Women Philosophers and Their Fate in History'. In Janet Kourany (ed.), *Philosophy in a Feminist Voice: Critiques and Reconstructions* (Princeton: Princeton University Press, 1998), 17–62.

O'Neill, Eileen. 'Early Modern Women Philosophers and the History of Philosophy'. *Hypatia* 20(3) (2005): 185–97.

Pollok, Anne. 'The Role of Writing and Sociability for the Establishment of a Persona: Henriette Herz, Rahel Levin Varnhagen, and Bettina von Arnim'. In Corey W. Dyck (ed.), *Women and Philosophy in Eighteenth-Century Germany* (Oxford: Oxford University Press, 2021), 195–210.

Preuss, Peter. 'Translator's Introduction'. In J. G. Fichte, *The Vocation of Man*, trans. Peter Preuss (Indianapolis: Hackett, 1987), vii–xiv.

Printy, Michael. 'The Determination of Man: Johann Joachim Spalding and the Protestant Enlightenment'. *Journal of the History of Ideas* 74(2) (2014): 189–212.

Rahm, Berta. 'Nachwort'. In Amalia Holst, *Über die Bestimmung des Weibes zur höhern Geistesbildung*, ed. Berta Rahm (Zurich: ALA Verlag, 1983), 153–61.

Reinert, Erik S. 'Johann Heinrich Gottlob von Justi: The Life and Times of an Economist Adventurer'. In *The Beginnings of Political Economy. The European Heritage in Economics and the Social Sciences*, vol 7, ed. Jügern G. Backhaus (Boston: Springer, 2009), 33–74.

Sellner, Timothy. 'A Paradoxical Life' In *The Status of Women: Collected Writings*, ed. Theodor Gottlieb von Hippel (Bloomington: Xlibris, 2009), 21–59.

Sotiropoulos, Carol Strauss. 'Scandal Writ Large in the Wake of the French Revolution: The Case of Amalia Holst'. *Women in German Yearbook* 20 (2004): 98–121.

Spalding, Almut. *Elise Reimarus (1735–1805), The Muse of Hamburg: A Woman of the German Enlightenment* (Würzburg: Königshausen & Neumann, 2005).

Trouille, Mary Seidman. *Sexual Politics in the Enlightenment: Women Writers Read Rousseau* (Albany: SUNY Press, 1997).

Warner, Charles Dudley, et al. *The Library of the World's Best Literature. An Anthology in Thirty Volumes* (New York: Warner Library, 1917).

Weber, Max. *The Protestant Ethic and the Spirit of Capitalism*, trans. Talcott Parsons (London: Routledge, 2001).

Yuval-Davis, Nira. *Gender and Nation* (Sage: London, 1997).

Zammito, John. *Kant, Herder, and the Birth of Anthropology* (Chicago: Chicago University Press, 2002).

Index

Adam 43, 45
Adolphus, Gustavus 40
Aeneas 17
Alexander 21
Alexander, William 23, 130nn17–18, 130n23, 131n35, 138n3
Amaranthe 35
Anjou 26
Antisthenes 55
Antony 18
Apollo 21
Arc, Joan of 24
Aristotle 34, 55
Aspasia 21
Astell, Mary xxix, xxixn80
Artemis 18
Athena 12
Augustus 19

Babet 38, 136n89
Backhaus, Jügern xvin24
Bandettini, Teresa Landucci 86
Barbauld, Anna Laetitia xxix, 136n81, 143n12
Basedow, Johann Bernhard x, xxxvin102, 117
The Method Book xix, xx, 143n9
Holst's critique of xxiv, 75, 142n4, 143n8–9, 144n13
Bause, Friederike Charlotte 39
Beauvoir, Simone de xl
Berlepsch, Emilie von xxxiii, 33
Bertha 23
Blois, Charles de 25–26
Bonnet, Charles 35
Boursolt, Edmé 38
Brandes, Charlotte 39
Brandes, Ernst xxxi–xxxiii, xxxv, xlvii, 13, 118, 128n7, 138n1
Brun, Friederike 33
Brunhilda 23
Buffon, Georges 35
Büsch, Johann Georg 96

calling
as mother 73, 77, 87, 90
distinct from vocation lx
female lvi, 7
of human beings 7
of nature lv
particular xl–xli, 37, 49
threefold xxxiv–xxxv, xxxviii, xli, xlv, xlvii–xlviii, 9, 10n*, 14, 42, 62, 91, 104, 105, 119, 123
to education 68, 101, 108–109
Campe, Franz August xvii–xviii
Campe, Joachim Heinrich xix–xx, xxiv, xxxi, xxxv
elementary books of xxiv, 134n60
Holst's critique of xxiv, xxxviii, 70n*, 74, 77, 86, 134n62
on marriage xxxvi
on women's education xx–xxi, xxxii, lx, 128n3, 144n21
Charles VI 23–24
Du Châtelet, Émilie xliv–xlv, l–li, 40
Christiani, Ernst 38
Christina, Queen 40
Christ xliii, 23, 47, 55, 119
Cicero 34, 55
Cleopatra 18
Confucius 55
Coligny, Henriette de 33
Corday, Charlotte 25
Cornelia 19
Coriolanus 19
culture
as the completion of nature xxii
false xxxii, 10, 105
high 7, 15–16, 58, 67, 76, 82, 84, 103, 110
of humankind 30–31, 43, 78, 85
of men 119
of women 53n*
state of xxxix–xl, 12
transition from nature to 13, 54, 122

156 INDEX

Dacier, Anne 32
Daphne 18
Deborah 17
Demosthenes 55, 67
Descartes, René 34, 40
Deshoulières, Antoinette 33
Dido 17, 24
Dohm, Hedwig xl
Du Barry, Comtesse 24
duties
   contradiction of xxxiv, 41, 51
   equality of all 44
   female ix, xi, xxvii, xxxiv, xli, xlvii–lii, lvi–lvii, 9, 14, 41, 43, 52, 59, 74, 87–90, 93, 103, 118–119, 121
   fulfilment of 65, 68, 71, 73, 87, 91–92, 98–99, 103–104, 109
   human l, 43, 60
   individual 10, 41, 104
   learnedness and moral 58
   male 49, 56
   professional 49
   priestly 21
   social 54, 62
duty
   highest xli
   of humankind xlii, 29, 31–32, 63, 84, 86, 101, 110
   of sociability 100
   principle of 28
   sense of 64, 75, 85, 87, 102, 108
Dyck, Corey xvin28

Ebbersmeyer, Sabrina xii, xxxvii
education
   and enlightenment xxx, xxxii
   and social reform lii
   arguments for restricting women's xi, xx–xxi, xxxiv–xxxv, xlvi, 9–10, 30, 74, 91, 119
   Holst's diagnosis of the errors of modern xxii–xxv, 117–118
   higher intellectual xvi, xxxvi, xlii, lxi, 17
   in relation to learnedness 54, 58–60
   influence of women on 27–28, 69, 72
   Locke's theory of xix
   neglected 39, 41
   of women xvi, xxv–xxviii, xxxvi, xl, xlv, l–li, 37
   of the lower classes 32, 90, 94–97
   principles of higher intellectual 31–32
   Rousseau's theory of xix, xxii, 117, 138n1
Edward III 25–26
Elagabalus 19
Elizabeth I 27
Elissa 17
l'Enclos, Anne de 38
enlightenment
   autonomy as the mark of ix, xxx, xxxiii
   danger of superficial xxv–xxvi, 10, 134n60
   gendered nature of xxxii, xl
   German ix–xii, xiv, xxx, xlix, lvii, lxi
   Holst's critique of x, xxxix, xlvii, 81–82, 103, 106, 129n11
   role of education in xix, xxii, 142n3
   role of women in xv, xxxviii, 35, 48, 60, 123, 139n4
Esther 17
Erxleben, Dorothee Christiane xxviii–xxix, xxxviii, 36–37, 51n[†], 113
Erxleben, Friedrich Georg Christian 36–37
Euler, Leonhard 40
Eustache de Saint Pierre 26
Ewald, Johann Ludwig xxxi, xlviii, 30, 62n[†], 119, 134n59, 141n23

La Fayette, Comtesse de 35
Felicia, Laberia 21
Feurer, Angelika xlixn115, l, liii
Fichte, Johann Gottlieb ix, xi, xxx, xxxin86, lix, 139n9
La Fontaine, Jean de 35
Foucault, Michel xxxii
Fredegund 23
Freya 22
Frederick the Great xv–xvi, liv, 16, 37, 40
Fraisse, Geneviève xn5
Fronius, Helen xviiin35

Genlis, Stéphanie de xxiii, xxxvin100, lii–liii, 36, 41, 91, 127n1, 136n80, 142n1, 145nn23–24
Gleim, Betty xlviin113
Göckingk, Leopold von 35
Goethe, Johann Wolfgang von 34
Gottsched, Johann Christoph xix, 71n[*], 142n4
Gouges, Olympe de xii, xxix, li, 127nn1–2, 129n13
Gray, Johanna 33

Halberstadt, Wilhelmine xlviin113, 1
Hannah 23
Hamburg und Altona xxxviii, xlvii–xlviii,
  120–125
Henry IV 24
Henry VI 26
Hebe 22
Herder, Johann Gottfried von xxx, 38–39
Hercules 12
Herodotus 131n30
Herschel, Caroline 40
Hippel, Theodor Gottlieb von liii–lvi, 7–8,
  10n*, 118, 133n57
  friendship with Kant ixn3
  on the education of women xlvi
  On Marriage xxxv, 138n104, 138n105, 138n2
  On Improving the Status of Women
    xliii–xliv, li, 10n*, 127n1, 128n9,
    133n56, 139n4, 139n8
Hobbes, Thomas 82
Hölty, Ludwig 80
Homer 12, 18, 34, 55
Hume, David 24, 26

Isis 21
l'Isle, Rouget de 33

Jacoby, Karl xviiin32
Jewell, William 141n26
John III 25
Judith 17
Juno 21
Jupiter 12
Justi, Heinrich Gottlob von xiv–xvi, liv,
  111–112, 114, 130n21

Kant, Immanuel ix–xi, xxx, xli, xliii–xliv, liii,
  lvin145, 34, 40–41, 138n105
Kauffmann, Angelika 38, 86
Klopstock, Friedrich Gottlieb 34, 79
Knigge, Philippine von 40
Korinna 33

Lais 21
learnedness xxviii–xxix, lxi
  as compatible with the female calling xxvi,
    xxxv, xli, 88–90
  in men xl, 11, 13, 119
  in relation to education xlviii–xlix, 34, 39,
    54–60, 120–122, 124–125

  in women xxxvii–xxxviii, 14, 37, 49–54,
    111, 114
  unsuitability of women for xiii, xl, 50, 63,
    120–122, 125
Leporin, Dorothea Christiane *see* Erxleben,
  Dorothea Christiane
Letters on *Elisa* xxv–xxvii, 140n15
Lichtenberg, Georg Christoph 16, 72
Linnaeus, Carl 35
literature
  and moral formation xxvi, 36, 135n76,
    136n90
  contribution of women to 33, 35–36
  see also poetry
Livy 17
Locke, John xviii–xix, xxii, 117, 142n3
Louden, Robert xxn43
Louis XIV 24, 37
Louis XV 24, 37
Lucretia 19
Luther, Martin 98, 119
luxury xxxiin92, 19, 56, 64–65, 74, 85–86,
  94, 105, 108, 141n25

Macaulay, Catherine xxiii, xxix, xxixn80, liii,
  128n3, 128n9, 138n2, 140n16,
  142n3, 145n23
Machiavelli, Niccolò 16
Maintenon, Françoise de 24, 37
Marat, Jean-Paul 25
marriage
  complementarian ideal of xxvi–xxvii, xxxvi
  desire and xxvii
  happiness in xxxiii
  Hippel's account of xxxv, li, liv, 138n2
  Holst's account of 44, 47–48, 58–61, 67,
    105–106
Martha 47
Marx, Karl xl, xlvii, 129n11, 141n20
Mary 23, 47
Mayer, Christine lxn1
Medici, Catherine de' 23
Medici, Marie de' 23
Meiners, Christoph xxxi, xlvii–xlviii, liii, 20,
  22, 118, 119, 131n29
Mill, John Stuart xiiin16, xxxix–xl, 128n6
Millot, Claude-François-Xavier 38
Minerva 12, 18, 21
Mohammed 55
Montfort, John of 25–26

More, Hannah xlv, liii
Moses 43–47, 55, 119, 124
Mouvillon, Jakob 13, 118, 128n7
Müller, Ernestine 35
Müller, Johann Gottwerth xxiv

Nantchen, *see* Sophie Vogel
nature
 adoration of 47, 80, 82
 and artistic expression 34–35, 86
 as the ground of duties xi, 41, 70, 88
 as the ground of happiness xxvi, 44, 63
 as the ground of social norms xxi, xxxii, xliv–xlv, 118, 124
 as the normative foundation of right lx, 12, 31
 capacities given by xxx, xlii, 29, 32, 43, 83, 92
 critique of liv, lv
 human 36, 85, 89
 in art 33, 38
 of children 71
 of marriage 67, 106
 of the sexes ix, xxii–xxiii, xxxi, xli, xlviii, 16, 50, 121
 state of xxxiv, xxxix, 12–15, 122, 128n5
 study of 56, 60, 73, 78–79, 81–82, 84
 violation of 53, 83
Nehalennia 22
Newton, Isaac 40, 79
Nietzsche, Friedrich xl, 128n5
Nimrod 12

O'Neill, Eileen xn5
Observations on the Errors of Our Modern Education xviii–xxv, xxxiv, xxxix, xlii, 117–118, 142n4
Octavian 18
Ovid 38

Paradis, Maria Theresia von 39
Paul xliii, 47, 50, 119
Pelias 21
Pericles 21, 55
Petrovna, Anna 27
Petrovna, Elizabeth 27
Philanthropin x, xxn43, lin121, 72n*, 143n5
Philanthropinism x–xi, xlviii, 139n4, 145n2
 Holst's critique of xviii, xxi–xxii, xxxiv–xxxvi, xxxix–xl, xlv, 127n1, 144n18

Philippa of Hainault 26
philosophy
 exclusion of women from xn5, xii, xivn17
 of history 76–78
 practical xli
 speculative ix, 41
 women and the study of xli, lvii, 31, 38–41, 74, 123
Phryne 21
Pindar 33
Plato 18n*, 34
Plutarch 131n35
Pockels, Karl Friedrich xi, xxxi, xxxv, xlvii–xlviii, 119, 121
 Holst's critique of 33–35, 44, 49, 52, 62
poetry
 and teaching xxii, 34–35, 74
 excellence of women in 33, 35
 inferiority of women in 33–34
Pompadour, Jeanne de 24
Pythagoras 34, 55
Pythia 21

Rahm, Berta xiin11, xivn18, xvin29, liii, lix
Raphael 67
reason
 as the foundation of right xxx, liv, 15–16
 and gender x, xxix, xxxi, xxxin86
 boundaries of 91
 faculty of xxiii, 29
 healthy 103
 in marriage 48, 65
 judgment seat of xxxix, xliii, xlvi, 43, 46–47, 122
 pedagogical xxii, 72, 117
 practical 12, 28
 public xix
Reiske Johann, Jakob 33
Robespierre, Maximilien 25
Roche, Sophie von la 36
Rochow, Friedrich Eberhard von xlv, 94, 124
Romulus 18, 57
Rousseau, Jean-Jacques
 Hippel on lv
 Holst's critique of xxiii, xxxiv–xxxv, xxxix, 13–14, 16, 54, 83, 122, 129n11
 influence on Philanthropinism x, xix, xx, xxx–xxxi

INDEX 159

on women's education xxii, 117, 138n1
women writers on xxiii, xxvii, lv, 128n3,
    128n9, 129n13, 136n79, 145n23
Rudolphi, Caroline 33

Sales, Jean-Baptiste-Claude Delisle de
    xliv, 10n*
Salzmann, Christian Gotthilf li, liii, 144n13
Sappho 29, 33
Saul 12
Schiller, Friedrich 34
Schulz, Joachim 59
Schurman, Anna Maria van 33
Schwamerdam, Jan 35
Schwarz, Sophie 37n*, 51n†
Scudéry, Madeleine de 33
Semiramis 17–18
Seneca 34
Sévigné, Marie de Rabutin-Chantal,
    marquise de 37
Sintenis, Christian Friedrich xin8, xiii, 62n*,
    139n5, 140n12
Solon 55
Sorel, Agnès 24
Sotiropoulos, Carol Strauss ixn1, xxxii, liii
Spalding, Johann Joachim xxx
sphere of influence xxi, xxvii, xxxi, xxxv, xlii,
    xlvi, l, lvi, 41, 74, 89, 93, 96, 99, 101, 107,
    108–109, 133n57, 134n62, 146n9
Staël, Germaine de xii, xxiii, xxviin75, xxxvi,
    xlviii, 38, 41, 128n9, 134n61
Stolberg, Louisa Maria von 33
Strinasacchi, Regina 39
Stuve, Johann 144n13
Sully, Duke of 24
Superbus, Tarquinius 19
system
    class xxxvi, liii
    of education xix, xxiv, l
    philosophical xli, lvii, 41, 122
    school x

Telemachus 12
Terence 105–106
Thais 71
Thales 34
Trapp, Ernst Christian 72n*

Valeda 22
Virgil 17, 24, 55
virtue
    and power 12, 62
    feminine xxv–xxvi, 9, 14, 121, 123,
        141n23
    unity of l, 25, 35, 48, 76, 106–107,
        128n9, 140n16
vocation
    and education 69, 96–97
    human xvii, xx, xxv, xxx, xxxiv, xxxviii,
        xli, xliin107, xlix, lii, 63, 83, 124
    in relation to calling lvi, lx
    of man xxxi, 53, 121
    of woman xvii, xx–xxii, xxvi, xxviii, xxxiii,
        xxxvii, xlviii, 11, 13, 48, 51n†, 53, 62, 90,
        101, 113
    threefold xi, 50, 121
Vogel, Sophie 33, 35
Voltaire 13, 24, 33, 40, 49

Warner, Charles Dudley 144n17
Weber, Max 145n1
Westenholz, Sophia Maria 39
Wieland, Christoph 34
Wobeser, Wilhelmine Caroline von
    xxv–xxvii, xlii, 134n60, 140n15, 146n9
Wollstonecraft, Mary xii, xxix
    on Rousseau xxviin75, liii
    possible influence on Holst li–liii, lv,
        127n2, 128n9

Zedler, Johann Heinrich lx
Zeno 34
Zenobia 18